CANADA FOR KIDS

CANADIAN
Geographic

CANADA F

OR **KIDS**

1000
Awesome Facts

AARON KYLIE

FIREFLY BOOKS

A Firefly Book

Published by Firefly Books Ltd. 2015
Copyright © 2015 Firefly Books Ltd.
Text copyright © 2015 Aaron Kylie

First printing

Publisher Cataloging-in-Publication Data (U.S.)
Kylie, Aaron.
Canadian Geographic Canada for Kids : 1000 awesome facts / Aaron Kylie.
[248] pages : color photographs, maps, graphs ; cm.
Includes index.
Summary: "A kid's reference featuring facts and trivia focusing on Canada's records,
achievements and "gee-whiz" accomplishments. The book looks at the country
and features, facts and figures for each province and territory within its borders" –
Provided by publisher.
ISBN-13: 978-1-77085-581-6 (pbk.)
1. Canada – History – Juvenile literature. 2. Canada – Geography – Juvenile
literature. 3. Canada – Miscellanea – Juvenile literature. I. Title. II. Canada for kids.
971 dc23   F1011.K955 2015

Library and Archives Canada Cataloguing in Publication
Kylie, Aaron, author
Canadian geographic Canada for kids : 1000 awesome facts
/ Aaron Kylie.
Includes index.
ISBN 978-1-77085-581-6 (paperback)
1. Canada--Miscellanea--Juvenile literature. I. Title.
FC58.K96 2015   j971   C2015-905491-5

Published in the United States by
Firefly Books (U.S.) Inc.
P.O. Box 1338, Ellicott Station
Buffalo, New York 14205

Published in Canada by
Firefly Books Ltd.
50 Staples Avenue, Unit 1
Richmond Hill, Ontario L4B 0A7

Cover and interior design: Gareth Lind, LINDdesign

Printed in Canada

The publisher gratefully acknowledges the financial support for our publishing
program by the Government of Canada through the Canada Book Fund as
administered by the Department of Canadian Heritage.

CONTENTS

INTRODUCTION

In my experience, both personally and through my children, the young at heart have a vast appetite for knowledge, particularly for stuff that's big, small, best or first, and the like. If that kind of trivia is of interest to you, this book's for you. It has 1,000 items that fit that theme. And it's all dedicated to Canada (it's organized in sections focused on the entire nation and then provinces and or regions).

So flip through the pages and you'll discover things like...

How Canada rules the dinosaur world: Alberta's Dinosaur Provincial Park, for instance is home to the richest area of dinosaur fossils on Earth— more than 40 dino species have been discovered there; the fossils of the world's oldest reptiles (which would become dinosaurs) are found at the Joggins Fossil Cliffs in Nova Scotia; Alberta's Royal Tyrell Museum of Paleontology has the largest display of dinosaurs on Earth; and the world's largest dinosaur monument (see the book's cover) is found nearby in Drumheller, Alberta.

Canada holds a pretty special place when it comes to video games: the nation is the largest producer of video games in the world per capita based on the number of employees (some 16,500); and you can even view a selection of the collection of the country's largest collector of video games, Syd Bolton of Brantford, Ontario, at the town's Personal Computer Museum.

Young Canadians hold some unique distinctions: a group of youngsters is behind the world's tallest mural, a bird that stretches 32-storeys of a building in Toronto's St. James Town community; singer Justin Bieber, of Stratford, Ontario, became the first musician with five Number One albums on the *Billboard 200* chart before he turned 19 years old; Canada's first supermodel, Monika Schnarre, was the youngest person to win the Ford Modeling Agency's Supermodel of the World competition, in 1986, at age 14, and she was also the youngest person to grace the covers of *American Vogue* and *Sports Illustrated*'s swimsuit issue, in 1987, at age 15.

There's much, much, much more, too, of course, from notable geographic facts to amazing wildlife feats to sporting benchmarks and beyond. Whether you're 9 or just feel that way (or want to!), this book is sure to tickle the curiosity of the kid in you—and feed its desire for knowing a lot of cool stuff about Canada.

Aaron Kylie, Editor, *Canadian Geographic*

The most widely accepted origin of the name Canada for our nation comes from explorer Jacques Cartier in 1536. Cartier noted that the local Aboriginals called their communities *kanata* (Iroquois word meaning "village" or "settlement"), which was interpreted by Europeans as referring to the term for the entire country.

AVRO ARROW

It's been called Canada's greatest aeronautical achievement. The Avro Arrow, or CF-105 jet fighter, was the only supersonic jet the country produced. It is said to have been faster (it had a maximum speed of 2,453 km per hour) and more advanced than any other comparable aircraft. Rising costs of production combined with the development of long-range missiles caused the government to cancel the aircraft (on February 20, 1959, a day known as "Black Friday" by some as a result), and all the existing jets were destroyed, along with all related plans and equipment.

Biggest heartfelt donation

Here's a gift from, er, for the heart. In November 2014, the family of the late Ted Rogers made the largest monetary donation to a Canadian health-care initiative when it gave $130 million for the creation of the Ted Rogers Centre for Heart Research. Toronto's Hospital for Sick Children, the University Health Network and the University of Toronto will each contribute facilities and expertise to the project, which aims to reduce hospitalization due to heart failure by 50 percent before 2024.

Longest parliamentary session

Canada's longest parliament? The 12th, which ran for 2,152 days, from November 15, 1911, to October 6, 1917. The prime minister at the time was Robert Borden, whose Conservative Party held a majority government.

Shortest parliamentary session

That didn't last long. Canada's 31st parliament lasted just 66 days. Prime Minister Joe Clark's minority Progressive Conservative government ruled from October 9 to December 14, 1979. The House of Commons sat only 49 times during the single session.

First Canadian-born prime minister

Can you believe it was almost 24 years after Canada became a nation before the country had a prime minister born in Canada? John Abbott, born on February 12, 1821, in St. Andrews, Lower Canada (present day Saint-André-d'Argenteuil, Que.), became prime minister on June 16, 1891.

A TIMELINE OF CANADA

Here are key events in the history of Canada—gathered in one place. You'll find some of these events elsewhere in this book. Others didn't qualify as the biggest, the first or perhaps the most fascinating—but that doesn't make them any less interesting or important.

12,000–30,000 YEARS AGO: The first people—the ancestors of Canada's Aboriginal peoples—cross over into Canada. Today the term "Aboriginal" peoples refers to three groups: Indian, First Nation and all Aboriginal people who are not Inuit or Métis. The Inuit, which means "the people" in the Inuktitut language, live in communities across the Arctic. The Métis are a distinct people of mixed Aboriginal and European ancestry who come from both French- and English-speaking backgrounds.

ABOUT 1,000 YEARS AGO: Leif Erikson leads a Viking expedition to the New World. The remains of a Viking settlement, L'Anse aux Meadows, in Newfoundland and Labrador, are a World Heritage Site.

1451 The Iroquois Confederacy is formed.

FIRST ROYAL VISIT

The first visit of the British king (the country's Head of State) to Canada happened more than 70 years after the country was formed. King George VI and his wife Queen Elizabeth made a six-week visit and toured the nation from coast to coast in 1939. Here they arrive in Vancouver.

First Canadian-born GG

If you think it took a long time for the nation to have a Canadian-born prime minister, you won't believe how long it took before the country had a native citizen appointed governor general. Vincent Massey, became the first Canadian-born GG in 1952, almost 90 years after the nation was born. Since 1952, all of Canada's governors general have been, and must be, Canadian citizens.

Longest serving politician

Here's serious dedication to Canada. Jean Chrétien, the nation's prime minister from November 4, 1993, to December 11, 2003, is also the country's longest-serving federal politician. Chrétien was first elected to the House of Commons on April 8, 1963, and served as a member of parliament for 35 years, 10 months and 25 days.

← **John Cabot**

1534-1542

Jacques Cartier makes three voyages across the Atlantic, claiming the land for France. In 1535 he becomes the first European to sail into the St. Lawrence River. Cartier hears two Indian guides talk about the route to "Kanata," the Iroquoian word for "village" or "settlement," and by 1547 maps designate everything north of the St. Lawrence as "Canada."

1497 Italian-born explorer John Cabot leads an English expedition to what is thought to have been Newfoundland and Labrador or Cape Breton Island. He claims a new continent for the King of England.

1576 In search of the Northwest Passage to Asia, British explorer Martin Frobisher reaches Baffin Island in what is now Nunavut. The Northwest Passage refers to a water route from the Atlantic to the Pacific Ocean and through Canada's Arctic Archipelago.

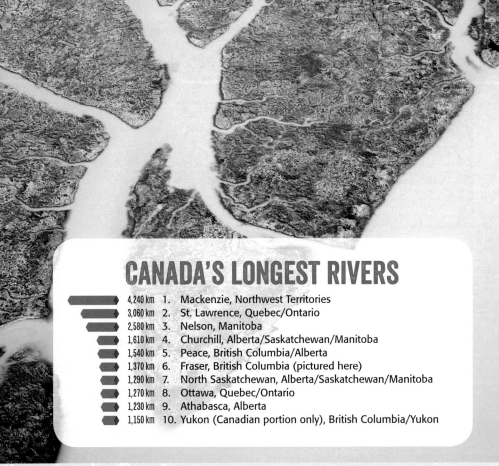

CANADA'S LONGEST RIVERS

4,240 km	1.	Mackenzie, Northwest Territories
3,060 km	2.	St. Lawrence, Quebec/Ontario
2,580 km	3.	Nelson, Manitoba
1,610 km	4.	Churchill, Alberta/Saskatchewan/Manitoba
1,540 km	5.	Peace, British Columbia/Alberta
1,370 km	6.	Fraser, British Columbia (pictured here)
1,290 km	7.	North Saskatchewan, Alberta/Saskatchewan/Manitoba
1,270 km	8.	Ottawa, Quebec/Ontario
1,230 km	9.	Athabasca, Alberta
1,150 km	10.	Yukon (Canadian portion only), British Columbia/Yukon

1608 Samuel de Champlain sets up a fur-trading post at the site of what is now Quebec City — Canada's oldest city.

1642 Montreal is founded as a mission and becomes a base for the fur trade.

1663 New France becomes a royal colony of the French Crown.

1670 The Hudson's Bay Company is established to trade for furs in what is today northern and western Canada.

1690-91 Henry Kelsey, a Hudson's Bay Company fur trader, becomes the first European to see the western prairies.

1713 The Treaty of Utrecht leaves Hudson Bay, Acadia and Newfoundland to Britain, and Cape Breton and St. John's Island (now Prince Edward Island) to France. (Acadia, founded in 1604, was a region in present-day Nova Scotia, New Brunswick, Prince Edward Island and the coastal area from the St. Lawrence River south into Maine.)

1725 Canada's population is just over 39,000.

Largest freshwater ecosystem

Looking for fresh water? Look no farther than the Great Lakes. Lake Ontario, Lake Erie, Lake Huron, Lake Michigan and Lake Superior form the world's largest freshwater ecosystem. It's estimated that a drop of water takes 400 years to travel from the system's headwaters in Lake Superior to the point where Lake Ontario meets the St. Lawrence River.

Biggest continuous body of fresh water

The Great Lakes are the world's biggest continuous body of fresh water. The Great Lakes basin contains about 18 percent of the world's fresh lake water.

More lakes

There are millions of lakes in Canada, so it's hardly surprising that our nation has more lake area than any other country. They're often big, too, with 563 lakes larger than 100 square km.

Largest freshwater lake

The greatest of the Great Lakes, Lake Superior is the largest freshwater lake in the world. It covers 82,100 square km, 28,700 of which are in Canada. It is 563 km long, 257 km wide and 406 m deep at its deepest point.

Most Canadian Great Lake

Canada shares four of the Great Lakes with the United States (Lake Michigan is wholly in the United States). But do you know which lake has the largest portion in Canada? Lake Huron, with a total of 36,000 of its 59,600 square km north of the border.

The Death of General Wolfe at the Battle of the Plains of Abraham. ➤

1755 The expulsion of the Acadians begins. About 10,000 Acadians who refuse to pledge allegiance to the British Crown must forfeit their property and are forced to leave the region.

1756 The Seven Years' War begins in North America and then spreads to Europe as Britain declares war on France.

1759 Quebec City falls to the British following the Battle of the Plains of Abraham. This is the key battle for North America and marks the end of France's empire in America. The commanders of both armies — Brigadier General James Wolfe and the Marquis de Montcalm — are both killed leading their troops in battle.

1763 The Seven Years' War ends with the Treaty of Paris. New France is formally ceded to Britain.

1774 The Quebec Act restores French laws and institutions in Quebec and extends the provincial boundary.

CANADA'S 10 BIGGEST LAKES

1. Lake Huron, Ont.
2. Great Bear Lake, N.W.T.
3. Lake Superior, Ont.
4. Great Slave Lake, N.W.T.
5. Lake Winnipeg, Man.
6. Lake Erie, Ont.
7. Lake Ontario, Ont.
8. Lake Athabasca, Sask.
9. Reindeer Lake, Sask./Man.
10. Smallwood Reservoir, Nfld.

Oldest part of North America

The Canadian Shield, which is about 4.4 million square km in size, covers about half of Canada and encircles Hudson Bay, was the first part of North America permanently above sea level. It is also the oldest section of the continent's crustal plate (a layer of the Earth's surface) and the largest area of exposed Precambrian rock (formed about 500 million years ago) on the planet.

1775 Loyalists (American colonists who supported the British during the American Revolution) begin to arrive in what are now the Maritime Provinces, Ontario, and Quebec. About 30,000 will eventually flee to Canada.

1783 The Treaty of Versailles officially marks the end of the War of American Independence as Great Britain recognizes the sovereignty of the United States. According to the terms of the treaty, the United States is granted a clearly defined border with Canada and the equal partition of the Great Lakes, except for Lake Michigan, which is granted to the Americans in full.

1791 The Province of Quebec is divided into two separate colonies—Upper Canada (roughly today's southern Ontario), in the western portion of the province; and Lower Canada (roughly today's southern Quebec), in the eastern portion.

1793 The Town of York (now Toronto) is established as the capital of Upper Canada.

Greenland

Nunavut

Northwest Territories

Hudson's Bay

CANADA'S 10 LARGEST ISLANDS

Eight out of 10 of Canada's largest islands are in Nunavut.

1. Baffin Island, Nunavut 507,451 km²
2. Victoria Island, Nunavut/ Northwest Territories, 217,291 km²
3. Ellesmere Island, Nunavut, 196,236 km²
4. Newfoundland, 111,390 km²
5. Banks Island, Northwest Territories, 70,028 km²
6. Devon Island, Nunavut, 55,247 km²
7. Axel Heiberg Island, Nunavut, 43,178 km²
8. Melville Island, Northwest Territories, 42,149 km²
9. Southhampton Island, Nunavut, 41,214 km²
10. Prince of Wales Island, Nunavut, 33,339 km²

Largest country with single border

Canada is the world's largest nation with only one land border with another country (the United States).

The Underground Railroad →

1812 The War of 1812 (1812–14) begins as U.S. forces invade Canada. The attempt to conquer Canada fails as the result of the efforts of Canada's volunteers and First Nations, supported by British soldiers. The present-day Canada–U.S. border is partly a result of that war.

1833 The British Parliament abolishes slavery throughout its empire. Thousands of slaves escape from the United States and reach Canada by way of the Underground Railroad, a secret network for fugitive slaves.

1834 York goes back to its original name, Toronto, and is incorporated as a city.

1837-38 Rebellions against British rule take place in Upper and Lower Canada.

LONGEST RECREATIONAL TRAIL

The Trans Canada Trail is the world's longest recreational trail. It is a 17,000 km network of close to 500 trails that runs across the country from the Atlantic to the Pacific oceans, connecting hundreds of communities. The trail, established in 1992, is still being expanded and will measure 24,000 km and go through every province and territory once completed.

Longest undefended border

Who says good fences make good neighbours? Since the War of 1812, Canada and the United States have shared the world's longest undefended border—8,890 km. The border is marked on land by a 6-m wide, tree-free swath and 5,528 boundary monuments. There are also 2,457 reference monuments marking the water boundary.

1839-49

Reformers such as Louis-Hippolyte La Fontaine and Robert Baldwin work together toward responsible government. Under responsible government, the support of the majority of elected representatives is required. This system, which is responsible to the people, is the one that Canada has today.

← Canada's first postage stamp

1841 Upper Canada (renamed Canada West) and Lower Canada (renamed Canada East) are united as the Province of Canada.

1851 The Three-Pence Beaver, Canada's first postage stamp, is issued.

1857 Queen Victoria chooses Ottawa to be the capital for the Province of Canada. Although it is a logging town far from the colony's main cities, it is the only sizable settlement located on the border of Canada East and Canada West.

First marine protected area

Canada's first federal marine protected area is considered to be Bird Rocks Migratory Bird Sanctuary. Located in the Gulf of St. Lawrence near the Magdalen Islands, the Bird Rocks and a 1-km zone around them (including the water) was established as a sanctuary in 1919.

First Canadian atlas

In 1906, the first edition of the *Atlas of Canada* was published by the federal Department of the Interior. It was one of the first national atlases in the world. At the time, Canada's population was seven million. Thirty percent of the people lived in 15 towns and cities with populations of more than 25,000. The sixth edition, published online in 1999, was one of the world's first online atlases.

Highest Arctic land area ⤵

Canada's Arctic Archipelago is the largest high-Arctic land area in the world, apart from Greenland (which is almost entirely covered in ice and geologically part of the archipelago). The chain is made up of 94 islands larger than 130 square km and 36,469 smaller islands. It has six of the world's 30 largest islands.

1864-67

Representatives of Nova Scotia, New Brunswick and the Province of Canada work to establish a new country. These men, known as the Fathers of Confederation, create two levels of government—federal and provincial. The Province of Canada is split into two new provinces—Ontario and Quebec—which, with New Brunswick and Nova Scotia, form the Dominion of Canada.

1866 The two western colonies of Vancouver Island and the British Columbia mainland unite to form the single colony of British Columbia.

1867 The British Parliament passes the British North America Act, and the Dominion of Canada is officially born on July 1. John A. Macdonald is selected the country's first prime minister.

1869-70

The Hudson's Bay Company sells Rupert's Land to the Government of Canada but fails to consider the existing residents—mainly Métis and Indians. The Métis of the Red River Colony are concerned that they will lose their land rights and culture. Under Louis Riel they mount a rebellion.

"Great" Canadian places

These are literally "Great" Canadian places:

- Great Barachois Lake, NS
- Great Barasway Lookout, NL
- Great Barasway Pond, NL
- Great Barren Lake, NS
- Great Bear Lake, NT
- Great Bear River, NT
- Great Bear Creek, BC
- Great Beaver Lake, BC
- Great Black Island, NL
- Great Brook, NL
- Great Burnt Island, NL
- Great Buse, NL
- Great Calf Island, NS
- Great Chain Island, BC
- Great Coat Island, NL
- Great Colinet Island, NL
- Great Cormorandier Island, NL
- Great Denier Island, NL
- Great Duck Island, NB
- Great Duck Island, ON
- Great Eastern Pond, NL
- Great Falls, NS
- Great Falls, MB
- Great French Beach, NL
- Great Gulch River, NL
- Great Gull Lake, NL
- Great Gull River, NL
- Great Hill, NS
- Great Island, NL
- Great Island, NS
- Great Island, MB
- Great Jervis Island, NL
- Great La Cloche Island, ON
- Great Lake, ON
- Great Manitou Island, ON
- Great Mountain, NL
- Great Mountain Lake, ON
- Great Northern Mountain, NL
- Great Pike Lake, ON
- Great Pine Lake, NS
- Great Pond, NL
- Great Pond, NB
- Great Portage Lake, ON
- Great Pubnico Lake, NS
- Great Rattling Brook, NL
- Great Ridge, NS
- Great Rock Peak, BC
- Great Sacred Island, NL
- Great Sand Hills, SK
- Great Seal Island, NL
- Great Slave Lake, NT
- Great Snow Mountain, BC
- Great Thrum, NS
- Great Tinker Island, NL
- Great Verdon Island, NL
- Great Village River, NS
- Great West Ridge, AB

1870 Canada adds the provinces of Manitoba (1870), British Columbia (1871) and Prince Edward Island (1873).

1871 The first census of the Dominion of Canada lists the population at 3,485,761 (Ontario—1,620,851; Quebec—1,191,516; Nova Scotia—387,800; New Brunswick—285,594).

1873 The North-West Mounted Police (now the Royal Canadian Mounted Police) is formed.

1875 The first recorded indoor ice hockey game takes place at the Victoria Skating Rink in Montreal.

1876 Alexander Graham Bell makes the first one-way long-distance telephone call.

1879 Canadian engineer Sandford Fleming devises the concept of Universal Standard Time (UST), which divides the world into 24 time zones. UST goes into effect in 1885.

1885 The five-month-long North-West Rebellion, fought mainly by Métis and their Aboriginal allies against the Canadian government and led by Louis Riel, is forcibly ended. Louis Riel is hanged for high treason.

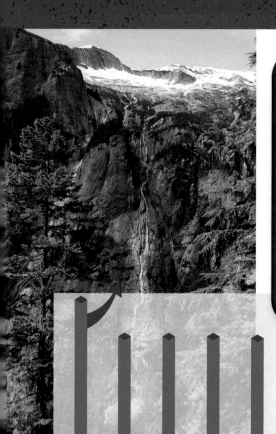

HIGHEST WATERFALLS

When it comes to waterfalls, much debate surrounds the question of which are the tallest. After all, many of them fall in a series of cascades, so where to start and end when measuring them is often a matter of discussion. Here's the list of the 10 highest waterfalls in Canada from worldwaterfalldatabase.com. All of them are in British Columbia.

James Bruce Falls	Gold Creek Falls	Unnamed waterfall	Unnamed waterfall	Lady Peak Falls	Madden Falls	Rugged Glacier Falls	Daniels River Falls	Swiftcurrent Falls	Marion Falls
840 m	610 m	610 m	610 m	600 m	579 m	560 m	540 m	537 m	527 m

1885 The Canadian Pacific Railway links Montreal to Port Moody, British Columbia. Donald Smith hammers in the "last spike"—a symbol of unity. The railway was built by both European and Chinese labour. The Chinese faced discrimination, which included an entry fee called the "Head Tax." The government apologized in 2006.

1885 Canada's National Park system begins at Banff in Alberta.

1896 Gold is discovered in the Klondike region near Dawson, Yukon, leading to the Gold Rush of 1897–99.

1896 Wilfrid Laurier becomes Canada's first French-Canadian prime minister.

1898 The Yukon is split from the North-West territories and enters Confederation.

1905 The provinces of Alberta and Saskatchewan are carved out of the North-West territories and enter Confederation.

1908 Governor General Earl Grey strikes the first coin produced in Canada, a 50-cent piece. Currency is no longer imported from England.

Longest place names

Sympathies if one these place names, the nation's longest, is in your address.

	Place name	Type	Prov.	Characters
1.	Dysart, Dudley, Harcourt, Guilford, Harburn, Bruton, Havelock, Eyre and Clyde	Township municipality	ON	68
2.	Cape St. George-Petit Jardin-Grand Jardin-De Grau-Marches Point-Loretto	Community	NFD	65
3.	L'Annonciation-de-la-Bienheureuse-Vierge-Marie-de-Nazareth	Geographical area	QC	58
4.	Stanley Bridge, Hope River, Bayview, Cavendish and North Rustico	Village	PEI	56
5.	L'Immaculée-Conception -de-la-Bienheureuse-Vierge-Marie	Geographical area	QC	54
6.	Cours d'eau du Cordon des Terres des Sixième et Septième Rangs	Stream	QC	52
7.	Cours d'eau de la Concession Sud-Est du Rang Saint-David	Stream	QC	48
8.	Décharge des Neuvième Dixième et Onzième Concessions	Stream	QC	46
9.	Lower North Branch Little Southwest Miramichi River Embranchement des Rangs Saint-Georges et Séraphine (tie)	Stream Stream	NB QC	45
10.	Cours d'eau des Cinquième et Sixième Rangs de Milton	Stream	QC	44

The original edition of *Anne of Green Gables* ➤

1908 Lucy Maud Montgomery publishes *Anne of Green Gables*, the first of several novels about Anne Shirley, who becomes a famous literary character.

1910 Canada's population is recorded at about seven million.

1912 The Northwest Territories (which entered Confederation in 1870 as the North-West Territories) assumes new boundaries. These boundaries remain until 1999, when Nunavut is created.

1914-18 The First World War. Canada makes great contributions but suffers great losses, with more than 65,000 dead and 175,000 wounded. More than 650,000 Canadians and Newfoundlanders (Newfoundland was not yet a province) serve in the war, out of a population of only eight million. The Canadian Corps captures Vimy Ridge in 1917—a major victory over German forces, but at a great cost, with more than 10,000 killed and wounded.

How is rain measured?

Rain, drizzle, freezing rain, freezing drizzle and hail are usually measured by using different gauges, depending on the network reporting the totals.

The Environment Canada networks use automated total precipitation weighing gauges (Geonor & Pluvio) which determine precipitation amounts through weight change. These gauges report total precipitation amounts hourly, in millimetres.

Staffed reporting stations use the standard Canadian Type B rain gauge, a cylindrical container 40 cm high and 11.3 cm in diameter. The precipitation is then funnelled into a plastic measuring tube that is calibrated to show the precipitation amount in millimetres. Precipitation is typically measured every six hours with a total amount reported at the end of the day.

How is snow measured?

At Environment Canada, snow is measured by automated observing stations which register the snowfall and snow-on-ground amounts, using an acoustic snow sensor (SR-50). The automated sites report snowfall amounts hourly in centimetres.

At staffed stations, the snow amount or the depth of accumulated snow-on-ground is measured using a snow ruler or a ruler calibrated to centimetres. The measurements are made at several points which appear representative of the immediate area, and then averaged. Snow is normally measured in "centimetres".

Also note that snowfall amounts are not measured at a number of Environment Canada and partner's stations as the automated equipment is not capable of this measurement.

A Canadian machine gun emplacement on the crest of Vimy Ridge, April 1917

1916 Women win the right to vote in Manitoba, Saskatchewan, and Alberta. (They win the right in the other provinces and territories in 1917 (British Columbia and Ontario); 1918 (Nova Scotia); 1919 (New Brunswick and Yukon); 1922 (Prince Edward Island); 1925 (Newfoundland and Labrador); 1940 (Quebec); and 1951 (Northwest Territories). At the time of Confederation, the vote was limited to property-owning white males. The effort by women to achieve the right to vote is known as the women's suffrage movement. Its founder in Canada was Dr. Emily Stowe, the first woman to practise medicine in the country.

Coldest year

It seems fair to call it Canada's coldest year: in 1972, every weather-reporting station in the country reported annual temperatures below average, the only time on record this ever happened.

Cold in 1947

1947 was a particularly cool year in northwestern Canada. Check out these other Canadian low temperature records:

Location	°C	Date in 1947
Mayo, YT	−62.2	February 3
Watson Lake, YT	−58.9	January 31
Norman Wells, NWT	−54.4	February 4
Whitehorse, YT	−52.2	January 31
Fort Nelson, BC	−51.7	January 30
Dease Lake, BC	−51.2	January 31
Yellowknife, NWT	−51.2	January 31
Fort McMurray, AB	−50.6	February 1

Canada is pretty cool

Canada is just about the coolest country—literally. It vies with Russia for first place as the coldest nation in the world, with an average daily annual temperature of −5.6°C.

Killing cold

Deadly cold. More Canadians die each year from exposure to extreme cold temperatures than from other natural events, according to Statistics Canada. An average of 108 people die annually from the cold, while only 17 succumb to other nature-related events.

Hottest year

The hottest year: 1998. Canada recorded its second warmest winter and warmest spring, summer and fall. Temperatures that year were an average 2.4°C higher than typical.

Crowd gathered outside old City Hall during the Winnipeg General Strike, June 21, 1919.

1917 A fire on a French munitions ship sets off the Halifax Explosion, killing about 1,600 and injuring another 9,000.

1917 The National Hockey League is founded. Teams include the Montreal Canadiens, the Montreal Wanderers, the Ottawa Senators, the Toronto Arenas and Quebec Bulldogs.

1919 Women gain the right to vote in federal elections. (The Military Voters Act of 1917 had previously granted that right to nurses and women in the military.)

1919 The Winnipeg General Strike begins and lasts for six weeks. More than 30,000 workers stop working because of poor wages and conditions.

Warming country

All of Canada has become warmer since the mid-20th century. Between 1948 and 2007, the nation's average temperature rose by 1.4°C.

Provinces getting colder

Other places in Canada have also seen average seasonal temperatures that don't follow the overall warming trend. Since 1948, the Atlantic provinces have grown colder in winter, and in the months of September, October and November, average temperatures decreased in Alberta, Saskatchewan, Manitoba, the Yukon and northern British Columbia.

Invention of the UV index

For a nation that's undoubtedly well known for its cool climate, it seems somewhat surprising that Canadians invented the UV Index, a measure of the intensity of the sun's ultraviolet radiation in the sunburn spectrum. As UV increases, the sun's rays can do more damage to skin, eyes and the immune system. In 1992, scientists at Environment Canada developed the index as a health protection tool for Canadians, and it is now forecast for 48 locations across the country.

Cities ranked by climate

Here is the Climate Severity Index for select Canadian cities:

City	Index	City	Index	City	Index
Victoria	15	Saskatoon	42	Saint John	48
Vancouver	19	Montreal	43	Regina	49
Calgary	35	Ottawa	44	Winnipeg	51
Toronto	36	Whitehorse	46	Quebec City	53
Edmonton	37	Halifax	47	Yellowknife	57
Fredericton	41	Charlottetown	48	St. John's	56

Agnes Macphail

Banting and Best ↘

1920 The Group of Seven, known for their paintings of wilderness landscapes, is formed.

1921 Agnes Macphail becomes the first woman elected to Parliament.

1921 The fishing schooner *Bluenose*, launched in Lunenburg, Nova Scotia, wins the international schooner championship.

1922 Frederick Banting, Charles Best, and others discover insulin treatment for diabetes.

1924 The Royal Canadian Air Force is formed.

1929-39 The Great Depression—a period of severe economic hardship—finds up to 25 percent of the Canadian labour force out of work.

FEATHERED GIANTS

The giant Canada goose, a subspecies of Canada geese, is the largest goose species in the world. It can weight more than nine kilograms and is known to be long-lived, with one individual recorded to have lived more than 30 years.

Real snowbirds

Canada is better known for snowbirds (those who travel to warmer southern places in winter) than for lovebirds, but there is one—only one—feathered flyer that breeds only in Canada. The Harris' sparrow nests in regions across the nation where the boreal forest meets Arctic tundra.

National Horse

Did you know Canada has an officially recognized national horse species? The Canadian horse, a breed that was developed in the 17th and 18th centuries in New France (present-day Quebec), was declared the country's national breed in 1909, and in May 2002, it was recognized as our national horse. The Canadian is known for its great strength, endurance, resilience, intelligence and good temper.

1930 Cairine Wilson becomes the first woman appointed to the Canadian Senate.

1930-39 A severe drought, beginning in areas of Saskatchewan, spreads within the province and into Alberta and Manitoba. The period of the Great Depression—along with the drought and dust storms of the prairies—is known as the "dirty thirties."

1931 The Statute of Westminster is passed by the British Parliament. It grants Britain's former colonies, including Canada, full legal freedom.

1937 Joseph-Armand Bombardier invents the snowmobile.

1939-45 The Second World War. The Canadian military plays an important role in the war, with action in Dieppe, France; the invasion of Italy; D-Day landings; the liberation of the Netherlands; and the final defeat of Germany. More than one million Canadians and Newfoundlanders serve in the military—over 45,000 give their lives, and another 55,000 are wounded. Canada's population at the time is only 11.5 million.

Most widespread tree

It figures that an evergreen (coniferous) tree would be the most wide-spread in Canada. But do you know which species? The white spruce is found almost everywhere in the country.

Disappearing forests

Here's a disappointing distinction. Canada had the largest forest loss in the world per capita between 2000 and 2012. Two-thirds of a hectare disappeared for each person in the country in that time.

Largest wildlife conservation organization

World Wildlife Fund Canada is the nation's largest international conservation organization. More than 150,000 Canadians support the organization, whose mission is to "stop the degradation of the planet's natural environment and to build a future in which humans live in harmony with nature."

Greenpeace ship *Arctic Sunrise*.

Most visible environmental ↗ organization

Greenpeace, a well-known international environmental organization, was founded in Vancouver in 1971. It claims it's the most visible environmental organization on the globe, with offices in more than 40 countries and 2.8 million supporters around the world.

1941 The federal government allows women to enlist in the army.

1942 The Canadian government announces plans to move all Canadians of Japanese origin on the country's west coast to inland camps. Their property is sold without compensation. In 1988, the Canadian government apologized and compensated the victims.

↑ **Tommy Douglas**

1944 T.C. (Tommy) Douglas leads the Co-operative Commonwealth Federation to power in Saskatchewan. He introduces the universal health-insurance system that would eventually be adopted across Canada.

1946 The *Canadian Citizenship Act* is passed. Canadian citizens are no longer classified as British subjects first.

1947-54 Major oil strikes take place in Alberta and Saskatchewan.

1948 Japanese-Canadians, the last group of Canadians of Asian descent, are granted the right to vote.

Marine wildlife organization
Sea Shepherd Conservation Society, an international non-profit organization dedicated to marine wildlife conservation, was formed in 1981 by captain Paul Watson (born in Toronto on December 2, 1950). The idea for the organization stemmed from an earlier conservation group formed by Watson, the Earth Force Society, in 1977 in Vancouver. Watson was also one of the co-founders of Greenpeace.

LONGEST MAMMAL MIGRATION

The humpback whale makes the longest migration of any mammal on the planet. The species travels up to 8,500 km one way. The north Pacific population travels through Canadian waters journeys from Alaska to the tropical seas near Hawaii.

1949 Newfoundland (today, Newfoundland and Labrador) officially enters Confederation to become Canada's 10th province.

1951 Canada's population is recorded at about 14 million.

1952 Lester B. Pearson is named president of the United Nations General Assembly.

1952 Vincent Massey becomes the first Canadian-born governor general.

1957 Lester B. Pearson is awarded the Nobel Peace Prize for his role in settling the Suez Crisis in the Middle East.

1959 The St. Lawrence Seaway—a system of canals, dams, and locks—is completed. It stretches for 3,790 km inland from the Atlantic Ocean to Lake Superior and is the world's longest inland waterway connected to ocean shipping.

1959 The Avro Arrow—a supersonic fighter plane developed in Canada—is scrapped in a decision that remains controversial.

Fastest bird

You do NOT want to be the prey of the peregrine falcon. Why? When hunting, peregrines can dive at more than 300 km per hour, making them the fastest bird in the world. The highest recorded speed of a peregrine is reported to be 389 km per hour. Here's hoping the prey don't even see it coming.

Biggest animal

The biggest animal on Earth calls Canada home (at least part of the time). Blue whales, which can grow up to 27 m long and weigh up to 132 tonnes, are found in Canadian waters along Canada's east coast. Not only are blue whales the largest creature on the planet, they're also the loudest. Their cry can reach 186 decibels, louder than a jet plane.

Biggest fish

The largest fish swimming in Canadian waters is the basking shark, which can grow to more than 6 m long and weigh up to 4,500 kg. It's also the second-largest shark and fish in the world. Basking sharks are often seen in Canadian waters in the summer and fall near coastal areas of Atlantic Canada.

Longest bird migration

Too bad there are no frequent flyer miles for birds. If there were, the Arctic tern would earn lots of free flights. After all, the small seabird, which summers in Canada's north, has the longest migration of any bird in the world. It travels some 40,000 km from its Arctic breeding grounds to its winter home near Antarctica and back again.

1960 Aboriginal peoples are granted the right to vote in federal elections without losing their treaty status.

1960 The "Quiet Revolution" — a period of political, social and educational changes — begins in Quebec.

1960 The Canadian Bill of Rights, setting out the rights of Canadians, becomes law.

1962 The Trans-Canada Highway, which today links St. John's in Newfoundland with Victoria in British Columbia, opens at British Columbia's Rogers Pass. At 7,821 km, it is one of the world's longest highways.

1965 After months of debate, Canada adopts the maple leaf flag.

↟ Longest butterfly migration

It weighs about as much as a paper clip, but the monarch butterfly doesn't let its small size get in the way of travelling great distances. The monarch butterfly makes the longest migration of all insect species. Experts believe that monarchs travel at least 4,600 km, but it's possible that they fly twice as far as that. Individuals migrate from southern Canada to wintering areas in Mexico each fall.

Most polar bears

Canada has two-thirds of the Earth's population of polar bears, the world's largest terrestrial carnivore. Adult males average between 400 and 600 kg, with some exceeding 800 kg. Polar bears are also the largest species of bears.

World's deadliest creature

Believe it or not, what many consider the world's deadliest creature lives right here in Canada. And they're found virtually everywhere. Fortunately for Canadians, the mosquito's bite here is largely just itchy. Around the world, however, mosquitoes carry and pass along malaria-causing parasites. The World Heath Organization estimates that in 2010 malaria killed between 537,000 and 907,000 people, mostly children under five years old in Africa.

The Expo 67 ➤
Ontario pavilion.

1967 Canada celebrates the 100th anniversary of Confederation and hosts Expo 67 in Montreal. The World's Fair attracts more than 50 million visitors.

1969 The *Official Languages Act* comes into force, declaring English and French as the official languages of Canada.

1970 The October Crisis is triggered when the Front de libération du Québec, a revolutionary organization, kidnaps British diplomat James Cross and Quebec cabinet minister Pierre Laporte, who is later killed.

Largest rodent ↑

Know what Canada's largest rodent is? We're so proud of it we put it on our nickel, and it's celebrated as a symbol of Canadianism. Yes, the beaver—which attained official status as a national emblem on March 24, 1975.

Smallest mammal

They weigh just 12.4 g, so it's little wonder that the pygmy shrew is the smallest mammal in the Americas. Looking like something between a mouse and a mole, shrews are small: the pygmy's average length is about 5.1 to 6.4 cm. They can be found throughout most of eastern Canada.

Birds' deadliest enemies

Sorry cat lovers, but your cuddly kittens are actually brutal killers. According to a 2013 study by Environment Canada, predation by cats is the largest human-related cause of death for birds in Canada. Urban pet cats are estimated to be responsible for about one-sixth of all bird deaths in the country, while feral cats (just 25 percent of all cats) are responsible for 59 percent of bird deaths. Outdoor cats are estimated to be responsible for the deaths of between 105 and 348 million birds per year.

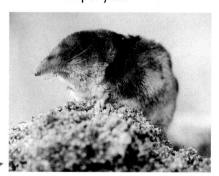

Canada's smallest mammal, the pygmy shrew, shown here life-sized. ↗

Paul Henderson celebrates scoring the ↙ "goal of the century."

Terry Fox in Toronto, ↙ July 12, 1980 during his Marathon of Hope.

1972 With 34 seconds remaining in the final hockey game, Team Canada defeats the Soviet Union four games to three, with one game tied. Paul Henderson scores the final goal in what has been called the "goal of the century."

1976 Montreal hosts the Summer Olympics.

1980 "O Canada" is officially proclaimed the national anthem, 100 years after it was first sung.

1980 British Columbian Terry Fox runs his Marathon of Hope, from St. John's in Newfoundland and Labrador to Thunder Bay in Ontario. Fox died in 1981, but not before realizing his dream of raising one dollar for every person in Canada. His legacy continues with fund-raising events in his name.

Most expensive office space

According to JLL, a commercial real estate and investment management company, the Canadian cities where offices are most expensive to rent, by square foot, are Toronto ($68.52), Calgary ($59.06) and Vancouver ($58.87).

Oldest company

The Hudson's Bay Company, founded in 1670, is North America's oldest continuously operating company. In its earliest days, the business was instrumental in European development in the country, particularly its eastern half, where numerous outposts were set up to trade goods. Today, HBC runs the country's largest department store, with 90 locations across the nation.

First Hudson's Bay blankets

The first of the now-famous, classic Hudson's Bay Company point blankets, known for their bands of colour, were shipped to HBC posts on a regular basis in the spring of 1780.

Largest private employer

Loblaw Companies Limited, whose offerings include grocery, pharmacy, health and beauty, apparel, general merchandise, banking and wireless mobile products and services, is considered the largest private-sector employer in Canada. The company, its franchises and associate-owners employ some 192,000 people across the nation.

Biggest uranium producer

Canada is the globe's largest producer of uranium, accounting for 18 percent of the world's production of the element. (Uranium is processed to create fuel for nuclear reactors.)

Marc Garneau ➤

1982 Canada adopts its Constitution, with a Charter of Rights and Freedoms. Among the rights found in the Charter are freedom of conscience and religion; Aboriginal peoples' rights; and mobility rights (the right of each citizen to enter, remain in and leave Canada).

1982 Jeanne Sauvé becomes the first woman appointed Canada's governor general.

1984 Astronaut Marc Garneau, aboard the space shuttle *Challenger*, becomes the first Canadian in space.

1987 Canada introduces the one-dollar coin, which, because of the loon on the reverse side, earns the nickname "loonie."

1987-90 The government tries to win Quebec's consent to the Constitution Act, 1982, through the Meech Lake Accord but does not receive the support of all the provinces.

First grain distillery

John Molson opened the nation's first industrial grain distillery. The Molson distillery became the first exporter of Canadian-made spirits to England, and it was the country's largest distillery until it closed in 1866.

Biggest zinc producer

Canada is one of the world's largest producers of zinc. Zinc is primarily used to galvanize steel against corrosion. The Teck Trail Operation in British Columbia is one of the world's largest, highest-margin, fully integrated zinc and lead smelting and refining operations.

MOST NEWSPRINT

With all that tree-covered hinterland, is it any wonder that Canada is the world's largest exporter of market pulp and newsprint? The forestry industry contributes up to three percent of the nation's gross domestic product; more than $34 billion in forest products are exported annually.

↖ **Confederation Bridge in PEI**

1988 Calgary hosts the Winter Olympics.

1992 The Charlottetown Accord, an attempt to amend the Constitution and obtain Quebec's consent to the Constitution Act, 1982, is rejected by a national referendum.

1994 Canada, the United States and Mexico sign the North American Free Trade Agreement (NAFTA).

1995 A referendum in Quebec, calling for the province's independence from the rest of Canada, is narrowly defeated.

1997 Confederation Bridge opens, linking Prince Edward Island and New Brunswick. The curved, 12.9-km bridge is the longest in the world crossing ice-covered waters.

↑ Biggest airline

It serves a customer base as large as the country's population. Air Canada is the nation's largest full-service airline. The company moves 35 million passengers each year to more than 175 destinations around the world.

Largest grocery chain

Grab a grocery cart. Loblaw Companies Limited is the country's largest food retailer, attracting more than 14 million shoppers to its stores every week. It operates more than 1,000 stores across the country, including Loblaws, Independent, Valu-mart, Zehrs, No Frills, Real Canadian Superstore, Maxi, SaveEasy and Extra Foods.

Biggest flaxseed producer

Canada is well known as a producer of a number of agricultural crops. Among them is flaxseed, and Canada is the world's largest producer, accounting for 40 percent of global production. Flaxseed is principally grown on the prairies and used for linseed oil, which is used as a drying oil in paints and varnish and in the production of linoleum and printing inks.

Oldest chartered bank

If you're looking for a Canadian financial institution with a long history, look no further than the Bank of Montreal, the nation's oldest chartered bank. Established in 1871, it served as the banker for the Canadian government from 1863 until 1935, when the Bank of Canada was formed.

Alexandre Bilodeau ↘

1999 Nunavut, the eastern part of the Northwest Territories, officially becomes a self-governing territory. Iqaluit, previously called Frobisher Bay, is its capital.

2001 The name of Newfoundland is changed to Newfoundland and Labrador to better reflect the province's geography and people.

2010 Vancouver hosts the Winter Olympics. Freestyle moguls skier Alexandre Bilodeau becomes the first-ever athlete to claim a gold medal on Canadian soil.

2015 Canada's population is recorded at about 35.7 million.

MOST COMMON COW

The Holstein is the most common dairy cow breed in Canada, accounting for 94 percent of the country's cows.

Biggest bulk food store

Bulk Barn is Canada's largest bulk food retailer. First opened in 1982, the company now has more than 200 locations across the country. Bulk Barn offers more than 4,000 products, everything from nuts and spices to pet food.

First international bank

The Bank of Montreal was the first Canadian financial institution to have agencies beyond the country's borders. In 1818 it established representatives in London and New York.

CANADA'S PRIME MINISTERS

This is a list of all of Canada's prime ministers, including their terms, their political parties, their birth places and other information.

1 John Alexander Macdonald
1815–1891

Birthplace: Scotland

Profession(s): Lawyer

Political party: Liberal-Conservative

Member of Parliament (MP) for: Kingston, Ontario; Victoria, British Columbia; Carleton, Ontario

Terms: 1867–73; 1878–91

Magazine with largest circulation

Maclean's has the largest circulation of any weekly magazine in Canada. Each of the publication's 44 issues per year are circulated to more than 310,000 people. The magazine reaches an estimated 2.4 million readers.

Biggest publisher

Rogers Publishing, a division of Rogers Media, is the nation's largest publisher. It produces both consumer and industry magazines, including well known Canadian titles such as *Maclean's*, *Chatelaine*, *Flare*, *Hello! Canada*, *Canadian Business* and *L'actualité*. In all, it publishes some 75,000 magazine pages annually.

TRANS-CANADA TELEPHONE SYSTEM

The first "trans-Canada" telephone system was completed in 1932. It covered Toronto, Montreal, Quebec City, Hamilton and Windsor.

---

2 Alexander Mackenzie
1822–1892

Birthplace: Scotland

Professions: Businessman, editor, stonemason

Political party: Liberal Party of Canada

MP for: Lambton, Ontario

Term: 1873–78

3 John Joseph Caldwell
Abbott 1821–1893

Birthplace: St. Andrews, Lower Canada

Professions: Dean, lawyer, professor

Political party: Liberal-Conservative

Senator for: Quebec

Term: 1891–92

4 John Sparrow David
Thompson 1845–1894

Birthplace: Halifax, Nova Scotia

Professions: Lawyer, lecturer

Political party: Liberal-Conservative

MP for: Antigonish, Nova Scotia

Term: 1892–94

First PM born in Canada

First trans-Canada broadcast

It was a special Canada Day. On July 1, 1927, Prime Minister Mackenzie King spoke to Canadians from Parliament Hill in the first trans-Canada radio broadcast. The milestone event included a variety of other speeches and performances in recognition of the Diamond Jubilee of Canada's Confederation.

First televised opening of Parliament

The opening of Parliament was broadcast on television in Canada for the first time in 1955.

First televised question period

The CBC began to broadcast question periods from the House of Commons live for the first time in 1977. In the first few weeks of broadcasts, several MPs wore sunglasses to avoid the bright television lights.

FIRST TELEVISED DEBATE

The first televised debate by leaders of political parties in Canada (involving Tommy Douglas, Pierre Trudeau, Robert Stanfield and Réal Caouette) took place on June 9, 1968.

5 Mackenzie Bowell
1823–1917

Birthplace: England

Professions: Editor, printer

Political party: Conservative

Senator for: Ontario

Term: 1894–96

6 Charles Tupper
1821–1915

Birthplace: Amherst, Nova Scotia

Professions: Diplomat, physician

Political party: Conservative

Did not serve in Parliament while Prime Minister

Term: 1896

7 Wilfrid Laurier
1841–1919

Birthplace: Saint-Lin, Canada East

Profession(s): Lawyer

Political party: Liberal

MP for: Quebec East, Quebec

Term: 1896–1911

First television satellite

Launched on January 17, 1976, Hermes, a collaborative effort between Canada and the United States, was the first satellite to broadcast television signals into homes. The most powerful satellite at the time, Hermes demonstrated direct broadcasting to Peru, Australia and Papua New Guinea, in addition to experiments conducted in Canada and the United States.

Third nation in space

Canada became the third nation in space—after the United States and the U.S.S.R.—on September 29, 1962, with the launch of the research satellite Alouette-I. Designed to last for one year, the satellite ultimately performed flawlessly for 10 years.

First Earth observation satellite ↑

The first high-resolution satellite image ever taken of the South Pole was captured in 1997 from Canada's first Earth observation satellite system, RADARSAT-1. Launched on November 4, 1995, RADARSAT-1 was capable of acquiring images of Earth in any conditions, day or night, rain or shine.

First communications satellite

The Anik A1 was the world's first domestic geostationary communications satellite system. It was launched on November 9, 1972. The system enabled Telesat Canada to provide high-quality telephone service to Canada's north and television service across the country.

---

8 Robert Laird Borden
1854–1937

Birthplace: Grand Pré, Nova Scotia

Profession: Lawyer

MP for: Halifax, Nova Scotia; Kings, Nova Scotia

Terms: 1911–17 (Conservative Party); 1917–20 (Unionist Party)

9 Arthur Meighen
1874–1960

Birthplace: Anderson, Ontario

Profession: Lawyer

MP for: Portage la Prairie, Manitoba

Terms: 1920–21 (National Liberal and Conservative Party); 1926 (Conservative Party)

10 William Lyon Mackenzie King 1874–1950

Birthplace: Berlin (Kitchener), Ontario

Professions: Author, editor, journalist, lawyer, senior public servant

Political party: Liberal

MP for: North York, Ontario; Prince Albert, Saskatchewan; Glengarry, Ontario

Terms: 1921–26; 1926–30; 1935–48

Halftone photographic printing

Canadians Georges-Édouard Desbarats and William Leggo are credited with the invention of halftone photographic printing. The process was first unveiled in print in 1869 in the *Canadian Illustrated News*, a publication Desbarats had founded.

William Leggo, co-inventor of halftone printing.

SUGAR-FREE POP AND POPCANS

A couple more firsts for the pop industry from the makers of Canada Dry: During the 1950s and 1960s, the company was the first of the major soft drink makers to market sugar-free beverages, and the first to put pop in cans.

11 **Richard Bedford Bennett**
1870–1947

Birthplace: Hopewell, New Brunswick

Professions: Lawyer, teacher

Political party: Conservative

MP for: Calgary West, Alberta

Term: 1930–35

12 **Louis Stephen St-Laurent**
1882–1973

Birthplace: Compton, Quebec

Professions: Lawyer, professor

Political party: Liberal

MP for: Quebec East, Quebec

Term: 1948–57

13 **John George Diefenbaker**
1895–1979

Birthplace: Neustadt, Ontario

Profession: Lawyer

Political party: Progressive Conservative

MP for: Prince Albert, Saskatchewan

Term: 1957–63

Strongest magnet

Here's a record that had a lot of pull. Until late in 2014, Canada was home to the world's strongest magnet dedicated to studying solids, and the strongest magnet in the nation, period. The magnet, housed at the Canadian National Ultrahigh-Field NMR Facility for Solids in Ottawa, was used by scientists from Canada and around the world, and had been operated since 2005.

First Canadian stamp

In 1851, the first Canadian postage stamp, the Three-Pence Beaver, was designed by Sir Sandford Fleming. The design was one of the first in the world to feature a pictorial, as opposed to a portrait of a monarch, a statesman, a geometric design or a coat-of-arms. The first of these stamps was issued on April 23 of that year.

Artificial fur

A Canadian project during the Second World War to develop better Arctic clothing for the military led to the first patent for artificial fur.

Alkaline battery

You'll get a charge out of this one. Canadian Lewis Urry invented the alkaline battery in 1959. About 80 percent of dry cell batteries in use in the world are based on Urry's invention.

Anti-torpedo gear

The Canadian Anti-Acoustic Torpedo (CAT) gear was created during the Second World War. This was a countermeasure to acoustic torpedoes and was deployed on a cable near the ship to deflect an attack. CAT is credited with saving many ships from torpedoes.

---

14 Lester Bowles Pearson
1897–1972

Birthplace: Newtonbrook, Ontario

Professions: Author, diplomat, professor, senior public servant

Political party: Liberal

MP for: Algoma East, Ontario

Term: 1963–68

15 Pierre Elliott Trudeau
1919–2000

Birthplace: Montreal, Quebec

Professions: Lawyer, professor, writer

Political party: Liberal

MP for: Mount Royal, Quebec

Terms: 1968–79; 1980–84

16 Charles Joseph ("Joe") Clark 1939–

Birthplace: High River, Alberta

Profession(s): Journalist, lecturer

Political party: Progressive Conservative

MP for: Yellowhead, Alberta

Term: 1979–80

SHUTTLE REMOTE MANIPULATOR SYSTEM

Quick, name the famed Canadian invention known as the Shuttle Remote Manipulator System. The device, more commonly known as the Canadarm, debuted on the space shuttle Columbia on November 13, 1981. It subsequently performed 90 shuttle missions over 30 years, before being retired with NASA's shuttle program. The technological advances it inspired live on in a family of robotics developed for the International Space Station.

17 The Right Hon. John Napier Turner 1929–

Birthplace: England

Profession: Lawyer

Political party: Liberal

Did not serve in Parliament while Prime Minister

Term: 1984

18 (Martin) Brian Mulroney 1939–

Birthplace: Baie-Comeau, Quebec

Professions: Author, corporate executive, lawyer

Political party: Progressive Conservative

MP for: Manicouagan, Quebec; Charlevoix, Quebec

Term: 1984–93

19 (A.) Kim Campbell, 1947–

Birthplace: Port Alberni, British Columbia

Professions: Lawyer, lecturer

Political party: Progressive Conservative

MP for: Vancouver Centre, British Columbia

First female PM

Term: 1993

✓ Canola

Its name kind of gives it away. Canola, the globe's only made-in-Canada crop, was created in the 1970s by researchers from Agriculture and Agri-Food Canada and the University of Manitoba. Today, canola is considered one of the most important oilseed crops in the world and has proven to be the most lucrative for Canadian farmers. Vegetable oil made from canola plant seeds also lays claim to being the healthiest vegetable oil on the planet.

Marquis wheat

In the early 1900s, a Canadian-produced wheat called Marquis replaced Red Fife as the nation's top wheat. It was a cross between Red Fife and Hard Red Calcutta. Marquis matured seven to 10 days earlier than Red Fife and produced a great yield of 41.6 bushels per acre, while retaining the baking quality of Fife. The yield and quality of Marquis made Canada the largest wheat-exporting nation on the planet.

Geographic Information System

Canadian geographer Roger Tomlinson is known as the "Father of GIS" for his role in developing the first Geographic Information System. GIS, developed in the 1960s, is a program that combines spatial analysis and digital mapping to process large quantities of data. Essentially, GIS combines cartography, statistical analysis and databases.

20 Jean Chrétien
1934–

Birthplace: Shawinigan, Quebec

Profession: Lawyer

Political party: Liberal

MP for: Saint-Maurice, Quebec

Term: 1993–2003

21 Paul Edgar Philippe Martin 1938–

Birthplace: Windsor, Ontario

Profession(s): Businessman, lawyer

Political party: Liberal

MP for: LaSalle–Émard, Quebec

Term: 2003–06

22 Stephen Harper
1959–

Birthplace: Toronto, Ontario

Profession(s): Author, economist, lecturer

Political party: Conservative

MP for: Calgary Southwest, Alberta

Term: 2006–

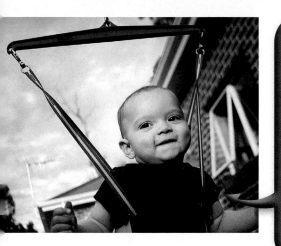

JOLLY JUMPER

The Jolly Jumper, a swing-like device that babies use for jumping, was invented by Canadian Susan Olivia Poole in 1910. The original was made for Poole's first child Joseph. It wasn't until 1948 – and after all seven of Poole's children had used the device – that the Jolly Jumper was mass-produced for retail.

Walkie-talkie

Canadian Donald L. Hings invented the walkie-talkie in 1937. The first versions of the device were designed as portable radios for bush pilots working for Consolidated Mining and Smelting (now Cominco), where Hings was employed. It wasn't until the Second World War, when the company lent Hings to the Department of National Defence and the National Research Council, that the walkie-talkie became widely used.

Most popular sailboat

It figures that the country with the longest shoreline in the world would invent a sailboat that's the world's most popular. In 1969, Bruce Kirby and Ian Bruce invented the Laser, a race-worthy vessel that could be carried on top of a car. They subsequently varied the size of sails to accommodate racers of various skills, and introduced two other versions of the boat, the Radial and the 4.7. Today, these vessels are popular with Olympic-calibre sailors around the world.

Fathometer

Canadian Reginald Fessenden created the fathometer, a device that measured the depth of water under a ship's hull. The invention won him the *Scientific American*'s Gold Medal in 1929.

✓ Laser sailboat

Variable-pitch propeller

Aeronautical engineer Wallace Turnbull, born in Saint John, is perhaps best known for inventing the variable-pitch propeller, which was first tested in flight in 1927. This propeller adjusts the angle at which its blades cut the air and became an aircraft standard that was safe and efficient at all engine speeds. Turnbull licensed the production of the invention and it was perfected by others.

Crash Position Indicator

The Crash Position Indicator, an emergency beacon locator for aircraft, was invented in 1957 by the National Research Council's Harry Stevinson. It was used for the first time that year by the military to locate a downed airplane. By the 1960s, the device was in use on commercial airlines.

Instant replay

Did you see that? Now you did, thanks to the invention of instant replay by the CBC in 1955. The technique was first used (where else?) on a broadcast of *Hockey Night in Canada*.

Panoramic camera

Talk about taking a wide-angled view of the world! Canadian John R. Connon patented the panoramic camera in 1888. Although there are earlier patents for similar devices, Connon's was the first to capture vistas of up to 360 degrees in a single exposure.

IMAX ↗

IMAX, a movie format that can record and display motion pictures at a far greater size and resolution than traditional film systems, was developed by a group of Canadian filmmakers and unveiled at the Fuji Pavilion at EXPO '70 in Osaka, Japan. The first IMAX projection system debuted at Toronto's Ontario Place in 1971. The world's first IMAX 3D system was revealed at Vancouver's EXPO '86. There are now more than 728 IMAX theatres in 53 countries.

Java

Here's an invention to make you sit up and take notice. Java, the programming language at the root of virtually every networked application, was invented by Canadian James A. Gosling. Sun Microsystems released the first version of Java in 1995.

WEEVAC 6

Here's proof big things can come in small packages. The WEEVAC 6, the world's first evacuation stretcher designed for infants, was created in 1987 by Canadian Wendy Murphy.

T-cell receptor

This could get complicated, so let's keep things simple. In 1984, Canadian Dr. Tak Wah Mak co-discovered the T-cell receptor. This led doctors to a better understanding of how the immune system recognizes and fights infections, allowing them to create new, more effective drugs. The discovery is considered the Holy Grail of immunology.

WonderBra

It's a name synonymous with lady's undergarments: WonderBra. And in 1939, the Canadian Lady Corset Company was the first to begin marketing bras under that brand name.

Strapless bra

The WonderBra brand had more firsts in women's underwear. The brand introduced the first strapless bra, the Winkie, in the 1940s. It also developed the diagonal shoulder strap in the same decade.

First bra ads on television

In 1972, WonderBra ran the first television ads in North America to feature a model wearing a bra. Before that, women's underwear had been displayed on mannequins or bust forms.

A WonderBra ad ↗

Standard time ↗

Imagine having to wear six watches to keep track of what time it is in different places. That's exactly what some people did before Canadian engineer Sandford Fleming devised the concept of Universal Standard Time in 1879. UST divides the world into 24 times zones. In each zone clocks indicate the same time, with one-hour difference between adjoining zones. At first, governments and the scientific community dismissed the idea, but eventually UST was accepted and went into effect on January 1, 1885.

Explosive Vapour Detector

While working at the National Research Council in the 1980s, chemist Lorne Elias developed the portable Explosive Vapour Detector, a device capable of sniffing out hidden bombs. In 1984, the RCMP used a prototype of the device during a visit by the Pope. When security officials were checking the Pope's baggage, a detector went off—triggered by a revolver one of the pontiff's bodyguards had packed in his luggage.

FIRST TRANSCONTINENTAL RAILWAY

The nation's first transcontinental railway, the Canadian Pacific Railway, was completed on November 7, 1885. The last spike was driven in at Craigellachie, British Columbia.

First trans-continental train

On June 28, 1886, the country's first transcontinental train left Montreal for Port Moody, British Columbia. It arrived on July 4.

Molson railway

The final legacy of John Molson was his key role in the construction of Canada's first railway, which was just starting when he died in 1836. Molson financed the Champlain and Saint Lawrence Railroad, which ran between La Prairie and Saint-Jean-sur-Richelieu.

First trans-border railway

The Grand Trunk Railway, incorporated in 1852, was the first trans-border railway in North America. It ran from Sarnia, Ontario, to Portland, Maine. Trains began running from Montreal to Portland on the route in 1853.

First trains with Wi-Fi

Canada's VIA Rail was the first railway company in North America to make Wi-Fi service available to passengers, in 2006.

First Canadian steamboat

John Molson, founder of the Molson brewery, was responsible for the construction of the first entirely Canadian-made steamboat in 1809. Molson eventually extended the endeavour to a fleet of 22 ships. The venture helped open the St. Lawrence and Canada to trade and settlement.

Northwest Passage ↗ west to east

The RCMP auxiliary schooner *St. Roch* holds a special place (or two or three!) in Canadian maritime history. Designed to avoid being crushed by ice, the wooden, sail-powered *St. Roch* was the first ship to sail the Northwest Passage from west to east in 1940–42 The ship was trapped in the ice for two seasons, before it completed its journey on October 11, 1942.

Northwest Passage east to west

Norwegian explorer Roald Amundsen was the first person to navigate Canada's Northwest Passage by ship, from 1903–06. Amundsen sailed his ship *Gjoa* west and south of Lancaster Sound through Peel Sound and through Queen Maud and Coronation gulfs in the western Arctic.

Northwest Passage west to east in one season

The HMCS *Labrador*, an icebreaker of the Royal Canadian Navy, was the first vessel to travel the Northwest Passage west to east in a single season, in 1954.

Northwest Passage east to west in one season

The *St. Roch* was the first vessel to travel the Northwest Passage in one season, which it did, east to west, in 1944, between July 22 and October 16. It travelled a "new" route, sailing through Lancaster Sound, through Prince of Wales Strait and along the northern Alaska coast.

Northwest Passage both ways

Thanks to its two voyages through the Northwest Passage in 1940–42 and 1944, the *St. Roch* became the first ship to sail the legendary route in both directions.

First through the Northwest Passage ↓

Canada's Northwest Passage has long transfixed explorers searching for a navigable route across the top of North America. In 1853–54, British explorer Robert McClure was the first recorded person to complete the route, partly by sledge, from west to east.

First to sink U-boat

On September 10, 1941, the *Chambly* and the *Moose Jaw* were the first Canadian warships to sink a U-boat. In a coordinated attack, the *Chambly* heavily damaged the German sub U-501 with five depth charges. The sub's captain opened its hatches when it surfaced, and it quickly sank, killing 11 Germans and one Canadian member of a boarding party.

Circumnavigating North America

To complete its maritime milestones, the *St. Roch* also became the first ship to circumnavigate North America, in 1950.

FIRST AIRPLANE

The Baddeck No. 1 was the first made-in-Canada powered aircraft. Built by the Canadian Aerodrome Company, its first flight was on August 12, 1909.

Seventh pilot

He wasn't the first, but he was darn close. Frederick Baldwin "Casey" Walker became the seventh person to pilot a plane (and the first Canadian and Commonwealth subject to do so). On March 12, 1908, at Hammondsport, New York he flew a plane called the "Red Wing," a biplane with the propeller located behind the wing. It flew a distance of 97.2 m before flipping to its side and crashing.

Firsts in aviation ↗

J.A.D. McCurdy was a man of many firsts. Some highlights:

- He co-founded the first aircraft manufacturing company in Canada, The Canadian Aerodrome Company, in April 1909.
- He performed the first figure-eight manoeuvre in an airplane in the world on August 28, 1908.
- He was the first Canadian to be issued a pilot's licence.
- He established the first aviation school in Canada.
- He was the first to fly a "flying boat," on May 1, 1910.
- At the time of his death, June 25, 1961, when he was 75, he was the world's oldest pilot.

More people take cars ↗
According to 2010 data from Statistics Canada, 82 percent of Canadians commute to work by car (12 percent take public transit, while six percent walk or cycle).

First water bomber
It figures that the only plane in the world built specifically to fight forest fires would be Canadian. The Canadair CL-215 was the world's first amphibious water bomber. Its first flight was October 23, 1967. The plane features two 2,271-litre tanks, which take eight to 10 seconds to scoop water and just two seconds to dump.

First metal bush plane ↗
The de Havilland DHC-2 Beaver was the first all-metal bush plane designed and built in Canada. It was particularly well-known for its ability on short takeoffs and landings. More Beavers were built than any other Canadian aircraft to date: 1,692 between 1947 and 1968.

First trans-Canada flight
The first trans-Canada flight took 10 days. It began on October 7, 1920, in Halifax and involved five different planes and six pilots. The journey ended in Richmond, British Columbia. It was also Canada's first transcontinental airmail run, as packages were dropped (literally in some cases!) off along the route.

First non-stop trans-Canada flight
On January 14, 1949, the first non-stop trans-Canada flight, from Vancouver to Halifax, took place. A Canadair North Star airplane took eight and a half hours to make the flight.

Black boxes and safe airplanes
First Air, a Canadian airline that principally services Canada's Arctic region, is the only airline in the world that can stream aircraft black box information (records of a plane's flight path, fuel and engine levels, etc.) to the ground in real time. First Air uses a system called FLYHTStream, which is activated by a predefined unusual event or can be triggered by flight crew.

Largest Canadian art collection

The Canada Council Art Bank is home to the world's largest collection of Canadian art. Its more than 17,000 paintings, prints, photographs and sculptures are loaned out to public and private organizations.

Longest running TV drama

Heartland, the story of a Western family that airs on CBC, is the longest running one-hour Canadian drama on TV ever. The program, which debuted in 2007, won the Directors Guild of Canada Award for Best TV Series: Family for five straight years from 2009 to 2013.

First documentary ↑

Nanook of the North, a silent movie from 1922 about a group of Inuit living on the coast of Hudson Bay, is widely regarded as the first full-length documentary film.

First talkie

Warner Bros. Pictures Inc., co-founded by Canadian Jack L. Warner, released the first movie with synchronized sound, *The Jazz Singer*, in 1927.

First documentary Oscar

Following in that tradition, the National Film Board's *Churchill's Island*, a documentary about the Battle of Britain, won the first Oscar for the category in 1941.

LARGEST VIDEO GAME MAKER

Game on! Canada is the largest producer of video games in the world per capita based on the number of employees according to the Entertainment Software Association of Canada. About 16,500 people work in the industry in Canada.

YOUNGEST COVER GIRL

Supermodel Monika Schnarre, was the youngest person to appear on the cover of *American Vogue* and in *Sports Illustrated*'s swimsuit issue, in 1987 at age 15.

Oscars for Canadian siblings

Here's a unique Canadian milestone from the Oscars: brother and sister Douglas and Norma Shearer are the only siblings to ever win Academy Awards in the same year. In 1931, Douglas took the Oscar for Best Sound Recording for The Big House, while Norma captured Best Actress for her role in *The Divorcee*.

Most Governor General Awards

Looking for Governor General–approved literature? Look no further than the work of author Hugh MacLennan or Michael Ondaatje. Each has won more Governor General Awards for literature than anyone else: a total of five each.

First Governor General Awards

The Governor General's Literary Awards were first presented in 1936. The first recipients were Bertram Brooker (fiction), for his book *Think of the Earth*, and T.B. Roberton (non-fiction), for a series of newspaper pieces.

King of Kid-Lit ↘

Quick: name the best-selling Canadian author of all time. Did you know it was Canada's "King of Kid-Lit" Robert Munsch? Munsch, who lives in Guelph, Ontario, has penned more than 40 books, with total sales of more than 30 million copies.

First Booker
Author Michael Ondaatje was the first Canadian to win the Man Booker Prize, a £50,000 literary award for the best novel of the year written by a citizen of the United Kingdom, the Commonwealth or the Republic of Ireland. Ondaatje and his novel *The English Patient* shared the 1992 Booker with Barry Unsworth and his work *Sacred Hunger*.

Superman
Superman, created by Canadian Joe Schuster and American Jerome Siegel, made his first appearance in the June 1938 issue of *Action Comics*.

Most blooms
Get your garden on. Canada Blooms is the largest flower and garden festival in Canada. Held annually in March since 1997, the exhibition now attracts more than 200,000 visitors.

Largest opera company
The Canadian Opera Company (COC) was the nation's first opera company, and it is the largest. It began as the Canadian Opera Festival in February 1950, and today the COC attracts about 140,000 patrons each season.

First Canadian published orchestral work
The first Canadian orchestral composition to be published was Guillaume Couture's Rêverie, which was performed in Paris in 1875 and then published.

First Canadian orchestral work played in Europe
The first Canadian orchestral work to be performed in Europe is thought to be Patrie, written by Calixa Lavallée (also the composer of O Canada). It was performed in 1874.

QUADRUPLE PLATINUM
Musician Burton Cummings, born on December 31, 1947, and a member of The Guess Who, was the first Canadian to have a quadruple platinum-selling album in Canada: his 1978 album *Dream Of A Child*.

Golden girl

Take that boys! Calgary's Kaillie Humphries became the first woman to compete with men in a four-man bobsled race on November 15, 2014. Humphries and her teammates placed sixth at a North American Cup event at the Utah Olympic Park. Humphries won a gold medal in two-person women's bobsleigh at both the 2010 Vancouver Olympics and the 2014 Games in Sochi.

World's oldest hockey stick

Just how important could a hand-hewn, nearly 200-year-old curved piece of wood be? If it's the world's oldest known hockey stick, it would be pretty darned special. Known as the Moffatt stick, the historic piece of gear is believed to have been crafted from a single piece of sugar maple from Cape Breton, Nova Scotia, in the 1830s. In early 2015, the Canadian Museum of History in Gatineau, Que., purchased the stick for $300,000.

Biggest multi-sport event

The Canada Games, held every two years, alternating between summer and winter, are the nation's biggest multi-sport event. Since their inception in 1967, almost 100,000 athletes have participated.

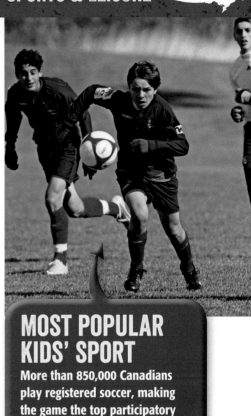

MOST POPULAR KIDS' SPORT

More than 850,000 Canadians play registered soccer, making the game the top participatory sport in the nation for kids between the ages of 5 and 14. Indeed, almost 44 percent of children in the country participate in soccer.

Skating for gold

The first Canada Games (see previous) were held in Quebec City from February 11 to 19, 1967. Among the most notable athletes who performed at the games was figure skater Toller Cranston, who won gold in the figure skating at the event.

Most popular sport ↗

More Canadians of all ages play golf than any other sport in the country. According to federal government statistics, about 1,465,000 Canadians play golf.

Top sports by participation among Canadians of all ages	
Golf	1,456,000
Hockey	1,239,000
Soccer	981,000
Baseball	581,000
Volleyball	531,000
Basketball	512,000
Skiing (downhill)	441,000
Cycling	395,000
Swimming	381,000
Badminton	312,000

First hockey game

Hockey is so popular in Canada that a number of Canadian cities claim to have hosted the first game, if not invented the game outright (such as Halifax; Windsor, Nova Scotia; and Kingston, Ontario). Regardless, one of the first reliable records of a form of the game being played is from a journal of Arctic explorer John Franklin, who notes a game on Great Bear Lake at Fort Franklin, Northwest Territories, on October 25, 1825.

First goalie mask

The first person known to wear a goalie mask in a hockey game? Bet you didn't know it was Elizabeth Graham. In 1927, Graham used a fencing mask to protect her face.

First father and son in Hockey Hall of Fame

Bobby Hull and his son Brett became the first father and son inducted into the Hockey Hall of Fame, when Brett joined the Hall on November 9, 2009. Brett recorded 1,391 points in 1,269 regular-season games. Bobby tallied 1,170 points in 1,063 regular-season games.

First Winter Olympic games

While it wasn't technically referred to as such, the 1924 International Winter Sports Week, organized by the International Olympic Committee and held in Chamonix, France, is widely considered the first Winter Olympic Games. It could be said that Canada won its first Winter Olympic medal at the event—gold in hockey (the 1920 gold in hockey had been won at the summer games).

Best hockey player ↗

Wayne Gretzky—'nuff said! But if you need more, the man who many consider to be the greatest hockey player ever holds or shares 61 records in the National Hockey League. Some highlights:

- Most points: 2,856 (1,485 games, 894 goals, 1,962 assists)
- Most points, including playoffs: 3,238 (2,856 regular season, 382 playoff)
- Most goals: 894
- Most goals, including playoffs: 1,016 (894 regular season, 122 playoff)
- Most assists: 1,962
- Most assists, including playoffs: 2,222 (1,962 regular season, 260 playoff)
- Most consecutive 40-or-more-goal seasons: 12 (1979–80 to 1990–91)
- Most consecutive 60-or-more-goal seasons: 4 (1981–82 to 1984–85)
- Most consecutive 100-or-more-point seasons: 13 (1979–80 to 1991–92)

Single Season Records
- Most points, one season: 215 (1985–86, 80-game schedule)
- Most points, one season, including playoffs: 255 (1984–85; 208 points in 80 regular-season games and 47 points in 18 playoff games)
- Most goals, one season: 92 (1981–82, 80-game schedule)

- Most goals, one season, including playoffs: 100 (1983–84, 87 goals in 74 regular-season games and 13 goals in 19 playoff games)
- Most goals, 50 games from start of season: 61 (1981–82 and 1983–84)
- Most three-or-more-goal games: 10 (1981–82, six three-goal games; three four-goal games; one five-goal game)
- Longest consecutive point-scoring streak: 51 games—61 goals, 92 assists for 153 points (October 5, 1983, to January 28, 1984)

Career Records: Playoffs
- Most playoff goals: 122
- Most playoff assists: 260
- Most playoff points: 382 (122 goals, 260 assists)
- Most game-winning goals in playoffs: 24
- Most points, one playoff year: 47 (1985, 17 goals and 30 assists in 18 games)
- Most points in final series: 13—three goals and 10 assists (1988, four games plus suspended game vs. Boston)

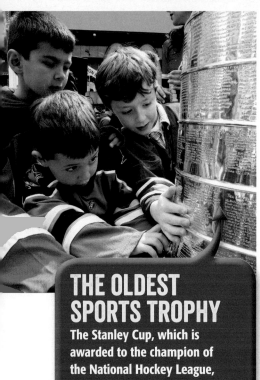

National summer sport

While many consider hockey Canada's national sport — and the federal government named it the country's national winter sport — lacrosse is considered the national summer sport. It's believed the game has been around for centuries, played in North America long before Europeans arrived. People have speculated that Native Americans invented the game as long ago as the 12th century.

Run of eight world championships

Talk about a sports dynasty. The first eight women's World Hockey Championship tournaments were won by Canada. Canada beat the American team in each championship game, from the inaugural tournament in Ottawa in 1990 to the Halifax/Dartmouth event in 2004. (The 2003 tournament slated for Beijing, China, was cancelled.)

Longest-running television sports program

Television trivia time. Name the longest-running sports program in television history. It's CBC's *Hockey Night in Canada* (*HNIC*). The show made its television debut (the brand has been on the radio since 1933) on October 11, 1952, airing a game between the Montreal Canadiens and the Detroit Red Wings. HNIC has broadcast a regular-season National Hockey League game every Saturday night since.

THE OLDEST SPORTS TROPHY

The Stanley Cup, which is awarded to the champion of the National Hockey League, is the oldest trophy competed for by professional athletes in North America. The trophy was established in 1892 by Sir Frederick Arthur Stanley (Lord Stanley), to be presented to the top hockey club in the Dominion of Canada. NHL teams became the exclusive competitors for the Cup in 1926.

Most traded players

These guys have a lot of sweaters in their closets. Canadian hockey players Mike Sillinger and Brent Aston are tied for the most-traded National Hockey League player. Each was traded nine times during his career.

MULTIPLE MEDALS

There are few athletes that reach the pinnacle of multiple sports. Canadian Olympic athlete Clara Hughes, however, is one of the world's finest exceptions. Hughes is the only Olympian ever to win multiple medals at summer and winter games. In speed skating she captured gold in the 5,000 m and silver in the team pursuit at the games in Turin, Italy, in 2006. As a cyclist, Hughes won bronze in both the road race and time trial events in Atlanta in 1996.

First Triple Crown

In 1919, Canadian-owned racehorse Sir Barton was the first to win the American Triple Crown—capturing first in each of the Kentucky Derby, Preakness and Belmont Stakes races—although the title didn't exist at the time. Sir Barton, owned by J.K.L. Ross, was officially awarded the honour in 1948.

First Olympic team

The 1904 Olympic Games in St. Louis marked the first time Canada sent an official team to the event. The 43-member team won six medals: four gold, a silver and a bronze. The gold medals came in soccer, lacrosse, 56-pound weight throw and golf.

First gold and silver in same event

The 1908 Olympic Games in London, England, marked the first time Canada captured gold and silver in the same event. Walter Ewing and George Beattie took first and second in the clay pigeon event.

Most medals

Clara Hughes (see above) and fellow speed skater Cindy Klassen are tied as the most-decorated Canadian Olympians. Each won six medals: Hughes captured four bronze (two in speed skating, two in cycling), one silver and one gold (both speed skating); Klassen nabbed three bronze, two silver and one gold, all in speed skating.

CRAZY CANUCK CHAMPIONSHIP WIN

"Crazy Canuck" Steve Podborski of Toronto, was the first male non-European skier to win the World Cup Downhill Championship, which he accomplished in 1982. Over his career, Podborski captured eight World Cup race wins and a bronze medal in downhill at the Lake Placid Olympics in 1980.

Most medals at one Olympics

Cindy Klassen holds the Canadian record for winning the most medals (five) at one Olympic Games. She reached the podium in the following long-track speed skating events in Turin, Italy in 2006: 1,000 m, 1,500 m, 3,000 m, 5,000 m and team pursuit. Her haul is also the most ever won by a female speed skater.

First death spiral

Canadian figure skating duo Suzanne Morrow and Wallace Distelmeyer were the first team to execute the modern-day death spiral in an international competition. They performed the move at the 1948 World Figure Skating Championships in Davos, Switzerland.

Largest fitness club company

GoodLife Fitness, a fitness club company, is the largest in the nation. Established in 1979, it has more than 877,000 members who visit its 300-plus clubs across the country.

First Canadian pro ballplayer

You've got to look back nearly 150 years to find the record of the first Canadian to play professional baseball. William B. (Bill) Phillips, born in Saint John in 1857, played his first game for the National League's Cleveland Blues on May 1, 1879. The first baseman also played for the league's Brooklyn Grays and Kansas City Cowboys, with a total of 1,881 games played.

First Canadian in Baseball Hall of Fame �‿

Pitcher Ferguson Jenkins was the first Canadian elected to the American National Baseball Hall of Fame in Cooperstown, New York, in 1987. Jenkins won 284 games—including a stretch of 20 a year for six straight seasons—and is the only pitcher in the game's history to strike out more than 3,000 batters and walk less than 1,000 batters.

First black ballplayer

Jackie Robinson, the first black baseball player in Major League Baseball in the modern era, played his first professional games for the Montreal Royals in 1946. A minor-league affiliate of the Brooklyn Dodgers—the team Robinson would debut within majors—the Royals won the International League title that season.

First Western woman to climb Everest

A Canadian also set a significant milestone on Everest. Sharon Wood, born in Halifax on May 18, 1957, was the first woman from the Western Hemisphere to reach the summit of Mount Everest. She completed the climb on May 20, 1986.

Tennis champ extraordinaire

He's a tennis virtuoso. Daniel Nestor, born on September 4, 1972, is the only player in the game's history to win all four Grand Slams, all of the Master Series events, the year-end Masters Cup and an Olympic gold medal in doubles.

Fastest run across Canada (woman)

The fastest trip across Canada on foot by a woman (Canadian Ann Keane), took 143 days. According to Guinness World Records, Keane travelled 7,831 km from St. John's to Tofino, British Columbia between April 17 and September 8, 2002.

Fastest run across Canada (man)

The fastest trip across Canada on foot by a man (Al Howie of England), took 72 days, 10 hours and 23 minutes, according to Guinness World Records. The 7,295.5-km trek from St. John's to Victoria took place from June 21 to September 1, 1991.

Fastest bike relay across Canada

The fastest cycling relay across Canada, according to Guinness World Records, is eight days, eight hours and 14 minutes. A team of five Canadians—Matt Young, Kyle Bagnano, Willie Cormack, Richard Alm and Keith Nicoll—set the record between September 4 and 22, 2007, cycling from Halifax to Vancouver. Their average speed? Forty km/hour.

FASTEST BIKE RIDE ACROSS CANADA

Here's a long, fast bike ride. According to Guinness World Records, the fastest time to cycle across Canada is 13 days, six hours and 13 minutes. Canadian Arvid Loewen set the mark between July 1 and 14, 2011, travelling 6,037 km from Vancouver to Halifax.

↵ First wheelchair gold in non-disabled competition

Chantal Petitclerc, born December 15, 1969, holds a truly unique athletic distinction. Petitclerc was the first athlete to claim gold in a wheelchair event as part of a major international non-disabled competition. She captured top spot in the 800 m event in July 2002 at the Commonwealth Games in Manchester, England.

Canada's coat-of-arms ↑

Can you name the official Canadian symbol that features a lion and a unicorn? Canada's Coat of Arms, of course, which boasts the lion of England holding the Royal Union Flag and the unicorn of Scotland carrying the flag of Royal France. The emblem also has fleurs-de-lis, maple leaves, an Irish harp, the floral symbols associated with the Canadian monarchy—the English rose, the Scottish thistle, the French lily and the Irish shamrock—and the Royal Crown. It also includes the country's motto: *A mari usque ad mare* (from sea to sea).

Provincial and territorial floral emblems

Newfoundland and Labrador	pitcher plant
New Brunswick	purple violet
Nova Scotia	mayflower
PEI	lady's slipper
Quebec	blue flag
Ontario	white trillium
Manitoba	prairie crocus
Saskatchewan	western red lily
Alberta	wild rose
British Columbia	Pacific dogwood
Yukon	fireweed
Northwest Territories	mountain aven
Nunavut	purple saxifrage

Provincial and territorial birds emblems

Newfoundland and Labrador	Atlantic puffin
New Brunswick	black-capped chickadee
Nova Scotia	osprey
PEI	blue jay
Quebec	snowy owl
Ontario	common loon
Manitoba	great gray owl
Saskatchewan	sharp-tailed grouse
Alberta	great horned owl
British Columbia	Stellar's jay
Yukon	raven
Northwest Territories	gryfalcon
Nunavut	rock ptarmigan

Provincial and territorial tree emblems

Newfoundland and Labrador	black spruce
New Brunswick	balsam fir
Nova Scotia	red spruce
PEI	red oak
Quebec	yellow birch
Ontario	eastern white pine
Manitoba	white spruce
Saskatchewan	white birch
Alberta	lodgepole pine
British Columbia	western red cedar
Yukon	sub-alpine fir
Northwest Territories	tamarack
Nunavut	none

Official dirt

Just how important can dirt be? So important, it turns out, that two provinces have proclaimed a provincial soil. The Holmesville Soil Series is the provincial soil of New Brunswick, while the iconic red Charlottetown soil is the provincial soil of Prince Edward Island.

Official grass

Three Canadian provinces have recognized an official grass species. Manitoba recognizes big bluesteam as its provincial grass, Saskatchewan proclaimed needle-and-thread grass its official grass and Alberta designated rough fescue as its grass emblem.

Provincial and territorial mineral/gemstone/stone emblems

Newfoundland and Labrador	Labradorite
New Brunswick	none
Nova Scotia	agate (gemstone); stilbite (mineral)
PEI	none
Quebec	none
Ontario	amethyst
Manitoba	none
Saskatchewan	potash (Sylvite)
Alberta	petrified wood
British Columbia	jade
Yukon	lazulite
Northwest Territories	gold (mineral); diamond (gemstone)
Nunavut	none

Mammal emblems

Three provinces and one territory have official animal or mammal emblems. The white-tailed deer is the official animal of Saskatchewan, the Rocky Mountain bighorn sheep is the official mammal of Alberta, the spirit bear (a white phase grizzly bear) is the official mammal of British Columbia, and the Canadian Inuit Dog is the official animal of Nunavut.

Official fish

Three provinces recognize an official fish species. The walleye is the official fish of Saskatchewan, Alberta's is the bull trout and the Northwest Territories recognizes the Arctic grayling.

Unofficial official national symbol

Is there a Canadian symbol more synonymous with the nation than the maple leaf? But did you know that it is not an official symbol of the country? Of course, it is featured prominently on the Canadian flag, and as part of numerous other official and unofficial national symbols.

First official document

The first and oldest known official document from what is modern-day Canada, is the pardon of Aussillon de Sauveterre, who had killed a sailor. The pardon was granted in September 1542, by Jean-François de La Rocque de Roberval, Canada's lieutenant-general at the time.

First Canadian Nobel Prize ↘

You're undoubtedly familiar with author Alice Munro snagging the 2013 Nobel Prize in Literature and becoming the first Canadian to do so. But do you know who was the first Canadian to win any Nobel Prize? That would be Sir Frederick Banting, who discovered insulin (along with his assistant Charles Best and other colleagues), thereby changing the lives of millions of people with diabetes. In 1923—the year after he first injected a patient with insulin—he was awarded the Nobel Prize in Medicine.

Canadian Nobel Prize winners

1923	Frederick Grant Banting (1891–1941)	Medicine
1949	William Francis Giauque (1895–1982)	Chemistry
1966	Charles Brenton Huggins (1901–97)	Medicine
1957	Lester Bowles Pearson (1897–1972)	Peace ↘
1976	Saul Bellow* (1915–2005)	Literature
1981	David H. Hubel (1926–)	Medicine
1983	Henry Taube (1915–2005)	Chemistry
1989	Sidney Altman (1939–)	Chemistry
1990	Richard E. Taylor (1929–)	Physics
1992	Rudolph A. Marcus (1923–)	Chemistry
1994	Bertram N. Brockhouse (1918–2003)	Physics
1996	William Vickrey (1914–96)	Economics
1996	Myron S. Scholes (1941–)	Economics
1999	Robert A. Mundell (1932–)	Economics
2009	Willard S. Boyle (1924–2011)	Physics
2011	Ralph Steinman (1943–2011)	Medicine
2013	Alice Munro (1931–) First Canadian woman	Literature ↗

*Saul Bellow was born in Quebec but later became an American citizen.

First Order of Canada recipients

The Order of Canada, created in 1967 in honour of the 100th anniversary of Confederation, is awarded to Canadians who demonstrate exemplary merit and achievement. Ninety people were appointed, including:

- Governor General Roland Michener, the first honourary member
- Montreal Symphony conductor Wilfrid Pelletier
- Quebec politician Thérèse Casgrain
- Author Hugh MacLennan
- Humourist Gregory Clark
- Neurosurgeon Dr. Wilder Penfield
- Former Prime Minister Louis St-Laurent
- Opera singer Pierette Alarie
- Hockey player Maurice Richard

First secret session of parliament

Keep it on the down low. On April 17, 1918, the House of Commons held its first secret session. Members were told that Allied forces in Europe faced possible defeat.

First vaccination

Dr. John Clinch is believed to have been the first doctor in North America to administer vaccinations. In 1798, the first person he vaccinated was his nephew Joseph Hart. Clinch later vaccinated 700 people for smallpox in Trinity, Newfoundland. Encouraged by the results, doctors in other communities in the province and in Halifax adopted the practice.

Oldest artists' association

The Royal Canadian Academy of Arts is the country's oldest national professional artists' association. Established in 1880, the organization's aim was the advancement and development of visual arts in Canada.

Largest library for the blind

The Canadian National Institute for the Blind Library is the largest library of accessible materials for people with print disabilities. The library's collection includes more than 80,000 books in braille, e-braille, printbraille, e-text, DAISY and online audio; popular audio magazines; research tools such as encyclopedias and dictionaries; and more than 50 regional, national and international newspapers.

Oldest Canadian club outside Canada

The Canada Club in London, England, founded in 1810, is the oldest Canadian club outside of Canada. Originally formed by fur traders of the North West Company, today the club is open to all with an interest in Canada. It hosts two dinners a year featuring keynote speakers of significance to Canadians. Every Canadian Prime Minister has addressed the club.

FIRST CANADIAN SPACE COMMANDER

Astronaut Chris Hadfield became the first Canadian to command a spaceship on March 13, 2013. Hadfield was Commander of the International Space Station during the second part of his five-month stay there. Hadfield's mission ended on May 13, 2013, after 146 days in space (144 on the ISS). He travelled nearly 99.8 million km during his mission.

Largest science lesson

Canada hosted the world's largest practical science lesson on October 12, 2012, organized by the federal government. The lesson, held at 1 p.m. EST at 88 locations across the country, focused on two experiments demonstrating Bernoulli's Principle on air pressure and included 13,701 students.

Longest-serving prime minister ↓

William Lyon Mackenzie King is Canada's longest-serving prime minister and the longest-serving prime minister in the Commonwealth. He served 21 years over three terms: December 29, 1921 to June 28, 1926; September 25, 1926 to August 7, 1930; and October 23, 1935 to November 15, 1948. King, a Liberal, oversaw the creation of old-age pensions and unemployment insurance and appointed the first woman to the Senate (in 1930), among other accomplishments.

First European to cross North America

Explorer Alexander Mackenzie was the first European to cross North America north of Mexico. He made the trip across present-day Canada to the Pacific on behalf of the North West Company, an English fur-trading company operating in North America. He completed his expeditions to the continent's northwest in 1793.

Last soldier killed in First World War

It's a terrible distinction. The last soldier killed in battle during the First World War was Canadian Private George Lawrence Prince. Prince died at Mons, Belgium, on November 11, 1918, about two minutes before the signing of the Armistice. He had enlisted in the army just over a year earlier, in October 1917.

Canadian life expectancy

The life expectancy of the average Canadian at birth is 81.1 years, according to the United Nation's Human Development Reports.

Last woman executed

The last woman executed in Canada under the Criminal Code, Marguerite Pitre, was hanged in 1953. Pitre had been convicted as a co-conspirator in Canada's largest mass murder at the time.

Biggest energy users

According to a 2013 report from The Conference Board of Canada (*How Canada Performs — Environment*), Canadians are the largest users of energy in the developed world.

Most garbage ↗

Here's a dirty secret. Canada produces more municipal waste than any other developed nation per capita, according to a 2013 report from The Conference Board of Canada (see above). Each Canadian produced 777 kg of municipal garbage in 2008, and the amount of waste generated by the country per capita has steadily increased since 1990.

Most salt ↘

That's salty. Canada has the world's largest per capita use of salt. It's estimated that each Canadian uses more than 360 kg of salt annually. Salt as a de-icing agent makes up a large part of this figure.

More Christians

More than 22 million people, roughly two-thirds of Canada's population, report affiliations with a Christian religion, based on the latest data from Statistics Canada. The largest Christian group is Roman Catholics, at 12.7 million people.

Most Asians

Canada is a nation largely built on immigration. Based on the latest data from Statistics Canada, the largest source of immigrants in recent years is from Asia (including the Middle East). About 57 percent of all immigrants who arrived between 2006 and 2011 came from Asia, a total of nearly 660,000 people.

Most South Asians

Canada is home to people from all over the world. Based on the latest data from Statistics Canada, nearly 20 percent of the country's population identifies as a visible minority. The largest group is South Asian. There are a total of 1,567,400 individuals who identify as such, which makes up one-quarter of all visible minorities in the country and nearly five percent of the nation's total population.

More Chinese speakers

Chinese languages are the most common among immigrants to Canada whose first language is other than French or English, according to the latest data from Statistics Canada. About 850,000 individuals reported a Chinese language as their mother tongue, 13 percent of all foreign-born residents for whom French or English isn't a first language.

Canadians' favourite American state

Canadians aren't shy about visiting our neighbours to the south. But do you know which American state is most visited by Canadians, according to Statistics Canada? New York State saw 3.4 million overnight visits from Canadians in 2010. Florida was second with 3.1 million overnight visits, while Washington State was third with 2.3 million.

Canadians' second-favourite destination

Do you know the most popular foreign destination for Canadians after the United States? Mexico. Canadians made nearly 1.4 million overnight visits there in 2010, according to Statistics Canada.

Most expensive state

Hmm, what could possibly be responsible for this? Based on Statistics Canada data from 2010, Canadians spent more money (an average $188 per night) in Nevada—home of Lost Wages, er, Las Vegas—than in any other American state.

Most compelling state

Canadians travelling to the United States stay longest in Florida (an average of 17.4 overnights per visit), according to 2010 data from Statistics Canada.

Most visited nation

The most-visited overseas nation by Canadians? United Kingdom, where Canadians made 880,000 overnight visits in 2010, according to Statistics Canada.

Worst epidemic

Canada's worst epidemic? Spanish influenza, brought home in 1918 by soldiers returning from the First World War. The Spanish flu killed some 50,000 Canadians. Worldwide, it's believed to have claimed the lives of more people than the Great War itself.

Worst forest fires

During what's considered the hottest recorded year in Canada (1988), the forest fires were the costliest in the country's history. An estimated 10,560 fires destroyed 4.6 million hectares of forests, approximately 50 percent more than an average year.

Most soccer ball touches – 60 seconds

According to Guinness World Records, Canadian Chloe Hegland holds the record for most touches of a soccer ball (while keeping it in the air) in one minute by a female – 339. She set the record on November 3, 2007, while filming a Guinness special in Beijing, China.

Most soccer ball touches – 30 seconds

Hegland also holds the record for most touches of a soccer ball (while keeping it in the air) in 30 seconds by a female (163), according to Guinness World Records. Hegland achieved the feat on February 23, 2008.

Heavy over 100

Kevin Fast of Cobourg, Ontario, holds the record for the heaviest vehicle pulled over 100 feet, according to Guinness World Records. On September 15, 2008, Fast pulled a 57,243 kg vehicle more than 30.48 m over level ground.

Chainsaw juggling ↓

Aaron Gregg of Victoria achieved the most chainsaw juggling catches ever (88), according to Guinness World Records. Gregg set the record on July 28, 2008.

WORLD'S LARGEST AXE
Nackawic, New Brunswick

World's largest beaver
Beaverlodge, Alberta

World's largest badminton racket
St. Albert, Alberta

World's largest bee
Falher, Alberta

World's largest blueberry
Oxford, Nova Scotia

World's largest bunnock
Macklin, Saskatchewan

World's largest burl
Port McNeill, British Columbia

World's largest chainsaw
Lillooet, British Columbia

World's largest adirondack chair
Varney, Ontario

World's largest muskoka chair
Gravenhurst, Ontario

World's largest chuck wagon
Dewberry, Alberta

World's largest claim post
Cobalt, Ontario

World's largest cookie jar
Deloraine, Manitoba

World's largest cross-Country skis
100 Mile House, British Columbia

World's largest curling rock
Arborg, Manitoba

World's largest Coke can
Portage La Prairie, Manitoba

World's largest conch
Caraquet, New Brunswick

World's largest cuckoo clock
Kimberley, British Columbia

World's largest dragonfly
Wabamun, Alberta

WORLD'S LARGEST DINOSAUR
Drumheller, Alberta

World's largest endangered ferrugious hawk
Leader, Saskatchewan

World's largest illuminated fiddle
Sydney, Nova Scotia

World's largest fiddleheads
Plaster Rock, New Brunswick

World's largest fire hydrant
Elm Creek, Manitoba

World's largest fly rod
Houston, British Columbia

World's largest gold pan
Quesnel, British Columbia

World's largest golf bag
Orangeville, Ontario

World's largest golf tee
Trochu, Alberta

Canada's largest goose
Wawa, Ontario

World's largest hockey stick and puck
Duncan, British Columbia

World's largest honeybee
Tisdale, Saskatchewan

World's largest inukshuk
Schomberg, Ontario

World's largest lamp
Donalda, Alberta

World's largest lobster
Shediac, New Brunswick

World's largest mallard
Andrew, Alberta

World's largest maple leaf
Millville, New Brunswick

World's largest moose
Moose Jaw, Saskatchewan

World's largest wooden nickel
Boiestown, New Brunswick

World's largest oil can
Rocanville, Saskatchewan

World's largest orchard ladder
Summerland, British Columbia

World's largest painting on easel
Altona, Manitoba

World's largest paper clip
Kipling, Saskatchewan

World's largest perogy
Glendon, Alberta

World's second largest smoking pipe
Saint Claude, Manitoba

WORLD'S LARGEST STARSHIP ENTERPRISE
Vulcan, Alberta

World's largest purple martin colony
Neepawa, Manitoba

World's largest putter
Bow Island, Alberta

The wall (world's largest photo-mosaic)
Port Carling, Ontario

CANADA
ROADSIDE ATTRACTIONS

World's largest railroad spike
Hines Creek, Alberta

World's largest rooster
Shediac, New Brunswick

World's largest silver fox
Salisbury, New Brunswick

World's largest snowman
Beardmore, Ontario

World's largest softball
Chauvin, Alberta

World's largest sturgeon
Dominion City, Manitoba

World's largest sundial
Lloydminster, Saskatchewan

World's tallest teepee
Medicine Hat, Alberta

World's largest tin soldier
New Westminster, British Columbia

World's largest tomahawk
Cut Knife, Saskatchewan

World's largest totem pole
Alert Bay, British Columbia

**World's largest totem
pole in diameter**
Duncan, British Columbia

**WORLD'S LARGEST
TOTEM POLE FROM
A SINGLE TREE**
Victoria, British Columbia

WORLD'S LARGEST UKRAINIAN EASTER EGG
Vegreville, Alberta

World's largest tree crusher
Mackenzie, British Columbia

World's largest turtle
Turtleford, Saskatchewan

World's largest wagon wheel and pick
Fort Assiniboine, Alberta

World's largest tractor weather vane
Westlock, Alberta

World's largest western boot
Edmonton, Alberta

BRITISH COLUMBIA

The name of the present-day province of British Columbia is thought to have come from Queen Victoria, and was introduced in 1858. The southern part of the colony had around that time been known to some as Columbia, after the river in the region, which had been named after the ship of American captain Robert Gray.

HELI-SKIING

Heli-skiing, in which a helicopter takes skiers to far-flung mountain runs, was invented in Canada in 1965. Hans Gmoser, who'd come to Canada from Austria in 1951, pioneered the concept in British Columbia's Bugaboo Mountians, where he built a lodge that still operates as a heli-skiing operation today.

PERFECT PEAK

It's Canada's perfect peak. British Columbia's Mount Assiniboine (3,618 m) is considered the Matterhorn of North America, due to its nearly symmetrical, pyramid shape.

Earliest settlement

The earliest known human settlement in Canada is found on British Columbia's Haida Gwaii. It is estimated that an archeological site at Nanu was inhabited between 15,000 and 12,000 years ago. Stone tools and remains of large butchered animals have been found at the site, which is thought to be the longest continuously occupied settlement in Canada.

Largest hot springs

The hot springs in the village of Radium Hot Springs, British Columbia, are the largest in the country. The pool's water, maintained at a temperature of 39°C, is odourless and clear.

Biggest spruce tree

So you think you're good at climbing trees? Try this one on for size. Canada's largest spruce tree, known as the San Juan Spruce, is 62.5-metres tall and has a circumference of 11.67 metres. A Sitka species of spruce tree, it grows along the San Juan River near Port Renfrew, BC It's also the second largest known Sitka in the world.

Highest point

The highest point in British Columbia is Mount Fairweather, which sits at an elevation of 4,663 m. It's located on the Alaska border at the southern end of the province's Tatshenshini-Alsek Wilderness Provincial Park. Captain James Cook named the mountain after he saw the peak in "fair weather" while exploring the region in 1778.

Largest high-elevation lake

The nation's largest, natural, high-elevation freshwater lake is British Columbia's Chilko Lake. The 158-square-km body of water sits at an elevation of 1,171 m.

Rain in the rainiest province

British Columbia certainly lives up to its reputation as a rainy province. Here's a chart showing the average annual precipitation for the province's wettest communities.

Days	City	mm	inches
205	Hartley Bay	4,673	184.0
169	Tahsis	4,305	169.5
207	Port Renfrew	3,505	138.0
225	Port Alice	3,427	134.9
206	Ucluelet	3,351	131.9
208	Tofino	3,271	128.8
229	Prince Rupert	3,060	120.5

Most consecutive rainy days ↗

Vancouver claims the record among large Canadian cities (those with a population of 100,000 and greater) for the most consecutive days of rain: 29, in 1953, between January 6 to February 3. The city nearly broke the record in January 2006, after 23 straight days of rain.

Highest Precipitation in the rest of Canada

Outside of BC, the Atlantic coast is Canada's wettest region. But it still gets nowhere near the amount of drizzle that deluges the Pacific coast. Here's how much precipitation falls at a sampling of the country's wettest spots:

Average total yearly precipitation			
Days	Place	mm	inches
164	Wreck Cove Brook, Nova Scotia	1,946	76.6
183	Red Harbour, Newfoundland	1,841	72.5
147	Pools Cove, Newfoundland	1,828	72.0
154	Guysborough, Nova Scotia	1,815	71.4
219	Forêt Montmorency, Quebec	1,583	62.3
236	St Fortunat, Quebec	1,542	60.7
172	Alma, New Brunswick	1,510	59.5
163	Allenford, Ontario	1,294	50.9
175	New Glasgow, PEI	1,258	49.5
149	Blyth, Ontario	1,247	49.1
162	Waterton Village, Alberta	1,096	43.2

Record rainfalls

A few places on BC's wet west coast have received more than 300 millimetres of rain in a single day. That's more than some areas of Canada get in a year. This table lists some of the biggest downpours ever recorded for one day in Canada:

Amount of precipitation in one day			
Days	Place	mm	inches
Jan. 26, 1984	McInnes Island, BC	319	12.6
Jan. 14, 1961	Seymour Falls, BC	314	12.4
Nov. 14, 1991	Mitchell Inlet, BC	306	12.1
Nov. 11, 1990	Tahsis, BC	300	11.8
Nov. 10, 1990	Seymour Falls, BC	300	11.8

Biggest snowfall

Get the shovel, er, shovels! The greatest single-day snowfall recorded in Canada was February 11, 1999, when Tahtsa, British Columbia, was blanketed with nearly a metre and a half of the white stuff (145 cm, to be exact). That broke a record of 118.1 cm of snow that fell on Lakelse Lake, British Columbia, on January 17, 1974. Neither is near the world record of 192 cm, set at Silver Lake, Colorado, on April 15, 1921.

Highest average snowfall

The highest average annual snowfall ever recorded at an Environment Canada weather station is 1,388 cm on Mount Fidelity, British Columbia. This mountain in Glacier National Park averages 141 days of snow a year.

Biggest snowfall in one year ↑

The heaviest annual snowfall the country has witnessed was in the Revelstoke-Mount Copeland area of British Columbia. The region spent the winter of 1971–72 digging out from a total of 2,446.5 cm, or nearly 24.5 m of snow.

Biggest blizzards

Canada's biggest blizzards, based on biggest single-day snowfalls on record:

Date	Place	cm	inches
February 11, 1999	Tahtsa Lake West, BC	145.0	57.1
December 4, 1985	Pleasant Camp, BC	127.0	50.0
March 20, 1885	Cap-de-la-Madeleine, QC	121.9	48.0
January 17, 1974	Lakelse Lake, BC	118.0	46.5
February 11, 1999	Terrace, BC	113.4	44.6
February 18, 1972	Kitimat, BC	112.3	44.2
January 16, 1976	Stewart, BC	105.7	41.6
February 5, 1988	Main Brook, NL	105.0	41.3
January 11, 1968	Kemano, BC	104.1	41.0
January 27, 2000	Unuk River, Eskay Creek Mine, BC	104.0	40.9
January 6, 1988	Nain, NL	103.4	40.7
February 17, 1943	Colinet, BC	101.6	40.0

Highest average snowfalls

Days	Place	cm	inches
141	Mount Fidelity, Glacier National Park, BC	1,388.0	546.4
114	Unuk River, Eskay Creek Mine, BC	1,298.6	511.3
104	Tahtsa Lake West, BC	975.7	384.1
78	Grouse Mountain, North Vancouver, BC	868.7	342.0
112	Rogers Pass, BC	864.7	340.4
78	Pleasant Camp, BC	723.8	285.0
90	Fraser Camp, BC	703.2	276.8
69	Hollyburn Ridge, West Vancouver, BC	654.6	257.7

Longest-lasting snowfalls

Outside of Canada's territories, here are the places with the highest number of average days each year with at least one cm of snow on the ground:

Location	Days
Mt. Fidelity, Glacier National Park, BC	271
Inukjuak, QC	228
Schefferville, QC	221
Churchill Falls, NL	221
Tahtsa Lake West, BC	216
Churchill, MB	215
Rogers Pass, BC	215
Unuk River, Eskay Creek, BC	212
Makkovik, NL	210
Nain, NL	205
Wabush Lake, NL	202
Kuujjuaq, QC	201
Poste Montagnais, QC	200

City with the least snow

So, do you want to live in a big Canadian city and avoid the snow? Victoria is the place for you. The capital of British Columbia receives only 33 cm of snowfall each year on average, and it lands over just seven days. The snow doesn't last long either. On average, accumulated snow is higher than 1 cm for just five days each year.

Three cities with the least snow

Of course, if you want to miss the snow, three of British Columbia's other major cities—Vancouver, Abbotsford and Kelowna—are also good bets, and rank second, third and fourth, respectively, as the nation's least snowiest. Vancouver gets just 44.6 cm of snow on average each year, Abbotsford sees an average of 55.2 cm annually, and Kelowna gets 63.5 cm.

Highest average temperature

Canada's West Coast is well known for being rainy, but not for being hot. Still, you could consider Victoria Canada's hottest major city. It has the country's highest recorded average daily maximum temperature at 15.3°C. Victoria also has the hottest recorded nights, with an average daily minimum temperature of 7.1°C.

Hottest cities

Canadian cities with more than 10 days a year where the temperature reaches at least 30°C or higher:

City	Days
Kelowna, BC	26
Windsor, ON	23
Hamilton, ON	18
Regina, SK	16
St. Catharines, ON	14
Winnipeg, MB	13
Saskatoon, SK	13
Brantford, ON	13
Ottawa, ON	12
Toronto, ON	12

Cities with the highest average temperatures

Canadian cities with the highest recorded average daily maximum temperature annually:

City	High °C	High °F
Victoria, BC	15.3	60
Abbotsford, BC	15.1	59
Kelowna, BC	14.7	59
Windsor, ON	14.4	58
Vancouver, BC	13.9	57
St. Catharines, ON	13.6	56
Brantford, ON	13.2	56
Hamilton, ON	13.1	56
Toronto, ON	12.9	55
London, ON	12.7	55
Oshawa, ON	12.1	54

Longest growing seasons

Canadian cities with the longest growing seasons based on the average number of frost-free days:

City	Days	City	Days
Vancouver, BC	237	Halifax, NS	182
Victoria, BC	211	St. Catharines, ON	179
Abbotsford, BC	208	Hamilton, ON	177
Toronto, ON	203	Oshawa, ON	168
Windsor, ON	195	Peterborough, ON	168

Hottest cities at night

The country's hottest cities at night, based on average daily minimum temperature annually:

City	Low °C	Low °F
Victoria, BC	7.1	45
Vancouver, BC	6.8	44
Toronto, ON	5.9	43
Abbotsford, BC	5.8	42
Windsor, ON	5.4	42
St. Catharines, ON	4.4	40
Kelowna, BC	4.1	39
Oshawa, ON	4.1	39
Hamilton, ON	4.0	39
Halifax, NS	3.6	38

Calmest city

Don't go fly a kite—at least not in Kelowna, British Columbia; because chances are slim you'll have enough wind for liftoff. Kelowna is Canada's least windy city, with 39 percent of wind observations per year indicating calm conditions.

Windiest place

Hold onto your hat! Cape St. James, located at the south end of Haida Gwaii, British Columbia, is Canada's windiest place. It sees more days with gale-force winds than anywhere else in the nation.

First protected area for grizzly bears

British Columbia's Khutzeymateen Provincial Park was the first area in the country specifically protected for grizzly bears. Established in 1994, and also known as the Khutzeymateen/K'tsim-a-deen Grizzly Sanctuary, or "Valley of the Grizzly," the 43,000-hectare park is located 45 km northeast of Prince Rupert and is home to about 50 grizzlies—one of the largest populations of the species in the province.

Tallest tree

You could call it the green giant. Canada's tallest recorded tree stands 56 m high. The western red cedar, located in British Columbia's Pacific Rim National Park, was discovered in 1988 and has been nicknamed "Cheewhat Giant" because of its proximity to Cheewhat Lake. The diameter of the tree is more than 6 m and contains an estimated 450 cubic m in timber volume.

LARGEST NUMBER OF BALD EAGLES

You don't need to be eagle-eyed to spy the famous birds that flock to British Columbia's Brackendale Eagle Provincial Park from November to February each year. That's because the park is home to the continent's largest concentration of bald eagles. Indeed, in 1994, there was a world-record count of 3,769 eagles.

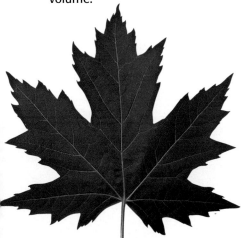

↵ Largest maple leaf

Here's a record with a special Canadian connection. The largest recorded maple leaf (actual leaf!) was found on December 14, 2010, in Richmond, British Columbia, by Vikas Tanwar and family. The leaf—53 cm wide, 52.2 cm tall, with a 32.5 cm stem—was confirmed by Guinness World Records as the biggest ever found.

First aquarium

Vancouver Aquarium, located in the city's Stanley Park, was the country's first. When it opened on June 15, 1956, the aquarium was a 830-square-m facility. Today, it's more than 9,000 square m.

First orca study

The Vancouver Aquarium (see First aquarium) was the first facility in the world to study an orca. The aquarium acquired killer whale Moby Doll, a young male, in July 1969.

Biggest salmon

With Canada's world-renowned salmon runs, is it any wonder the country holds a salmon angling world record? The International Game Fish Association all-tackle world record for chum salmon, a 15.87 kg fish, was caught on July 11, 1995, in Edye Pass, British Columbia.

Biggest Canada moose

This was one big moose. According to the Boone & Crockett Club, the world-record Canada species moose was taken in 1980 by Michael E. Laub near British Columbia's Grayling River. Based on the size of its antlers the moose scored 242.

Biggest cougar

Here's one colossal cat: according to the Boone and Crockett Club, the world-record cougar was taken in 1979 by Douglas E. Schuk near Tatlayoko Lake, British Columbia. It scored 164/16 (the score is based on the skull's width and length).

LARGEST AND OLDEST FRESHWATER FISH

The white sturgeon is the largest and longest-living freshwater fish in North America. In Canada, the species can be found in a number of rivers in British Columbia, including the Fraser, Kootenay, Nechako and Columbia. Specimens more than 6 m in length and estimated to be more than 100 years old have been recorded in the Fraser River.

TALLEST TIMBER TRESTLE BRIDGE

The Kinsol Trestle near the village of Shawnigan Lake on Vancouver Island is the country's tallest timber trestle. It is also one of the largest timber bridges in the world and the highest timber trestle remaining in the Commonwealth. The 44-m high, 188-m long bridge crosses the Koksilah River. It was built in 1920.

Longest cable-stayed bridge

The SkyBridge, which crosses British Columbia's Fraser River between New Westminster and Surrey, is the longest transit-only, cable-stayed bridge in the world. The double-tracked structure stretches 616 m. It opened in 1990.

First shopping mall

Attention shoppers: Park Royal Shopping Centre in Vancouver is considered Canada's first shopping mall. It opened in September 1950.

Highest small city

The city of Kimberley, located in southeastern British Columbia, is the nation's highest small city (a population less than 100,000). It sits 1,110 m above sea level.

Largest living roof

The two-hectare "living roof" on the West Building of the Vancouver Convention Centre is the largest of its kind in Canada, and the largest non-industrial such roof in North America. Landscaped with more than 400,000 indigenous plants and grasses, the living roof helps insulate the building, keeping it cool in the summer and maintaining heat in the winter.

Highest dam

The highest dam in Canada is the Mica Dam in British Columbia, in operation since 1977. Located on the Columbia River, about 135 km from Revelstoke, the dam at the Mica Generating Station is 243 m high. The power plant accounts for 15 percent of the province's hydroelectric capacity.

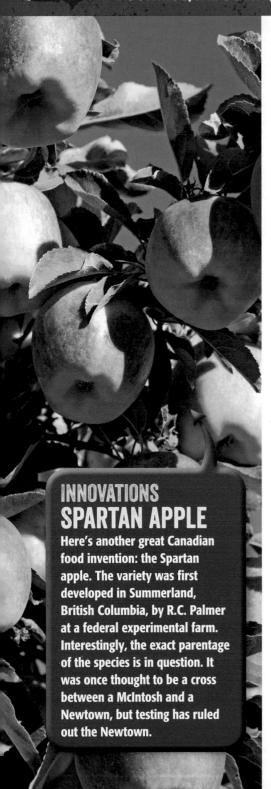

Most lumber

Not only does Canada lead the world as an exporter of softwood lumber, but British Columbia is the global export leader of the product. The province moves out more than 11.3 million cubic m of softwood, worth close to $11 million. The United States, China and Japan are the three largest importers of the wood.

Most Caterpillars

Finning International, headquartered in Vancouver, is the world's largest dealer of Caterpillar products, which include construction and mining equipment vehicles. Finning sells and rents the Cat equipment to mining, construction, oil and gas, and forestry industries around the world. In 2012 the company generated $3.3 billion in revenue.

Longest railway tunnel

Yes, there is a light at the end of the tunnel. Canada is home to the longest railway tunnel in North America, the 14.7-km Mount MacDonald Tunnel in British Columbia's Selkirk Mountains. Construction of the tunnel was completed in 1988.

Busiest port

Port Metro, Vancouver is the nation's largest and busiest port. More than 70 million tonnes of cargo, delivered from more than 3,000 different container ships, pass through the port each year.

INNOVATIONS
SPARTAN APPLE

Here's another great Canadian food invention: the Spartan apple. The variety was first developed in Summerland, British Columbia, by R.C. Palmer at a federal experimental farm. Interestingly, the exact parentage of the species is in question. It was once thought to be a cross between a McIntosh and a Newtown, but testing has ruled out the Newtown.

OLDEST STERNWHEELER

The SS *Moyie* is the world's oldest intact passenger sternwheeler. The ship was retired in 1957 after 59 years of service for the Canadian Pacific Railway's BC Lake and River Service. The *Moyie* performed a number of duties over its lifetime and was the last operating sternwheeler in Canada. The ship is a national historic site today at its home in Kaslo, British Columbia.

Worst streetcar disaster

The worst streetcar disaster in North America occurred on May 26, 1896, when a car plunged in the Victoria Harbour after a span fell out of the bridge at Point Ellice. Fifty-five people died.

Lowest road

The lowest point on a public road in Canada is in the George Massey Tunnel under the Fraser River near Vancouver International Airport (it's 20 m below sea level). The 629-m tunnel, which opened in 1959, was considered an engineering marvel. It was the first project in North America to use immersed-tube technology. Six concrete segments, each 105 m long and weighing 16,783 tonnes, were built on dry land, joined, sealed and sunk into place.

Fastest highway

The Alaska Highway, which runs from Dawson Creek, British Columbia, to Fairbanks, Alaska, was built faster than any other highway in the world. The entire 2,451-km freeway was built in less than a year, through 1942 and 1943.

↙ First gas station

Here's a fill 'er up first: the nation's first gas station opened in Vancouver in June 1907. Prior to the development of specialized gas stations, drivers had to fill up at distribution sites, which were typically located on the edges of towns or cities.

Biggest dump truck

In Sparwood, British Columbia, they call it simply "The Truck." The truck in question, a 1974 Terex Titan, is the largest tandem axel dump truck in the world. The 350-tonne, 20-m-long, 3,300-hp vehicle is so big, it can fit two Greyhound buses and two pickups in the box at the same time.

Fuel-cell factory ↘

The Mercedes-Benz plant in Burnaby, British Columbia, is the planet's first automated facility dedicated to producing automotive fuel cells. It opened in June 2012.

First fuel-cell car

The world's first fuel-cell car, Daimler-Benz's NECar I, used fuel-cell technology created by British Columbia's Ballard Power Systems. Invented in 1994, the car required 12 fuel-cell stacks to create 50 kW of power.

First fuel-cell bus

British Columbia-based Ballard Power Systems unveiled the world's first fuel-cell bus in 1993. The 9.75-m shuttle bus could carry 20 people, and created less greenhouse gas emissions than conventional buses.

Fuel-cell bus

The world's largest fleet of fuel-cell buses were part of BC Transit's fleet at the Vancouver 2010 Winter Olympics. The 20 buses (still operating in Whistler and representing 87 percent of that city's fleet), have a top speed of 90 km per hour and are estimated to stay in service for 20 years.

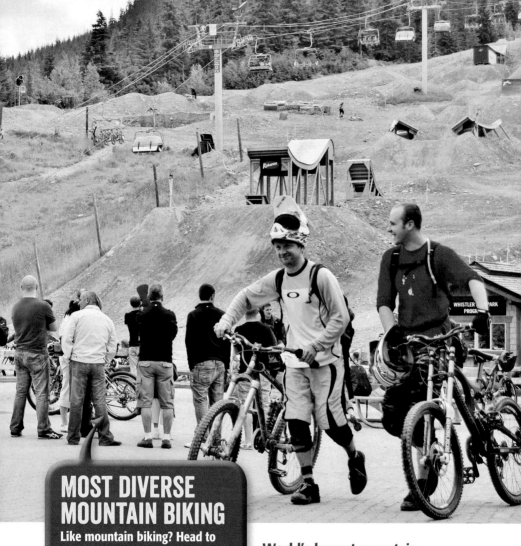

MOST DIVERSE MOUNTAIN BIKING

Like mountain biking? Head to Whistler, British Columbia, home to what's claimed to be the most-diverse mountain biking terrain on the planet. The town is home to 241 km of single-track trails, 200 km of lift-accessed downhill runs at the Whistler Mountain Bike Parks, trail parks and 32 km of paved trails in the Valley Trail system.

World's largest mountain bike festival

Whistler, British Columbia, is well known for its skiing. Its likely not very well known for its mountain biking, but maybe it should be, given that it's home to the world's largest freeride mountain bike festival. Crankworx Whistler is held for 10 days each August and attracts the globe's best amateur and professional mountain bikers.

Steepest vertical drop

If you like downhill skiing in one really long run, British Columbia's Revelstoke Mountain Resort is for you. It boasts the largest vertical drop of any ski resort on the continent at 1,713 m.

Youngest to swim Juan de Fuca Strait

On August 23, 1956, Marilyn Bell became the youngest person to swim across British Columbia's Juan de Fuca Strait. She completed the crossing in 10 hours and 39 minutes, after which she retired from marathon swimming.

Fastest cyclist

A native of Quadra Island, British Columbia, Sam Whittingham is considered the fastest bicyclist in the world. He holds five cycling speed records from the World Human Powered Vehicle Association and shares another. His fastest speed was recorded on September 18, 2009, at Battle Mountain, Nevada, when he clocked 133.28 km/hour in the men's 200 m flying start.

SKI ON A GLACIER

The Whistler Blackcomb Ski Resort, in Whistler, British Columbia, is the only ski resort in North America where you can ski or ride on a glacier. The Horstman Glacier is typically open to skiing through June and July, helping Whistler Blackcomb achieve the country's longest ski season.

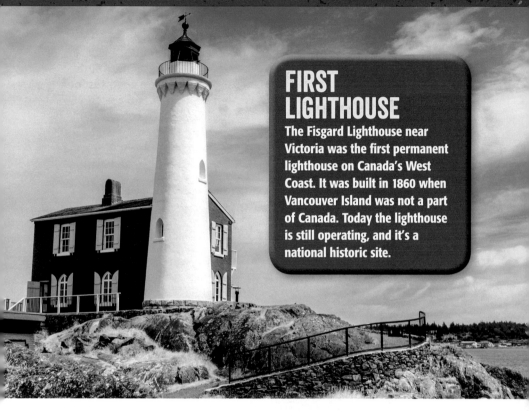

FIRST LIGHTHOUSE

The Fisgard Lighthouse near Victoria was the first permanent lighthouse on Canada's West Coast. It was built in 1860 when Vancouver Island was not a part of Canada. Today the lighthouse is still operating, and it's a national historic site.

First McDonald's restaurant

Richmond, British Columbia, was home to the first McDonald's restaurant outside of the United States. It opened on June 1, 1967.

First marine police

The Vancouver Police Department established the nation's first marine squad in 1911.

First women police officers

The Vancouver Police Department was also the first in the country—and the third in the world—to hire female offices. It hired two women officers on July 8, 1912.

Oldest western city

Quick, name the oldest city in Western Canada? Did you know it was New Westminster, British Columbia? The city was selected to become the first capital of the colony of British Columbia in 1859, and it was incorporated on July 17, 1860. It was named by Queen Victoria (after here favourite neighbourhood in London, Westminster), and was the capital of BC until 1866.

Miniature trees

The Gardens at the Horticulture Centre of the Pacific in Victoria are home to the nation's largest bonsai garden (made up of the miniature trees grown in containers), and the second largest on the continent.

Highest restaurant
Talk about dining at the height of style. Eagle's Eye restaurant at the Kicking Horse Mountain Resort near Golden, British Columbia, is the country's highest eatery. Located at the summit of the Golden Eagle Express gondola, it's 2,350 m above sea level. Reservations are highly recommended.

Oldest working birdcage elevator
The Maritime Museum of BC in Victoria features the oldest continuously operating birdcage elevator in North America. The building the museum is housed in was built as the home of the province's first Supreme Court, which opened February 1, 1889. The elevator was installed during a renovation in 1899–1900.

Lowest birth rate
British Columbia has the country's lowest birth rate, at an average of 1.42 children per woman, according to 2011 data from Statistics Canada.

Biggest planned explosion
Ripple Rock was a killer. More than 20 large ships and at least 100 smaller vessels were sunk or damaged by the underwater mountain in the Seymour Narrows near Campbell River, British Columbia, and 114 people lost their lives as a result. So on April 5, 1958, Ripple Rock became the site of the world's largest peacetime non-atomic explosion, when it was blown up to prevent further accidents.

FIRST WHEELCHAIR AROUND THE WORLD
Man in Motion, no doubt. Canadian Rick Hansen, born on August 26, 1957, in Port Alberni, British Columbia, became world famous in 1985 when he travelled more than 40,000 km around the world through 34 countries in his wheelchair to raise awareness for spinal cord injuries and research. Dubbed the Man in Motion World Tour, Hansen's feat—the first such ever—raised more than $26 million.

Deadliest avalanche

The deadliest avalanche in Canadian history occurred on March 5, 1910, when 62 railway workers were killed two km west of Rogers Pass, British Columbia. Their engine was hit by a snow slide and hurtled 500 m into Bear Creek. More than 600 volunteers dug through 10 m of snow with shovels and pickaxes in search of survivors.

Worst offshore earthquake

The largest recorded earthquake in the country was an 8.1 magnitude quake that struck offshore near British Columbia's Haida Gwaii islands on August 22, 1949. Considered one of the largest quakes ever, the tremor fortunately did not cause any deaths, although the shaking was so significant it was said to have knocked cows off their feet on Haida Gwaii.

Worst onshore earthquake

The largest recorded onshore earthquake in Canadian history occurred on June 23, 1946, on Vancouver Island. The epicentre of the 7.3 magnitude quake was in the Forbidden Plateau area in central Vancouver Island. It caused considerable damage in many island communities, including Comox, Port Alberni and Powell River, and resulted in one death (a drowning caused by a wave that capsized a small boat).

LONGEST BEARD

Sarwan Singh of Surrey, British Columbia, has the longest beard in the world according to Guinness World Records. Singh's beard, measured on March 4, 2010, was 2.37 m long.

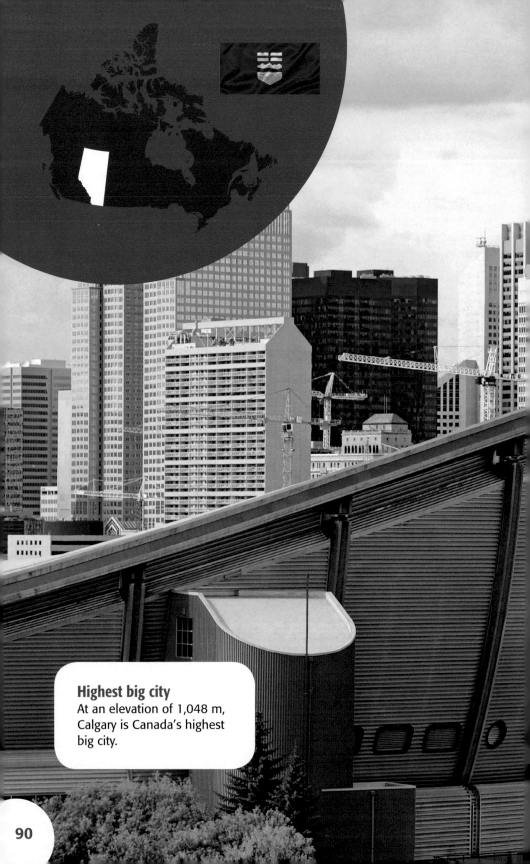

Highest big city
At an elevation of 1,048 m, Calgary is Canada's highest big city.

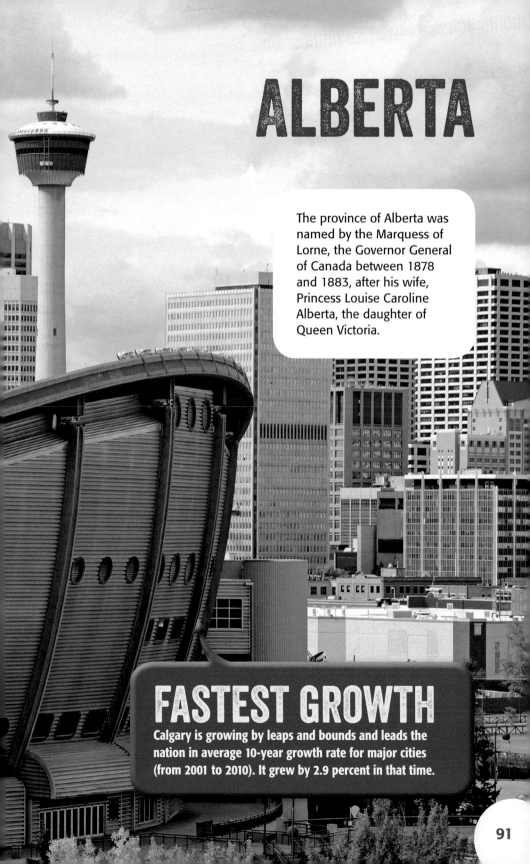

ALBERTA

The province of Alberta was named by the Marquess of Lorne, the Governor General of Canada between 1878 and 1883, after his wife, Princess Louise Caroline Alberta, the daughter of Queen Victoria.

FASTEST GROWTH

Calgary is growing by leaps and bounds and leads the nation in average 10-year growth rate for major cities (from 2001 to 2010). It grew by 2.9 percent in that time.

LARGEST ERRATIC

A big rock, indeed. Known as "The Big Rock," the Okotoks Erratic (a rock moved from its original location by a glacier) is the largest known glacial erratic in the world. Weighing an estimated 16,500 tonnes, and measuring about 9 m high, 41 m long and 18 m wide, the Big Rock is located southwest of Okotoks, Alberta. It's believed the erratic was originally part of a mountain in what is now Jasper National Park, some 450 km away.

Longest river system
It could be the nation's longest winding trail. The Mackenzie River system is Canada's longest waterway, from its origins in the Columbia Icefields in Alberta's Jasper National Park and the deep snowfields of the upper Peace River in northeastern British Columbia to its mouth on the Beaufort Sea of the Arctic Ocean on Nunavut's coast. Including all the rivers and lakes of the system's 1.8-million-square-km drainage basin, it stretches 4,241 km in total, ranking as the world's 13th-longest river system.

Highest point
At an elevation of 3,747 m, Mount Columbia in Banff National Park is the highest point in Alberta. (It's also the second-highest point in the Canadian Rockies.)

Largest cave

The country's largest known cave system, Castleguard Cave, is located in Alberta's Banff National Park. The cave extends for 23 km below the Columbia Icefields. It is the world's only cave where some passages are plugged by ice pushed in from the surface. The cave's entrance tends to flood unexpectedly, so the cave can only be safely explored in winter.

Second-largest glacier-fed lake ↗

Located in Alberta's Jasper National Park, Maligne Lake is the second-largest glacier-fed lake in the world. The lake is 22 km long and 97 m deep.

Greenest city ↘

It's nicknamed "Festival City" owing to its year-round slate of cultural events, but an equally apt moniker for Edmonton might be "City of Green." Alberta's capital lays claim to the largest urban green space in North America. The "Ribbon of Green" winds its way through the city along the shores of the North Saskatchewan River, with nature areas and more than 150 km of trails.

First national park

Canada's first national park, Banff National Park, was created in 1885, and was the world's third national park. The 6,641-square-km protected area in Alberta is the most-visited national park in the country.

First international peace park

Except for that war we won in 1812, Canada and the United States have had a relatively cordial relationship. Indeed, in 1932, the nations joined to create the world's first international peace park, Waterton-Glacier International Peace Park. (There are now 170 peace parks around the globe.) Designated a UNESCO world heritage site on December 6, 1995, the 4,556-square-km cross-border park joins Alberta's Waterton Lakes National Park and Montana's Glacier National Park.

Most dinosaur fossils

Where will you find the richest area of dinosaur fossils in the world? Why, Alberta's Dinosaur Provincial Park, naturally. Since the 1880s, more than 150 complete dinosaur skeletons have been unearthed from a 27-km area near the Red Deer River. More than 40 dinosaur species have been found here, as well as the fossils of 450 other organisms.

↑ Most petroglyphs and pictographs

Alberta's Writing-on-Stone Provincial Park, located in the southeast corner of the province, is home to the largest concentration of First Nation petroglyphs (rock carvings) and pictographs (rock paintings) on the great plains of North America.

Largest mountain park

Looking for a park full of mountains? Look no further than Alberta's Jasper National Park, the largest mountain national park in the country. The 11,228-square-km park, boasts stunning mountain vistas, a plethora of wildlife and more than 1,200 km of hiking trails.

Hydrographic apex

The hydrographic apex of North America — the only spot on the continent where water flows to three different oceans from one point — is the Columbia Icefield in Alberta's Jasper National Park.

BEST BUFFALO JUMP

Talk about a literal place name! Alberta's Head-Smashed-In Buffalo Jump is considered one of the Earth's oldest, largest and best-preserved buffalo jumps. Now a UNESCO world heritage site, the spot was used by Aboriginal peoples for close to 6,000 years to drive plains bison to their deaths by stampeding them off the edge of the cliffs.

Head-Smashed-In Buffalo Jump Interpretive Centre

Hours of Operation: Open 9 a.m. to 6 p.m.

Alberta
COMMUNITY DEVELOPMENT

MOST EXPENSIVE FLOODS

It's still fresh in the memory of most Canadians and certainly in the minds of southern Albertans. The Insurance Bureau of Canada has called the floods that hit the southern area of the province from June 20 to June 24, 2013, the costliest insured natural disaster in Canada. Property damages from the flooding were estimated at more than $1.7 billion dollars.

Snowiest May

Calgary receives more snow in May, September and October than any other Canadian city. On average, Calgary has two to three days of snow in May, one or two in September and four (!) in October.

Sunniest big city

Looking for a staycation suntan? Move to Calgary. It is the nation's sunniest large city, getting 2,396 hours of sunshine on average annually. And it comes over 333 days. That's more than half of the city's daylight hours.

City	Days
Calgary, AB	333
Edmonton, AB	325
Regina, SK	322
Saskatoon, SK	319
Winnipeg, MB	316
Victoria, BC	308
Montreal, QC	305
Toronto, ON	305
Thunder Bay, ON	305
Kelowna, BC	304

Percentage of sunshine

Here's a list of the country's sunniest cities, as measured by the percentage of the daylight hours the sun shines on average:

City	% sunshine
Calgary, AB	52
Winnipeg, MB	51
Edmonton, AB	50
Regina, SK	50
Saskatoon, SK	49
Thunder Bay, ON	46
Hamilton, ON	45
Ottawa, ON	45
Toronto, ON	44
Montreal, QC	44

Driest city in Canada

Conserve the water. Medicine Hat, Alberta, has more dry days than any other Canadian city, with 271 days per year without measurable precipitation.

Biggest mercury jump

There's a saying in Canada that if you don't like the weather, wait five minutes. Never could that have been truer than in Pincher Creek, Alberta, where Canada's most extreme temperature change was recorded. The mercury soared from −19°C to 22°C in just one hour.

Largest beaver dam

DAM! The world's largest beaver dam (spotted on satellite images by the scientists who discovered it) is found in Wood Buffalo National Park.

SMALLEST BIRD

Keep your eyes peeled: Canada's smallest bird is the calliope hummingbird, which is about 7 cm long (shown life size here) and weighs just 2.5 g. It's found in central British Columbia and southwestern Alberta.

FASTEST ANIMAL

The pronghorn antelope, found in southern Alberta and Saskatchewan, is the fastest land animal in North America, capable of reaching speeds up to 72 km per hour in short bursts and sustaining speeds up to 60 km per hour over longer distances. Its speeds over longer distance lead some to consider it the fastest land animal in the world.

Biggest bighorn sheep

This bighorn sheep really did have big horns. The world record bighorn sheep was taken near Luscar Mountain, Alberta, by Guinn D. Crousen in 2000. The Boone and Crockett Club, the international keeper of such records, scored the animal 2083/8. The score is based on a combination of characteristics of the horns.

Biggest mosque

Baitunnur Mosque in Calgary is the largest Muslim mosque complex in the country at 4,460 square m.

First planetarium

Sit back and enjoy the view. Canada's first planetarium, the Queen Elizabeth II Planetarium in Edmonton, opened on September 22, 1960. The planetarium closed on December 31, 1983.

Largest military training area

Canadian Forces Base Suffield, north of Medicine Hat, Alberta, is the nation's largest military training area in Canada. The base, which falls under the command of the 3rd Canadian Division, covers 2,690 square km.

Biggest jail

Go to jail, go directly to Canada's biggest jail—the Edmonton Remand Centre. The facility has space for 1,952 beds and is the size of 10 CFL football fields: 59,511 square m.

Largest pedestrian walkway network

Calgary's +15 Skyway is a system of pedestrian walkways (including a series of elevated, protected bridges) that connect buildings in the city's downtown core. It is the largest network of its kind on Earth. Called the "+15" because it's about 15 feet above the ground, the 18-km system now has 62 bridges.

Highest town

Look up, way up—to Banff, Alberta, Canada's highest town. It sits at an elevation of 1,383 m above sea level.

Biggest indoor lake

West Edmonton Mall is home to the world's largest permanent indoor lake. The lake includes an exact replica of the Santa Maria, the flagship of Christopher Columbus' 1492 expedition to North America.

Biggest indoor amusement park

The West Edmonton Mall's Galaxyland is the world's largest indoor amusement park. It features 24 rides and attractions.

Biggest parking lot

Looking for a parking spot? At West Edmonton Mall, that shouldn't be a problem. The mall boasts the planet's largest parking lot, with a capacity for 20,000 vehicles. A lot adjacent to the mall has space for another 10,000 cars.

↑ Biggest shopping mall

Edmonton is home to the largest mall in North America, the West Edmonton Mall, at 4.9 million square m. From 1981 until 2004 it was the largest mall in the world. The shopping centre boasts 800 stores and services, including 2 hotels and more than 100 restaurants. Approximately 30.8 million shoppers descend on it each year. That's serious retail therapy.

Biggest indoor miniature golf course

West Edmonton Mall is also home to the world's largest indoor miniature golf course. Professor WEM's Adventure Golf Course features 18 holes, complete with sand traps and water hazards.

Biggest indoor wave pool

West Edmonton Mall is also home to the globe's largest indoor wave pool, which is part of the mall's World Waterpark.

BIGGEST INDOOR TRIPLE-LOOP ROLLER COASTER

West Edmonton Mall boasts the world's largest indoor triple-loop roller coaster, the Mindbender, which is part of the mall's Galaxyland amusement park.

Highest gross domestic product

Further bolstering Calgary's rise as one of the country's financial centres is the fact that the city has had the highest total gross domestic product in Canada over the past 10 years (from 2001 to 2010), at 29.6 percent.

Most head offices

Despite being considered the country's financial capital, Toronto does not lead the nation in number of head offices. Calgary holds the distinction of the highest concentration of head offices per capita in Canada, at 9.3 percent.

Highest wages

Want to make some serious salary? Calgary's the place to be for that. It leads the nation in highest wages and salaries per employee for a decade (2001 to 2010). In 2010, the average annual wage per employee was $65,121.

Longest bike urban bike trail ↑

Ring, ring! Looking for a long bike ride? Head to Calgary, home of the longest network of urban bike pathways on the continent. The city boasts some 800 km of bike-riding routes, which of course can also be used by walkers, runners and rollerbladers, too. The city even provides snow-clearing services to nearly half the system, so it can be used throughout the year.

INNOVATIONS
BLOODY CAESAR

The Bloody Caesar cocktail was first created in 1969 at Marco's Italian restaurant at the Calgary Inn (which is now the Westin Calgary). The beverage was invented to celebrate the restaurant's grand opening.

The most horse-drawn vehicles ↘

The continent's largest collection of horse-drawn vehicles resides at the Remington Carriage Museum in Cardston, Alberta. The museum boasts more than 270 carriages, buggies, wagons and sleighs from the 19th and early 20th centuries.

The most manuals

Here's a unique niche achievement. The Reynolds-Alberta Museum, just west of Wetaskiwin, Alberta, is home to the nation's largest collection of publically held service and operation manuals for cars, trucks and planes. The museum's resource centre houses hundreds of books on parts, sales catalogues and brochures, magazines and other reference files. The museum is also home to the nation's second-largest collection of vintage aircraft (after the Canadian Aviation and Space Museum in Ottawa).

First landing pad for UFOs ↗

Who needs Area 51? Canada has the world's first UFO landing pad. The unique landmark was built in the town of St. Paul, Alberta, and opened on June 3, 1967. In 1996, a UFO interpretive centre was built to accompany the pad.

Longest runway

Slated to open in June, 2014, the new fourth runway at Calgary International Airport will become Canada's longest, at 4,267 m long and 61 m wide. It was planned as part of the airport's $2 billion development program, in response to passenger volume doubling in the last two decades. The new landing strip will be capable of landing the world's largest aircraft, the A380 and B747-800. One million square m of concrete will be used to pave the new runway and related taxiways, and more than 5,000 LED lights will illuminate the area.

First flight over Rockies

The first flight over the Canadian Rocky Mountains occurred on August 7, 1919. Pilot Ernest Hoy flew a Curtiss JN-4 from Vancouver to Calgary. The flight took 16.5 hours.

Most country music

It's possible they're biased, but Alberta Travel claims the Big Valley Jamboree is the largest outdoor music festival in North America. Held annually in mid-summer since 1993 in Camrose, southeast of Edmonton, the four-day country music fest has hosted a who's who of the genre's top acts.

Biggest Fringe

The Edmonton International Fringe Theatre Festival was the first such festival and it is the largest in North America and the second-largest in the world. It's been held each August since 1982.

First international winter event

Cool! The XV Olympic Winter Games, held in Calgary from Feb. 13 to 28, 1988, marked the first time the international winter event was held in Canada. A total of 1,423 athletes participated in 46 events.

FIRST QUADRUPLE JUMP

He put a whole new spin on things. In 1988, at the World Figure Skating Championships in Budapest, Hungary, Kurt Browning, born in Rocky Mountain House, Alberta, on June 18, 1966, performed the first quadruple jump in competition in the sport's history. Oh, he won the championship, too.

Winter Olympic firsts

The Calgary Olympics (see previous page) established a number of firsts in Olympics history. The super giant slalom skiing event was included in the games for the first time, the speed skating events were held in a covered facility for the first time, and curling, short-track speed skating and freestyle skiing were all demonstration events for the first time.

Fastest zipline

WinSport's Canada Olympic Park in Calgary is home to the fastest zipline on the continent. It's a drop of more than 100 metres from the top of the ski jump tower at the park travelling at a top speed of between 120 and 140 km per hour along the 500-m-long line. Don't forget to hold on tight!

Fastest ice

It's hardly surprising that the so-called "fastest ice in the world" is in Canada. Specifically, it's at the Olympic Oval in Calgary, built for the 1988 Winter Olympic Games. It's earned the honour thanks to the 258 long track and 30 short track world records set on the surface. Why so quick? The ice is made with demineralized water, which reduces the amount of dirt and mineral buildup that can create friction between ice and skate. Less friction equals faster ice. The track was also the first fully covered 400 m oval in North America.

Greatest basketball team

James Naismith called the Edmonton Grads "the finest basketball team that ever stepped out on a floor." Between 1915 and 1940, The Edmonton Commercial Graduates, a women's team often referred to as the greatest basketball team ever, played 522 games the world over and won 502, including 147 straight victories. The Grads also won seven of nine games against men's teams.

Crazy Canuck World Cup win

Considered the leader of the Crazy Canucks, Canada's team of top competitive skiers of the 1970s and 1980s, Ken Read was the first non-European to win a World Cup downhill race. Read, who calls Calgary home, achieved the milestone in Val d'Isere, France in 1975.

First concussion sensors in high school

There's no shortage of concussion talk these days in sports. And thankfully, lots of experts are doing their best to prevent the head injuries. In the fall of 2013, Calgary's Ernest Manning High School became the first secondary school in Canada to install specifically designed sensors (called the "Shockbox") in their helmets to measure the impact of collisions. Calgary's Canadian Football League team, the Stampeders, were the first pigskin club in the country to employ the device.

Longest golf hole

Fore! Actually, perhaps that's not necessary on Canada's longest golf hole. The 11th hole at The Nursery Golf and Country Club near Lacombe, Alberta, is a whopping 782 yards! The course's hole description notes: "Your first two shots are critical…" Indeed.

Longest luge ↓

The Skyline Calgary luge track is the world's longest, at 1.8 km. The warm-weather track, which uses wheeled sleds, drops more than 100 m over its entire length. Located at the city's Winsport Olympic Park, the summer track runs along the luge course built for the 1988 Winter Games.

BIGGEST SKI RESORT

If you're looking for a ski run, look no further than Alberta's Lake Louise Ski Resort, the nation's largest, and one of the biggest on the continent. The resort boasts 4,200 skiable areas, 145 named runs and 10 lifts. The resort's longest run is 8 km.

First cereal box appearance

Bet you'll never guess who was the first Canadian athlete to appear on the front of an American cereal box. Did you know it was Kurt Browning? Figure skater Browning graced the front of Special K boxes in 1998.

First Canadian to climb Everest

Talk about the height of sports. Laurie Skreslet, born in Calgary on October 25, 1949, was the first Canadian to climb to the summit of Mount Everest, the world's tallest peak. He did it on his 33rd birthday, October 5, 1982.

Official anthem

Alberta is the third province with an official provincial song. The tune, titled Alberta, was composed by Mary Kieftenbeld as part of a contest to create an official song for the province's centennial in 2005.

Flatlands, rollin' plains
Clear blue skies, prairie rains;
A tapestry of colours in the fall.
Snow covered mountain tops,
Wheat fields, canola crops;
Alberta has it all.

Chorus

Alberta is calling me.
Home sweet home, it's where I'm
    proud to be.
Alberta is calling me.
Livin' right I'm feelin' free.

Verse 2

First Nations built the land
Fur trade, way back then.
We've come a long way since that.
Agriculture, lumberjacks,
Oil derricks, natural gas;
There is no turnin' back.

Bridge

Culture diverse as it can be.
This is the land of opportunity.
Welcoming friends, night and day.
That's the way I pray Alberta stays.

Largest collection of troll dolls

Here's a real dedication to dolls. Ray Dyson of Edmonton owns the world's largest collection of troll dolls, with 1,754 unique versions of the collectible creatures. Dyson owns more than 4,000 troll-related items in total.

Biggest ice cream sundae

Here's a tasty world record. A group of Edmonton residents holds the record for creating the world's largest ice cream sundae. On July 24, 1988, the group filled an empty temporary swimming pool in the Edmonton City Centre Mall with 350-pound slabs of ice cream in 63 flavours, along with 45-gallon drums of various toppings. The sundae weighed a whopping 24.91 tonnes.

BIGGEST QR CODE

Increasingly, corn mazes are popping up across the nation each fall. And in 2012, a family in Lacombe, Alta., created a particularly memorable one in the shape of a giant QR code (a barcode that can be scanned by electronic devices). Indeed, it was so big (28,760-square metres), it was recognized as the world's largest QR code.

Longest dog's tail

Bet you this dog's tail is longer than your dog's tail! Finnegan, an Irish wolfhound owned by Reilly Smith from Calgary, Alta., hold's the Guinness World Record for longest dog tail. Finnegan's tail measured 72.29 cm long. The record was established on August 15, 2013.

Largest living history museum

Want to get a load of history? Try a visit to Fort Edmonton Park, known alternatively as "Canada's largest living history museum" or "the largest historical theme park in Canada." Among the attractions at the 63-hectare park: more than 80 historical buildings, a steam-engine train, four early-1900 streetcars and a stagecoach.

First Aboriginal senator ↘

The first Aboriginal appointed to Canada's Senate was James Gladstone in 1958. Gladstone, a member of the Blood Tribe of the Blackfoot Nation, represented the province of Alberta. When he was appointed, status Indians in the country did not have the right to vote — a right Gladstone helped to fight for, and which was granted in 1960.

Highest after-tax income

Want to keep more of your money? Move to Alberta. That province has the nation's highest median after-tax income.

Most dinosaurs ↗

Looking for dinosaur bones? The Royal Tyrrell Museum of Palaeontology, near Drumheller, Alberta, has the largest display of dinosaurs on Earth. It's Canada's only museum dedicated to palaeontology. The museum, which opened September 25, 1985, is named after Joseph Burr Tyrrell, who discovered the Albertosaurus in 1884, not far from the museum's site near Kneehill Creek.

Worst rockslide

The worst rockslide in Canadian history occurred on April 29, 1903, when 82 million tonnes of rock crashed down from the Turtle Mountain on the town of Frank, Alberta. The slide killed 70 people.

LARGEST CAPITAL BUILDING

The prairie vistas are not the only big things in Saskatchewan. The province's Legislative Building in Regina is the largest capital building in Canada. Planning for the building began less than a year after Saskatchewan became a province on September 1, 1905. The home of Saskatchewan's Legislative Assembly, the building opened on October 12, 1912, and is surrounded by one of the largest urban parks in North America. The façade and interior reflect the beaux-arts architectural style of the time.

SASKATCHEWAN

The name Saskatchewan is derived from Cree *kisiskâciwanisîpiy*, meaning "swift-flowing river." Saskatchewan became a province of Canada on September 1, 1905.

Highest point

Since Saskatchewan is known for its expanse of flat prairie, it seems suitable that the highest point in the province is referred to as a hill. The Cypress Hills to be exact, located in the province's southwestern corner. The so-called "West Block" of the Hills, lying along the border with Alberta, has an elevation of 1,392 m. This geographical region extends into Alberta, where the highest point rises 1,466 m above sea level.

Largest lake that drains two ways

Northeastern Saskatchewan's Wollaston Lake (2,681 square km) is the largest lake in the world that naturally drains in two directions. The Fond Du Lac River drains from Wollaston to the northwest into Lake Athabasca and the Mackenize River system, while the Cochrane River drains from the lake to the northeast into Reindeer Lake and the Hudson Bay basin.

Largest inland freshwater delta

While such things are debatable because of the range of criteria on which they're based, nonetheless the Global Institute for Water Security considers the Saskatchewan River Delta — a series of lakes, rivers and wetlands along the Saskatchewan-Manitoba border — to be the largest inland freshwater delta in North America and one of the largest in the world. This river delta is also known as one of the most biologically diverse regions in the country.

SALTY LAKE

Water so buoyant it's impossible to sink? Head to the Dead Sea, right? Or go to central Saskatchewan's Little Manitou Lake. Fed by underground springs, the 13.3-square-km lake has mineral salt concentrations of 180,000 mg per litre, making the water extremely buoyant.

COLDEST CITY

Canada's coldest city? A tie between Saskatoon and Regina, with –50°C recorded on February 1, 1893, and January 1, 1885, respectively. The most recent sub –40°C temperature recorded in a Canadian city? Sherbrooke, Quebec, at –41.2°C on January 15, 2004.

Largest dune fields

Think of long, sandy beaches and you probably don't think of Canada. You also probably don't think of Canada's north. But the Athabasca Sand Dunes, a series of dune fields running about 100 km along the south shore of Lake Athabasca in northwest Saskatchewan, is the largest active sand dune surface in Canada and one of the most northern dune fields on Earth.

Closest to centre

At a latitude of 50°26' and a longitude of 104°37', Regina is the Canadian city closest to the geographical centre of North America.

Non-geographic boundaries

Saskatchewan is the only province in the country that has no geographical features as boundaries.

Coldest big city

Saskatoon holds the record for the coldest major Canadian city, based on mean daily temperature (averaged over the year), at 2.2°C. Winterpeg, er, Winnipeg, is actually the third coldest major city at 2.6°C, following Saguenay, Quebec, at 2.3°C.

Major cities with the least snow

Here are the least snowiest major cities in the country, outside of British Columbia.

Annual average snowfall a year

City	cm	inches
Saskatoon, SK	73.4	28.9
Brantford, ON	98.4	38.7
Regina, SK	100.2	39.4
Oshawa, ON	105.8	41.6
Winnipeg, MB	113.7	44.8
Hamilton, ON	118.1	46.5

Hot day in Saskatchewan

On July 5, 1937, the mercury soared to 45°C in Yellow Grass, Saskatchewan.

Temperatures higher than 40°C

Here's a list of when and where temperatures 40°C and higher were recorded in Canada:

Location	°C	Day
Midale and Yellow Grass, SK	45.0	July 5, 1937
Lillooet and Lytton, BC	44.4	July 16 & 17, 1941
St Albans, MB	44.4	July 11, 1936
Emerson, MB	44.4	July 12, 1936
Brandon and Morden, MB	43.3	July 11, 1936
Regina, SK	43.3	July 5, 1937
Fort Macleod, AB	43.3	July 18, 1941
Oliver, BC	42.8	July 27, 1939
Osoyoos, BC	42.8	July 27, 1998
Spences Bridge, BC	42.5	July 23, 1994
Medicine Hat, AB	42.2	July 12, 1886
Moose Jaw, SK	41.7	August 6, 1949
Winnipeg, MB	40.6	August 7, 1949
Saskatoon, SK	40.6	June 5, 1988
Kamloops, BC	40.6	July 31, 1971
Atikokan, ON	42.2	July 11 & 12, 1936
Northwest River, NL	41.7	August 11, 1914
Windsor, ON	40.2	June 25, 1988
Temiscamingue, QC	40.0	July 6, 1921

Sunshine capital

Estevan, Canada's sunshine capital is in southeast Saskatchewan. It averages 2,540 hours of sunlight each year.

Deadliest tornado

Known as the "Regina Cyclone," the tornado that hit Saskatchewan's capital in the late afternoon of June 30, 1912, is considered the deadliest such storm in Canadian history. The whirlwind tore through six city blocks, killed some 40 people and injured 300 more. It destroyed 500 buildings and left a quarter of the city's population homeless. It took an estimated 46 years to pay for the damages of the three-minute storm.

Freezing cities in summer

Yes, it happens. Below zero temperatures in summer—yes, summer—in large Canadian cities. Here are the seven cities across the country that have seen the freezing mark in June, July or August:

City	Lowest °C	Date
Regina, SK	−5.6	June 12, 1969
Calgary, AB	−3.3	June 8, 1891
Saskatoon, SK	−3.3	June 9, 1903
Winnipeg, MB	−3.3	June 3, 1964
St. John's, NL	−3.3	June 1, 1970
Sherbrooke, QC	−2.2	June 3, 1965
Saguenay, QC	−2.2	June 12, 1946

The hottest and the coldest

As most Canadians know and have experienced, this country can deliver a wide range of temperatures, from cold winter nights to hot summer days. Interestingly, among Canada's large cities, Regina lays claim to both the country's lowest recorded temperature and its highest. The city sweltered at 43.3°C on July 5, 1937. Likewise, Winnipeg and Saskatoon, both holding cold-weather records themselves, also posted some of the highest recorded temperatures for large Canadian cities; they tied for second place at 40.6°C (Winnipeg on August 7, 1949 and Saskatoon on June 5, 1988).

Biggest lake trout

If there's a freshwater fish synonymous with Canada, it's got to be the lake trout. It should come as no surprise that the largest laker ever recorded was caught by a commercial angler in Saskatchewan's Lake Athabasca in 1961. The trout measured 126 cm long and weighed 43.6 kg.

Biggest rainbow trout

What's at the end of a rainbow? Who cares, when it's a world-record rainbow trout. The International Game Fish Association all-tackle world-record rainbow, a 21.77 kg specimen, was caught on September 5, 2009, in Saskatchewan's Lake Diefenbaker.

Biggest whitetail deer

With a name like Biggar, is it any wonder that the Saskatchewan town has the world record for the largest typical whitetail deer taken by a hunter? The Boone and Crockett Club scored the deer 213⅝. The score is based on a combination of the length of the antlers and the number of points they have. The big buck was taken by hunter Milo Hanson in November 1993.

FIRST WATERFOWL REFUGE

Saskatchewan's Last Mountain Lake Bird Sanctuary was the first waterfowl refuge in North America. It was established in 1887. More than 280 species of birds have been recorded in the 15,600-hectare sanctuary, and more than 100 of these species breed there. It's also an important area for migratory birds, and in the fall up to 50,000 sandhill cranes, 450,000 geese and several hundred thousand ducks pass through – often in flocks of tens of thousands.

Longest pedestrian bridge

Originally built as a railway bridge, the 914-m viaduct in Outlook, Saskatchewan, is the country's longest pedestrian bridge. Crossing the South Saskatchewan River and part of the Trans Canada Trail, the bridge operated as a railway bridge from October 23, 1912 until March 16, 1987.

Biggest geothermal mineral pool

Looking for natural relaxation? Try the Temple Gardens Mineral Spa Resort in Moose Jaw, Saskatchewan. It's home to the nation's largest therapeutic geothermal mineral water pool. The pool's waters are drawn from an ancient seabed more than 1,350 m underground and stay warm throughout the year.

One city, two provinces

Here's a unique geographical distinction: Lloydminster is the only city in Canada that straddles a provincial border. Located almost the same distance from both Edmonton and Saskatoon, Lloydminster was first settled in 1903. When the provinces of Alberta and Saskatchewan were formed in 1905, the settlement was split along the 4th meridian, the provincial boundary. On May 20, 1930, the two communities were reunited as a single municipality.

BIGGEST URANIUM MINE

Saskatchewan's McArthur River mine is the largest high-grade uranium mine on Earth. It can produce more than 8.16 million kg of uranium each year by mining just 150 to 200 tonnes of ore per day.

BIGGEST WHEAT-PRODUCING PROVINCE

Saskatchewan grows 45 percent of Canada's grain. It also produces more than 54 percent of the nation's wheat. Its production also accounts for 10 percent of the world's total exported wheat.

Biggest mustard producer

If you like your mustard, thank Saskatchewan. The prairie province is the world's largest mustard exporter. In 2013, the province produced 117,000 tonnes of mustard in three different types—yellow, brown and oriental.

Biggest fertilizer company

You could say it's a growing business. PotashCorp, based in Saskatoon, Saskatchewan, is the world's largest fertilizer company by capacity. It produces fertilizers from potash, phosphate and nitrogen. The company is aptly named, as it's the global leader in potash production, with 20 percent of the global capacity coming from its Canadian operations.

Longest fibre-optics network

SaskTel, a communications company based in Regina, created the world's longest commercial fibre-optics network, which was completed in 1984. The 3,268-km network connected 52 of the province's largest communities.

Automatic landing system

Electronics engineer Eric William Leaver, who grew up in Saskatchewan, invented an inertial guidance system (automatic landing system) for aircraft in the 1930s. Subsequent products based on his invention are used all over the world today.

Cobalt bomb ↓

Medical physicist Dr. Harold Johns and his graduate students at the University of Saskatchewan were the first researchers to successfully treat a cancer patient using cobalt-60 radiation therapy, in 1951. The technology, also known as the "cobalt bomb," significantly changed cancer treatment and saved and prolonged the lives of millions of cancer patients.

MOST ROAD

If someone tells you to hit the road in Saskatchewan, be prepared for a very long walk. The province has more road surface than any other in the country: a total of 250,000 km.

First film fest

Saskatchewan's Yorkton Film Festival, established as the Yorkton International Film Festival in 1947, was the first film festival in North America. The festival, held each May, was created by James Lysyshyn, a field officer for the National Film Board, and is still going strong today.

Canada's first fastest man ↓

He was Canada's first recorded fastest man: Harry Winston Jerome, born on September 30, 1940, in Prince Albert, Saskatchewan, was the first Canadian to officially hold a world track record. In 1960, at just 19, Jerome ran the 100 m in 10 seconds at the Canadian Olympic Trials to tie the world mark. Jerome held several sprinting world records through his career.

Aviation licence firsts

Roland J. Groome was a man of firsts. Along with Edward Clarke and Bob McCombie, Groome formed the Aerial Service Company in 1919 and built the first licensed aerodrome in Canada in Regina. Groome would become the first licensed commercial aviator in the nation. One of the company's aircraft became the country's first licensed commercial airplane: the *JN-4 Canuck* (registration number G-CAAA).

RCMP historic training site

All cadets of the Royal Canadian Mounted Police undergo their initial basic training at the RCMP Academy "Depot" Division in Regina. Established in 1885, the site was once the headquarters of the North West Mounted Police and then later, the Royal Northwest Mounted Police.

LARGEST NORTHERN INLAND SEA

Hudson Bay is considered the world's largest northern inland sea. It covers 822,324 square km. It's the world's second-largest bay, and the largest if measured by coastline, at 12,268 km. This satellite photo shows the Nelson (left) and Hayes rivers entering Hudson Bay. The lighter coloured shorelines are sandy beaches.

MANITOBA

It's believed there are two principle origins for the name of the province of Manitoba. The more likely inspiration for the name is from the Cree *maniotwapow*, or "the strait of the spirit or manitobau." This comes from the load sound made by pebbles on Manitoba Island in Lake Manitoba. The second possible origin is from Assiniboine words *mimi* and *tobow*, which combined mean "lake of the prairie."

HIGHEST POINT

The flat prairie plains of central Canada cover much of Manitoba. Still, Baldy Mountain in Duck Mountain Provincial Park is the province's highest point, at an elevation of 831 m. Visitors can drive to the top of the mountain and take in the surrounding region from a 12-m-high observation tower.

Coldest major cities

Canada's coldest major cities in winter, based on daily average temperature in December, January and February:

City	Daily Average °C
Winnipeg	−15.3
Saskatoon	−14.8
Saguenay	−13.9
Regina	−13.8
Sudbury	−11.5
Quebec City	−11.0
Sherbrooke	−10.1

Coldest temperatures in southern Canada

And the coldest recorded temperatures in southern Canada:

Location	°C	Date
Norway House, MB	−52.8	January 9, 1899
Esker 2, NL	−51.1	February 17, 1973
Schefferville, QC	−50.6	February 7, 1950
Sisson Dam, NB	−47.2	February 1, 1955
Upper Stewiacke, NS	−41.1	January 31, 1920
Kilmahumaig, PEI	−37.2	January 26, 1884

Winterpeg

Turns out Winnipeg may still have a legitimate claim to that Winterpeg moniker. Of Canada's large cities, the 'Peg leads when it comes to the average number of days when the temperature doesn't break 0°C, at 117. Perhaps it's not surprising that Saskatoon and Saguenay, Quebec, are second and third in the same category, with 112 and 110 days, respectively.

Most winter sunshine

Winnipeg has more hours of winter sunshine than any other Canadian city.

Most hours of sunshine

Despite the fact they're some of the country's snowiest and coldest cities, the following cities are also the sunniest. Here's the list of the nine cities (after Number One: Calgary) that received the highest average hours of sunlight annually:

City	Hours
Winnipeg, MB	2,353
Edmonton, AB	2,345
Regina, SK	2,318
Saskatoon, SK	2,268
Thunder Bay, ON	2,121
Hamilton, ON	2,111
Victoria, BC	2,109
Ottawa, ON	2,084
Toronto, ON	2,066

Deadliest heat wave

Environment Canada calls it the "deadliest heat wave in history." From July 5 to 17, 1936, temperatures in Manitoba and Ontario were more than 44°C and responsible for the death of 1,180 people (largely infants and the elderly). In an unfortunate twist of fate, 400 of those deaths were attributed to drowning from people trying to escape the heat. It was so hot that steel railways and bridge girders twisted, and crops dried up.

Most snakes ⬈

If you've got ophidiophobia (a fear of snakes), DON'T stop here. Manitoba's Narcisse Wildlife Management Area has the largest concentration of snakes in the world. It's estimated that up to 70,000 snakes use hibernacula (hibernation sites) here, particularly the red-sided garter snake. The snakes emerge in massive wriggly masses on the first warm days of May. In fact, Mother's Day, of all days, is often a prime time to see the spectacle.

Biggest land animal

The largest land animal in North America is the wood bison, which can be found in Alberta, Manitoba and the Northwest Territories. Mature males can reach 3.8 m in length, stand 2 m high at the shoulder and can weigh up to 900 kg. It's believed there were once more than 168,000 wood bison in Canada, but hunting and severe winters have decimated the population. Today the country is home to only about 10,000 of these animals.

LARGEST FOSSIL

Like dinosaurs? Like bugs? This is for you! The world's largest known complete fossil of a trilobite, a prehistoric multi-legged sea creature, was found along Hudson Bay in Manitoba. The trilobite specimen, which looks like a huge bug, is more than 70 cm long.

Polar bear capital of the world

Churchill, Manitoba, is world renowned as the Polar Bear Capital of the World, thanks largely to its accessibility to the polar bear habitat. Through October and early November, it's possible to see 40 or more bears a day.

Most historic downtown

Winnipeg's Exchange District, a national historic site, is considered one of the best preserved and largest collections of terra cotta and cut-stone architecture in North America. The 20-block area, the original core of Winnipeg, boasts about 150 heritage buildings, as well as a number of buildings that are national historic sites in their own right, including early skyscrapers.

Longest historical suspension bridge ⬈

Looking for a swinging good time? Try the Souris Swinging Bridge in Souris, Manitoba, the nation's longest historical suspension bridge. Open to pedestrian traffic, the 177.4-m bridge was originally built in 1904. The bridge was lost in 1976 when it was taken out by water and ice, but was rebuilt and has been commemorated on a Canada Post stamp.

Slurpee capital of the world ⬈

Winnipeg is famous for many things, but did you know it's considered the Slurpee Capital of the World? The crown is based on having the highest average number of Slurpee cups sold per store each year (400,000). The 7-Eleven store on Portage Avenue sells the second-most Slurpees in the country.

Pure gold coin (1)
In 1982, the Royal Canadian Mint's refinery produced the world's first 9999 (99.9 percent pure) gold bullion coin—the Gold Maple Leaf coin.

Pure gold coin (2)
In 2007, the Royal Canadian Mint one-upped itself by producing the world's first 99999 (99.999 percent pure) gold bullion coin. It is the only mint in the world to produce coins at this standard.

FIRST $1 MILLION COIN
Don't try making change for this coin. The Royal Canadian Mint created the world's first $1 million coin in 2007. The 100 kg, 99999 (99.999 percent) pure gold bullion coin was created to market the Mint's new standard for gold coin purity. However, a number of people came forward interested in purchasing the real McCoy. The Mint has subsequently sold five of the colossal coins, which at the time were the world's largest.

Most romance

Harlequin Romance, one of the world's leading publishers of books for women (it has sold an estimated 6.28 billion books since its inception), was founded in May 1949 in Winnipeg. In 1969, the company relocated to Toronto, where today it publishes more than 110 titles a month in 34 languages, which are sold in 110 countries on six continents.

✓ First emergency number

Who doesn't know the phone number 911 and what it's for? But did you know that Winnipeg was the first city in North America to implement a central phone number to contact emergency services? The number (the city used 999 at the time) was introduced on June 21, 1959, at the suggestion of Winnipeg mayor Stephen Juba. Most of North America adopted 911 as the emergency contact number on June 22, 1975.

Degaussing process

Sir Charles Goodeve, born in Neepawa, Manitoba, on February 21, 1904, invented the process of degaussing in 1940, which helped protect ships from magnetic mines by reducing the hull's magnetism.

Snow road

Winter driving here is recommended. The Wapusk Trail road is the longest seasonal winter road in the world, according to Guinness World Records. The 752-km road is constructed annually in January between Gillam, Manitoba, and Peawanuk, Ontario, on snow and ice.

First sounding rocket ↗

The Black Brant sounding rocket, invented in the 1950s, was the first industrial-scale rocket built in Canada. A high-altitude rocket typically used to launch research instruments, the first was launched in September 1959 from Fort Churchill, Manitoba. The Black Brant is still used today by both the Canadian Space Agency and NASA.

First Canadian movie hit

Considered by many as Canada's first filmmaker, James Freer immigrated to Canada from England in 1888 and settled in Brandon Hills, Manitoba. Freer was sponsored to tour Britain with his films starting in April 1898. His *Ten years in Manitoba*—25,000 instantaneous photos on half-a-mile of Edison films, depicting scenes of everyday Canadians—was considered a popular and commercial success.

First woman in Royal Society of Canada

Author Gabrielle Roy was the first woman to be admitted to the Royal Society of Canada—a collection of scholars, artists and scientists aiming to promote learning and research—in 1947.

First Canadian Prix Femina Étranger

Considered by many to be one of Canada's most important authors, Gabrielle Roy, born in St. Boniface, Manitoba, on March 22, 1909, was the first Canadian author to win the French Prix Femina Étranger. Roy captured the French literary award granted to the best novel by a foreigner for her first novel, *Bonheur d'occasion* (*The Tin Flute*) in 1945.

Oldest ballet company ↑

The Royal Winnipeg Ballet is the nation's oldest dance company and the second-oldest in North America. Founded as the Winnipeg Ballet Club by Gweneth Lloyd and Betty Farrally, the organization gave its first performance in 1939. The club received a royal charter from Queen Elizabeth II in 1953 to become the first "Royal" ballet company of the Commonwealth.

Number One hit

Guess who was the first Canadian-based band to have a Number One hit in the United States? The question's the answer. "American Woman" by The Guess Who, based in Winnipeg, Manitoba, hit the top of the Billboard Hot 100 list the weeks of May 9, 16 and 23 in 1970.

Most outdoor musicals

Winnipeg's Rainbow Stage, a musical theatre company that performs in the city's Kildonan Park, is the nation's largest and longest-running outdoor theatre. The company's 3,000-seat amphitheatre opened on July 7, 1954, and the first musical, Brigadoon, was performed in 1955. Today the Rainbow Stage attracts more than 40,000 patrons annually.

Biggest marine dinosaur

What a big mosasaur you have! The prehistoric marine dinosaur, from the late Cretaceous period 80 million years ago, on display at the Canadian Fossil Discovery Centre near Morden, Manitoba, is the largest of its kind on display in the world. Nicknamed Bruce (though it's actually a female), the beast measures more than 13 m in length.

↑ First Olympic gold for hockey

The Winnipeg Falcons were the first team to win an Olympic gold medal in hockey, in 1920 in Antwerp, Belgium. At the time, the winner of the Allan Cup, awarded to the nation's top senior men's amateur hockey club, was selected to represent the country at the games. The Falcons dominated the tournament, besting Czechoslovakia 15–0, the United States 2–0 and Sweden 12–1 to claim gold. At the time the event was held in the summer.

Largest western winter festival

The annual Festival du Voyageur, held each February since 1970 in Winnipeg's French-quarter, is the largest winter festival in Western Canada. The festival celebrates the rich culture and history of the voyageur with food, music, song and dance.

MILLION-DOLLAR HOCKEY PLAYER

Bobby Hull was the first hockey player to sign a $1 million-dollar contract. He accepted the contract with the Winnipeg Jets, then part of the World Hockey Association, on June 27, 1972, at the corner of Portage and Main in Winnipeg.

First human rights museum ↑

Opened in late 2014, the Canadian Museum for Human Rights in Winnipeg is the first museum "solely dedicated to the evolution, celebration and future of human rights." It is also the only national museum to be built outside Canada's National Capital Region (Ottawa and area).

First province where women could vote

In 1916, Manitoba was the first province in Canada to grant women the right to vote. First proposed by Manitoba's Icelandic community in the 1870s, the fight for women's suffrage was taken up by a team of women, including Dr. Mary Crawford, Lillian Beynon Thomas and Nellie McClung.

Nellie McClung ↑

Most Inuit art

Established in 1912, the Winnipeg Art Gallery claims a couple of Canadian superlatives. It's home to the world's largest public collection of contemporary Inuit art, with more than 10,730 works. The gallery also offers the largest program of art classes in the country, with professional artists teaching classes for children and adults.

Most Icelanders

Given its reputation as being particularly cold (temperature-wise), is it any wonder that Manitoba is home to the largest Icelandic population outside of Iceland? Between 1870 and 1915, 20,000 Icelanders immigrated to the province—nearly a quarter of Iceland's population at the time. Today Manitoba's provincial government continues to appeal to Icelanders to settle there.

Worst flood

The Red River Flood in the spring of 1950 is considered the greatest flood disaster in Canadian history. The river crested 9.2 m above its normal level in Winnipeg. Just one person drowned, but the flood forced the evacuation of 100,000 people from southern Manitoba, damaged 5,000 homes and buildings, and cost $550 million in property damage. Following the disaster, the provincial government decided to build the Winnipeg Floodway to mitigate future flooding.

ONTARIO

The name Ontario is likely derived from Amerindian and was first applied to the Great Lake bearing the same name. It may come from *onitariio*, which means "beautiful lake," or *kanadario*, meaning "sparkling or beautiful water." Europeans eventually began using the name to refer to the land along the lake, and over time to increasingly larger areas north of the lake.

MOST SHARKS

The Ripley's Aquarium of Canada in Toronto is home to the largest collection of sharks in North America. One of the facility's highlights is the Shark Lagoon, which features a 96-m tunnel walkway through a 2.84-million-litre tank, where you can see sand tiger sharks that measure 3 to 3.7 m.

Largest wetland

The Hudson Bay Lowland is the largest wetland area in North America and the third largest on Earth. Eighty-three percent of the ecozone lies in Ontario, with smaller portions in neighbouring Quebec and Manitoba. More than 85 percent of the region is mineral wetland or organic peat land. The area has very few trees.

Highest point

Ontario may boast the biggest and best of many things in the country, but its highest point is not one of them. Located in the Timiskaming area of northern Ontario, the Ishpatina Ridge is the province's highest spot, at an elevation of 693 m.

LONGEST FRESHWATER COAST

Lake Huron, including Georgian Bay, has the longest freshwater coast of any lake in the world. It boasts 6,157 km of shoreline.

Largest crater

The largest known impact crater in Canada (and the second-largest on Earth) is found near Sudbury, Ontario. Known as the Sudbury Basin, the crater is 130 km in diameter. It is believed that the impact of a 10-km-diameter meteorite created the Sudbury Basin in just seconds about 1.85 million years ago.

Highest hydraulic lift lock

Talk about moving up in the world! Lock 21 on the Trent-Severn Waterway in Peterborough, Ontario, is the highest hydraulic lift lock in the world. Opened on July 9, 1904, the lock lifts boats 19.8 m. It was also the first of only two lift locks ever built in North America.

Oldest canal system

The Rideau Canal, which runs from the Ottawa River to Lake Ontario and the St. Lawrence River at Kingston, is the oldest continuously operated canal system in North America. Opened in 1832, the Rideau is 202 km long and boasts 47 locks that connect lakes and rivers through the region. It is a national historic site and a UNESCO world heritage site.

Oldest water

With all the water in Canada, is it any wonder that the oldest known water on the planet was found here? University of Toronto geoscientist Barbara Sherwood Lollar and her colleagues discovered the 2.6-billion-year-old water some 2.4 km below the earth in a mine near Timmins, Ontario.

One-third of Earth's fresh water

Given that the Great Lakes host the world's largest supply of fresh water, it's little surprise that the province where the lakes are found, Ontario (which is also home to more than 250,000 other lakes), contains about one-third of the Earth's fresh water.

Highest point of departure

It seems hard to believe, but there's a lake in central Ontario that's the highest freshwater lake in the Americas from which a skipper can circumnavigate the world by ocean-going vessel. At 265.5 m above sea level, Ontario's Balsam Lake is considered the "summit" of the Trent-Severn Waterway, a canal system that crosses Ontario's cottage country from Lake Ontario's Bay of Quinte to Lake Huron's Georgian Bay.

Lake in a lake

A lake in a lake? You bet. Ontario's Manitoulin Island is home to the world's largest lake on a freshwater island (and the world's largest lake in a lake, too). Lake Manitou has a surface area of approximately 104 square km. There are also a number of small islands on Manitou, making them islands on a lake on an island in a lake!

Largest island in freshwater lake

The largest island in a freshwater lake in the world is Ontario's Manitoulin Island in Lake Huron. The 2,765-square-km island is a continuation of the Bruce Peninsula, the strip of land stretching into Lake Huron that separates Georgian Bay from the larger area of the lake. The Bruce Peninsula is part of the Niagara Escarpment, a massive ridge of fossil-rich sedimentary rock that began to form 450 million years ago.

ONTARIO GEOGRAPHY

Southernmost island

Relatively speaking, it's an unassuming island in the middle of Lake Erie. But Middle Island is actually Canada's southernmost point. In 1999, the island was purchased by the Nature Conservancy of Canada to protect the Carolinian habitat and the rare and endangered species that call it home. In 2000, the island's ownership was transferred to Parks Canada, and Middle Island became part of Point Pelee National Park.

Largest freshwater archipelago

With all the country's fresh water, is it any wonder Canada is home to the world's largest freshwater archipelago? Ontario's 13,000 square km Georgian Bay, part of Lake Huron, is home to some 30,000 islands.

First provincial park

The first provincial park in Canada was Queen Victoria Niagara Falls Park, which opened May 24, 1888 and lies near the famed falls themselves. Originally a 62.2-hectare park, the protected area has been expanded over the years to encompass 1,720 hectares along the Niagara River.

Slowest growing trees

The Niagara Escarpment, a ridge that runs east and west through south-central Ontario, is home to the world's slowest growing trees. Though the trees are the common eastern white cedar, the species grows particularly slowly in this environment, living up to 1,000 years.

↑ Southernmost land

While Middle Island in Lake Erie is Canada's most southerly piece of land, Point Pelee is the most southerly tip of Canada's main land mass. Stretching out into Lake Erie, the point is home to Point Pelee National Park and a major migration stopover for numerous bird species. Indeed, 42 of 52 regularly occurring warbler species have been spotted at Pelee.

Largest dune formation

Ontario's Sandbanks Provincial Park, on the shores of Lake Ontario near Picton, is home to the largest baymouth-barrier dune formation in the world. Some sections of the dune are 60 m high. The park's location and unique habitat make it a hot spot for migrating birds in the spring and fall.

Longest freshwater beach

That's a whole lotta sand! Ontario's Wasaga Beach is the longest freshwater beach in the world. It stretches 14 km along the shore of Lake Huron's Georgian Bay.

First dark-sky preserve

Are you afraid of the dark? Then best to avoid the Torrance Barrens Conservation Area in Ontario's Muskoka region. The 1,902-hectare park was named the world's first permanent dark-sky preserve in 1999. Trees and bushes are stunted in height in this area of bedrock and wetlands, and hence Torrance Barrens offers sky watchers clear views of the night sky, with very little light pollution.

Oldest and longest footpath

The Bruce Trail, which runs along the Niagara Escarpment from Niagara to Tobermory in Ontario, is the nation's oldest and longest marked footpath. The trail stretches for 890 km, with another 400 km of associated trails.

Largest botanical garden

The Royal Botanical Gardens in Burlington, Ontario, is the largest botanical garden in Canada, with 1,100 hectares of gardens and nature reserves and more than 27 km of trails.

First capital

The first capital of Upper Canada (present-day Ontario) was Newark, now Niagara-on-the-Lake. It was changed to York (present-day Toronto) in 1793 to protect it from American attack.

First marine conservation area ↗

Fathom Five National Marine Park was Canada's first national marine conservation area. Established in 1987, the park covers a 130-square-km area of water and 20 islands located off the end of Ontario's Bruce Peninsula, which separates Lake Huron from Georgian Bay. The park's waters are home to unique geology, plants, wildlife and 22 shipwrecks.

Most impressive waterfalls

It's been said Ontario's famous Niagara Falls are the world's largest by volume. However, that is simply not true. They may be the globe's most impressive, but they rank 11th on Earth by volume, with more than 168,000 cubic m of water going over the edge every minute. The falls have moved back 11 km in 12,500 years, due to erosion, and may be world's fastest moving waterfalls.

Most lightning

Flash! The north shore of Lake Erie near Highgate, Ontario, gets the greatest annual number of days (50 in 2006) with lightning of any inland place in Canada.

Most lightning in one year

Call it Canada's lightning capital. Windsor, Ontario, is the Canadian city that had the most lightning in any one year: 47 days with lightning in 2007.

Toronto's worst snowfall

There was that time Toronto called in the army (early January 1999), but the worst single-day snowfall in the country's largest city was actually December 11, 1944. The winter storm dropped 48 cm of snow on Toronto. It was accompanied by gale-force winds that created huge snowdrifts. In all, 57.2 cm of snow fell over two days, and 21 people died, including 13 from overexertion.

Toronto's snowiest January

Lest Toronto get too bad a rap for calling in the army, the series of snowstorms that struck the city in January 1999 hit the city with almost a year's worth of snow in two weeks, from the 2nd to the 15th. In total, it was the snowiest January in the city's history, with 118.4 cm of snow and the most snow on the ground at one time, at 65 cm.

Longest tracked tornado ↑

It was a deadly and disastrous day on May 31, 1985, when a total of 14 tornadoes hit a number of Ontario communities, including Barrie (pictured above), Grand Valley, Orangeville and Tottenham. The storms killed 12 people and damaged more than 1,000 buildings. Of particular note was the Grand Valley tornado, which started near Arthur and travelled east to Campbellford. It is considered one of the longest tracked tornadoes in Canada, wreaking havoc over 115 km.

← Famous shipwreck

Immortalized in singer Gordon Lightfoot's song "The Wreck of the Edmund Fitzgerald," a severe storm on November 10, 1975 — accompanied by 20-m-high waves on Lake Superior — sank the largest bulk ore carrier on the Great Lakes, the Edmund Fitzgerald. The ship's crew of 29 was lost. Pictured here is the ship's bell.

Fly away home

William Lishman, of Blackstock, Ontario, joined by photographer Joseph Duff and Dr. William Sladen, were the first researchers in the world to use aircraft to teach birds to migrate. In 1993, the three men used ultralight planes to lead 18 Canada geese 644 km from Ontario to Virginia. The geese returned to Ontario the following spring. The project proved that people could use planes to teach birds to migrate.

First migratory waterfowl refuge

Jack Miner, known as the "Father of Conservation," is considered the founder of the migratory waterfowl refuge system. He founded the first such reserve, the Jack Miner Migratory Bird Sanctuary, in 1904 in Kingsville, Ont.

First banded birds ↗

Five years after Jack Miner (see previous) established the world's first migratory bird reserve, he created the concept of banding birds to trace the migratory periods and routes of waterfowl. Ever since, the practice has been instrumental in the protection of migratory birds in North America and the world.

Longest snake

No matter what you call it, this is one long snake. And the longest native snake you'll find in Canada. Once known as the black ratsnake, but today called the gray ratsnake, the species is known to grow to 1.5 m and even longer. It is an excellent climber and is sometimes found in the cavities of hollow trees. It is typically found in southwestern Ontario north of Lake Erie and in the Rideau Lakes area from Kingston to Smith Falls.

LARGEST ZOO

The Toronto Zoo is the largest zoo in Canada. Opened on August 15, 1974, today the 284-hectare facility is home to 5,920 animals of 484 species. It attracts about 1.5 million visitors annually.

HELPING WILDLIFE

African Lion Safari, a wildlife park near Hamilton, Ont., is a national leader in research to protect and reintroduce threatened species, both Canadian and international. Indeed, in 1980, the facility's staff helped hatch the nation's first Peregrine falcons in captivity.

Test-tube giraffes

On December 31, 2013, Safari, the first artificially inseminated giraffe born in Canada was born at African Lion Safari. Safari was also the second such giraffe born in the world.

Baby giraffes

Here's one tall order. African Lion Safari is home to the nation's largest herd of Rothschild giraffe, with 14 of the animals. Since 1977, more than 25 giraffes have been born at the park.

Largest captive elephant herd ➘

African Lion Safari hosts the largest herd of Asian elephants of any zoo on the continent. Twelve of the animals currently call the facility home.

Test-tube elephants

On November 2, 2009, Jake, the first artificially inseminated elephant born in Canada was born at African Lion Safari. Nellie, the first Asian elephant with parents born in Canada, was born at African Lion Safari on August 2, 2013.

Oldest maple tree

Canada's known for many things, and a big one is maple syrup. The oldest known sugar maple tree in the country is estimated to be at least 500 years old, and it's found in southwestern Ontario's North Pelham area. The Comfort Maple, as it's known, stands about 30.5 m tall and has a trunk circumference of 6 m.

Biggest brook trout

If you're an angler in Canada, you're undoubtedly familiar with the legendary Cook brook trout. Caught in July 1916 by Dr. J.W. Cook in Ontario's Nipigon River, the 6.6-kg brookie has stood as the world record for the species for nearly a century. In fact, it's one of the longest-standing angling records on Earth.

Biggest lake sturgeon

Another big fish story. The International Game Fish Association all-tackle world-record lake sturgeon was caught in Ontario's Georgian Bay on May 29, 1982. The behemoth weighed a whopping 76.2 kg.

Biggest splake

Given that it's somewhat of a uniquely Canadian species, it's hardly surprising that the International Game Fish Association all-tackle world record for splake was caught here. The 9.39-kg fish was hauled from Ontario's Georgian Bay on May 17, 1987.

Biggest Aurora trout

It figures that the International Game Fish Association all-tackle world record for Aurora trout comes from Canada. The 2.21-kg fish was caught in Ontario's Carol Lake on October 8, 1996.

Biggest rock bass

What a big red eye you have! One of the two fish tied for the International Game Fish Association all-tackle world-record rock bass—a species recognizable by its distinctive red eye—was caught in Ontario's York River on August 1, 1974. The rock weighed 1.36 kg.

Biggest lake whitefish

The International Game Fish Association all-tackle world record lake whitefish was caught on May 21, 1984, in Meaford, Ontario. The fish weighed 6.52 kg.

Largest indoor aquarium ∨

Ripley's Aquarium of Canada in Toronto is the nation's largest indoor aquarium. The 12,500-square-m attraction, which opened on October 16, 2013, boasts more than 16,000 marine animals and more than 450 species.

First retractable roof

Toronto's Rogers Centre boasted the world's first fully retractable roof when the building opened in June 1989 (at the time it was called SkyDome). The 11,000-tonne roof is made of four sections and opens (and closes) in a semi-circular motion in 20 minutes. The current home of Major League Baseball's Toronto Blue Jays and the Canadian Football League's Toronto Argonauts, the stadium also hosts numerous other sporting and entertainment events. Indeed, more than 60 million people have passed through the building's turnstiles.

Tallest tower

It's since been eclipsed, but for 34 years (1976–2010) Toronto's CN Tower put the country on the world map as home to the globe's tallest tower, building and freestanding structure. Though it now ranks third tallest, at a mere 553.33 m, it's still no less impressive. Approximately 1.5 million people visit the tower each year, for attractions that include a lookout, a glass floor, a revolving restaurant and the EdgeWalk (the world's highest, hands-free walk on a 1.5 m ledge encircling the building, 365 m up).

Scraping the sky

Toronto has 8 of Canada's 10 tallest buildings.

	1. First Canadian Place	2. Scotia Plaza	3. Aura	4. Canada Trust Tower
City	Toronto	Toronto	Toronto	Toronto
Storeys	72 storeys	68 storeys	78 storeys	53 storeys
Height	298 m	275 m	273 m	261 m
Built	Built: 1975	Built: 1988	Built: 2014	Built: 1990

Tallest building

At 72 storeys and 298 m high, Toronto's First Canadian Place is the country's tallest building (not tower, please note). The 2.6 million-square-m skyscraper was considered ahead of its time when it opened in 1975, and extensive interior and exterior rejuvenation was completed in October 2012. With the highest rooftop in Canada, it also serves as a prime communications site, second only to the nearby CN Tower.

Tiny house ↑

It's hard to say what record, if any, the tiny house at 128 Day Avenue in Toronto holds, but there's no doubt it's one small house. Measuring 2.2 m wide and 14.3 m long, the home was built in 1912. It's still lived in today.

Largest sports complex

Whitby, Ontario, located about an hour east of Toronto, is the home of the country's largest municipally owned and operated multi-use sports complex. The Iroquois Park Sports Centre houses six arenas, a 25-m-deep swimming pool, six tennis courts, four baseball diamonds, one lit soccer field, and a strength and conditioning training centre. It is surrounded by 20 hectares of parkland.

Biggest seats

Those seats at your local stadium feeling small? Time to visit Hamilton's Tim Hortons Field, the home of the Canadian Football League's Hamilton Tiger-Cats, which opened in 2014. The stadium's luxuries include the largest individual seats of any outdoor sports building in Canada (53 cm to 61 cm wide, depending on their location in the facility) and more leg room than any other comparable stadium.

First Canadian mosque

The Baitul-Islam Mosque in Vaughan, Ontario, just north of Toronto, was the first Muslim mosque in Canada. It opened on October 17, 1992.

5.	6.	7.	8.	9.	10.
Trump International Hotel & Tower	Commerce Court West	The Bow	Le 1250 Boulevard René Lévesque	TD Tower	Bay Adelaide West
Toronto	Toronto	Calgary	Montréal	Toronto	Toronto
57 storeys	57 storeys	58 storeys	47 storeys	56 storeys	51 storeys
257 m	239 m	236 m	226 m	223 m	218 m
Built: 2012	Built: 1972	Built: 2012	Built: 1992	Built: 1967	Built: 2009

First drive-in
The nation's first drive-in theatre opened in Stoney Creek, Ontario, in 1946. The Skyway had a 750-car capacity.

First milk pasteurization
The Hospital for Sick Children installed the first milk pasteurization plant in Canada in 1908 — 30 years before the process was mandatory.

First two-screen cinema
Ottawa's Elgin Street Theatre was the first in the world to have two screens, allowing customers to choose between watching one of two movies in one venue. The second screen was added in 1957 by owner Nathan Taylor, who would go on to create the Cineplex Odeon chain.

First opera and ballet theatre
One of a kind: the Four Seasons Centre for the Performing Arts in Toronto was the first theatre in Canada built specifically for opera and ballet performances. Opened in 2006, the facility features a modern take on the traditional horseshoe-shaped auditorium, which delivers great sightlines and acoustics. The building is the permanent home of the Canadian Opera Company.

Last double-decker theatre ↑
Toronto's Elgin and Winter Garden Theatre Centre is the last operating double-decker theatre (two separate and distinctive theatres on top of one another) on the planet. It is also considered one of the most beautiful theatre complexes in the world. The complex was built in 1913 as the flagship of Marcus Loew's theatre chain.

LARGEST CHILDREN'S HOSPITAL
If buildings had a heart, this one's would be pretty big. Toronto's Hospital for Sick Children, known as SickKids, is the country's largest facility dedicated to children's health. The hospital dates back to 1875 (shown here is a photo of a child being wheeled into an operating room in 1915), and today about 15,000 youngsters stay at the facility each year. There are also more than 100 clinics that see nearly 300,000 visitors each year.

LARGEST LIBRARY SYSTEM

The Toronto Public Library is the largest public library system in Canada, and in 1998, after seven library boards of Metropolitan Toronto merged, it was the largest library system in North America at the time, serving 2.3 million. It is still one of the world's busiest library systems, with more than 18 million people visiting its 98 branches in 2012.

Smallest jail

Hope you're not a claustrophobic crook. The Rodney Jail, in Rodney, Ontario, bills itself as the smallest jail in North America. Built in 1890, the jail is 4.57 m by 5.49 m.

Biggest snow playground

Like to play in the snow? Check out the largest snow playground in North America, which is created annually each winter for Winterlude, held in Ottawa and Gatineau, Quebec. The Snowflake Kingdom, as the playground is known, is built in Gatineau's Jacques Cartier Park and features gigantic snow slides, a winter obstacle course, a giant maze and much more.

Biggest water park

The Calypso water park near Ottawa is the nation's largest. The 40-hectare park, which opened on June 7, 2010, features 100 different water attractions to keep visitors cool.

Biggest convention centre

Looking for a place to show off? Try Toronto's Direct Energy Centre, the nation's largest convention and exhibition facility. Located at Exhibition Place, on the west side of the city's downtown, the centre boasts 99,592,000 square m of exhibit space in eight halls, plus the Ricoh Coliseum, an 8,200-seat arena.

Most multicultural city

Talk about your united nations. Toronto is considered by many to be the most multicultural city in the world. More than 100 languages and dialects are spoken there.

Most immigrants

There's no doubt that Toronto is Canada's most multicultural city. It's home to the largest percentage of immigrants in the country, with 37 percent of the nation's foreign-born residents, according to Statistics Canada. More than 2.5 million immigrants call Toronto home, making up 46 percent of the city's population.

BIGGEST AMUSEMENT PARK

The name is bang-on. Canada's Wonderland, located in Vaughan, Ontario, just north of Toronto, is the nation's largest amusement park and one of the largest in North America. Opened on May 23, 1981, the park features more than 200 attractions, 69 rides, an eight-hectare water park and live shows.

Most roller coasters

Looking for a roller coaster? Canada's Wonderland is home to the continent's largest variety of roller coasters, with 16. The park's longest and fastest coaster is the Leviathan, which measures 1,672 m and reaches a top speed of 148 km/hour.

One-of-a-kind thrill ride

Looking for a unique thrill? The Sledge Hammer ride at Canada's Wonderland is one of a kind. The attraction, which debuted in 2003, lifts riders 24.3 m in the air in four- to eight-person gondolas, then takes them through a series of jumps and freefalls that lasts one minute and 43 seconds, reaching a top speed of 65 km per hour.

First WindSeeker swing ride

Canada's Wonderland's WindSeeker swing ride, which ascends 91.75 m and swings riders at a 45-degree angle at speeds of up to 50 km per hour, was the first such ride in the world. The ride lasts three minutes.

Biggest outdoor wave pool

White Water Bay at the Splash Works water park in Canada's Wonderland is the largest outdoor wave pool in the nation. It would take 90 gallons of paint to paint the bottom of the pool.

Largest underground shopping complex ⤹

You could call it the walkway to retail heaven. The PATH system in Toronto, an underground pathway that links 30 km of shops under a large portion of the city's downtown core, is considered the largest underground shopping complex in the world. PATH boasts 371,600 square m of retail space, houses about 1,200 shops and services, and connects more than 50 buildings.

Biggest entertainment venue

Toronto's Exhibition Place is the nation's largest entertainment venue. The 77-hectare site is home to a variety of exhibition buildings, conference facilities and sporting venues, such as the Direct Energy Centre, the Better Living Centre, Ricoh Coliseum and BMO Field. It attracts more than 5.2 million visitors each year. Exhibition Place also hosts big events, including the Canadian National Exhibition and the Royal Winter Fair.

TSE firsts

The Toronto Stock Exchange has been a world leader. In 1977, it was the world's first stock exchange to introduce computer-assisted trading, and in the late 1990s it was the first exchange to introduce decimal trading (as opposed to fractions). It was the largest North American exchange to rely completely on electronic trading and the first to have a female president, Barbara G. Stymiest.

Biggest stock exchange

The Toronto Stock Exchange is the largest stock exchange in Canada, the third-largest in North America and the seventh-largest in the world. It opened on October 25, 1861, and 18 stocks could be traded. The TSE became a publicly traded company in 2000 (two years later adopting the abbreviation TSX). In 2008 it acquired the Montreal Exchange.

Richest vein of silver

The world's richest vein of silver was found in Cobalt, Ontario in 1903. In the following 60 years, silver mines in the area produced a total of almost 1.2 million tonnes of silver ore and concentrates, and the total production over that time was more than 11,921 million grams of silver. The silver rush ended somewhat abruptly in the mid-20th century, and the town turned its mining attention to the mineral it was named after. Thanks to improved technology, cobalt had become more useful.

Deepest ↖

That's one deep hole. The Macassa gold mine in Kirkland Lake, Ontario, is the deepest mine shaft in Canada, at 2,200 m. Until the mid-1990s, it was the deepest shaft in the Western Hemisphere). Operations at the Macassa mine closed down in 1999.

Oldest mines

The oldest operating mines in Canada are the Stobie Mine and the Copper Cliff North Mine near Sudbury, Ontario. Both mines began operation in 1886.

Biggest salt mine

Need salt for that? Then head to Goderich, Ontario, home of the world's largest salt mine. Owned by Sifto Canada, 6,577,089 tonnes of salt are mined from the site every year.

First oil company

Oil! The first oil company in North America was founded in the aptly named community of Oil Springs, Ontario, southeast of Sarnia. On December 18, 1854, Charles Tripp received approval for his commercial oil company.

CN Tower: 553 m

Mancassa gold mine: 2,200 m deep

Best farmland

Think of farming in Canada and you probably think of the prairies or Prince Edward Island potatoes. But Ontario has more than half of the nation's "Class 1" agricultural land (the highest quality farming property). The province's 51,950 farms contribute almost one-quarter of the country's farm revenue.

First hydroelectric transmission

The Barber Paper Mill of Georgetown, Ontario, has a powerful place in the country's history. In 1888, the mill's John R. Barber commissioned the Cleveland Brush Company to build a 60-hp motor and a 100 hp generator for him. He built a power plant called the "Dynamo," which transmitted power from a dam on the Credit River to the mill three km away. This is believed to be the first transmission of hydroelectric power over a distance in North America.

Most manufacturing

Ontario is considered part of the manufacturing heartland of North America. The province has more manufacturing employees than anywhere else in Canada and ranks third in North America to California and Texas.

MOST WIND POWER

Boasting more than 1,000 wind turbines with a capacity of more than 2,000 megawatts, Ontario is the nation's leader in wind-power production.

Most cars

When it comes to cars, there's a good chance it comes from Ontario. The province is the largest regional automotive assembly jurisdiction in North America. In 2011, Statistics Canada reports that 88 percent of the province's vehicle production was exported, almost entirely to the United States.

Largest youth employer

Help wanted. Canada's Wonderland, the nation's largest amusement park, located just north of Toronto, is the single largest employer of youth in Canada. It's also the top employer in York Region, the municipality where it's located. The park employs more than 4,000 seasonal staff.

Biggest hotel

Toronto's Eaton Chelsea is the country's largest hotel. It boasts 1,590 guestrooms and more than 2,200 square m of meeting and event space, including two ballrooms. The hotel also has four dining options.

First 100-kilovolt

In 1910, the Hydro-Electric Power Commission of Ontario built the first 100-kilovolt transmission line. The line ran from Niagara Falls to power a number of communities in southern Ontario, including Toronto.

Biggest mining province

When it comes to mining in Canada, images of the Yukon gold rush come to mind. Ontario, however, is the country's leading metal producer. Twenty-five different metal and non-metal mineral products are produced in the province, including 43 percent of the nation's nickel, 52 percent of its gold, 38 percent of copper and 84 percent of platinum metals.

Biggest solar farm

The Sarnia Solar Project in Sarnia, Ontario, is the country's largest solar farm. The facility boasts 1.3 million individual solar modules, which combined are capable of producing 80 megawatts of electricity, or enough to power 10,000 homes annually. This saves about 22 tonnes of carbon dioxide emissions each year.

BIGGEST CREATIVE OUTPUT

Ontario is the country's hotbed of creativity, at least when it comes to its entertainment and publishing industries, which are the largest in Canada and the third-largest in North America (after California and New York). Ontario leads the nation in film and television production, book and magazine publishing and sound recording.

First stratospheric balloon

In September 2013, the Canadian Space Agency, in partnership with the French space agency (Centre national d'études spatiales), completed the first launch of a stratospheric research balloon in Canada. The remote-controlled balloon was launched from Timmins, Ontario. It can haul up to 1.58 tonnes of equipment, requires no fuel and is fully recoverable.

Biggest farmers' market

With a population of only about 2,000, it's hard to believe that St. Jacobs, Ontario, located west of Toronto, is the home of the nation's largest year-round farmers' market. Approximately 4,000 Old Order Mennonites from the surrounding area are key to the market's size and success. Open Thursdays and Saturdays, the market has hundreds of vendors.

Largest chocolate seller

Laura Secord, the chocolate company formed in 1913, is the nation's largest chocolatier. Today the company boasts more than 120 stores across the country and more than 400 products.

First coin

The first domestically produced Canadian coin was struck on January 2, 1908, at the opening ceremony for the Royal Mint in Ottawa. The silver 50-cent piece bore the effigy of King Edward VII.

Newspaper with the most readers

The *Toronto Star* is the nation's largest daily newspaper. Established as The Evening Star on November 3, 1892, the paper now has more than three million readers every week (in print and online). Its weekday editions are circulated to nearly 350,000 people, while its Saturday paper reaches more than 470,000 readers.

Oldest student publication

Toronto's Upper Canada College private school is home to the nation's oldest continuously running student publication. The *College Times* has been published since 1871.

Oldest newspaper in Ontario

The Kingston Whig-Standard of Kingston, Ontario, is Canada's oldest continually published daily newspaper. It was first established in March 1810 as the *Kingston Gazette* and adopted its present moniker in 1849.

Oldest magazine

Based in Toronto, the *United Church Observer* is the oldest continuously published magazine in North America, and the second oldest continuously published English-language magazine in the world. It was established in 1829 as the *Christian Guardian* and has had several name changes since then.

First newspaper published by a black woman

Mary Ann Shadd was the first black woman in North America to publish a newspaper, the *Provincial Freeman*, which she established in 1853 in Windsor, Ontario, and later published in Toronto and Chatham, Ontario. The paper provided information about the successes of black people living in freedom in Canada. Shadd herself had emigrated to Canada from the United States.

First phone call

Alexander Graham Bell was a man of many firsts, not the least of which was making the first one-way, long-distance telephone calls between the Ontario communities of Brantford and Paris, and Mount Pleasant and Brantford, on August 10, 1876. Bell received that first call from Brantford in Robert White's Boot and Shoe Store and Telegram Office in Paris.

LARGEST NUKE

The Pickering Nuclear Generating Station in Pickering, Ont., is the largest nuclear generating facility in Canada and one of the largest in the world. The station's six reactors produce 3,100 megawatts of electricity, which is enough to serve 500,000 people.

First telegraph

The first electric telegraph message sent in Canada was from Toronto to Hamilton on December 19, 1846. The early means of electronically sending encoded messages was sent between Toronto City Hall and Hamilton on a line owned by the Toronto, Hamilton and Niagara Electric-Magnetic Telegraph Company. The transmission: "Advise Mr. Gamble [president of the telegraph company] that Mr. Dawson will speak to him at half-past one."

Paint roller ⤵

It's oh, so simple! And saves countless backbreaking hours of work. Plus, it's hardly changed in more than 80 years: the paint roller. It was invented by Norman Breakey of Toronto in 1940. Unfortunately, Breakey never got to roll in the profits, as he was never able to make enough rollers to profit from it before competitors made slightly different variations and sold it as their own invention.

Green plastic garbage bag

Three Canadians lay claim to the invention of an indispensible household product: the green plastic garbage bag. Harry Wasyluk of Winnipeg, Larry Hanson at Union Carbide in Lindsay, Ontario, and Frank Plomp of Toronto all came up with variations of the polyethylene bags in the 1950s, which were originally sold to hospitals and businesses.

Acetylene gas

Here's another bright idea. Electrical engineer Thomas Wilson, who was born in Princeton, Ontario, developed the first commercial process to produce calcium carbide, a chemical used to make acetylene gas, in 1892. At the turn of the 20th century, acetylene gas was widely used for lighting.

First light bulb

Thomas Edison gets all the recognition, but a Toronto medical student named Henry Woodward, with help from a city innkeeper named Matthew Evans, developed and patented a predecessor to Edison's light bulb in 1874. The duo didn't have the money to produce and sell the bulbs, and sold the patent in 1875 to Edison. His light bulb debuted in 1879.

Snowplow

What else would a Canadian dentist invent, but the first rotary snowplow? Huh? Indeed, Toronto's Dr. J.W. Elliot invented the machine in 1869. But one was never built until the winter of 1883–84 after another Canadian, Orange Jull, improved on the original design. Designed for trains, the invention became standard on trains through the winter.

Batteryless radio

The Rogers batteryless receiver, created by E.S. Ted Rogers, was unveiled at Toronto's Canadian National Exhibition in 1925. The radio was one of the first successful batteryless sets on the market.

Painted road lines ↗

Sometimes you just have to draw a line. Indeed, in the 1930s, engineer John D. Millar of the Ontario Department of Transport came up with the idea of painting lines on roads to ensure traffic stayed in its own lane. The world's first road lines were painted on a stretch of highway near the Ontario-Quebec border, and within three years the lines were commonplace throughout the continent.

Electric railway

John Wright is credited with building the first electric railway in Canada. In 1883, an engine owned by Wright was used in an electric railway demonstration by the Toronto Industrial Exhibition at the Canadian National Exhibition, but it proved unable to move any cars. The following year, however, a similar demonstration using a motorized Grand Truck flatcar worked.

First hexagonal wind tunnel

Blow me down! The Windee Dome at Western University in London, Ont., is the world's first hexagonal wind tunnel. The unique structure, which boasts a 25-m-diameter inner dome and a 40-m-diameter outer dome, allows scientists to recreate real wind systems at a large scale under controlled conditions. Opened in 2013, the facility will test models of wind farms and transmission lines and the dispersion of pollutants.

Pressure suit

Wilbur Franks, born in Weston, Ontario, and a graduate of the University of Toronto, was a medical researcher who invented the pressure suit, which allows pilots to perform high-speed acrobatics without passing out. The suit was first used in 1942 by Allied fighter pilots. Today's space suits are considered subtle refinements of Franks' invention.

Human centrifuge

Franks was responsible for the construction of the nation's first human centrifuge (also the first in Allied nations), which was built for the pressure-suit project in 1941. The lab in Toronto, which was used to test the suit and train jet pilots to withstand g-forces, eventually became the RCAF Institute of Aviation Medicine.

Electronic organ

A Canadian pioneer of electronic music? Frank Morse Robb invented the first electronic organ in Belleville, Ontario. His Robb Wave Organ didn't hit the market until 1936, although news of his creation had been covered in the *Toronto Star* as early as 1927. Designed to reproduce the sounds of a cathedral pipe organ and considered to sound better than the competing Hammond Organ, the device didn't last long. Its higher price led to its demise by 1941.

Voltage-controlled synthesizer

Electronic music owes a lot, if not its entire existence, to Canadian Hugh Le Caine. In 1945, while working for the National Research Council in Ottawa, Le Caine spent his spare time working on the development of electronic musical instruments, including the Electronic Sackbut, which is considered the first voltage-controlled synthesizer. He went on to create voltage-control systems for a range of uses.

Mobile blood transfusion

Norman Bethune, born in Gravenhurst, Ontario, in 1890, devised the world's first mobile blood transfusion service during the early days of the Spanish War, which began in 1936. Blood was collected in cities and transported to the front lines. The service is considered the greatest innovation in military medicine to arise from that war.

▲ Norman Bethune's graduation photo, 1922.

Mobile operating theatre

Bethune also created the globe's first mobile operating theatre, in 1938 while working for the Chinese Communist Party during the Second Sino-Japanese War. The facility, which could be carried by two donkeys, was put to good use. Bethune is reported to have operated on 115 soldiers during a 69-hour period without pause under heavy artillery fire.

Bethune rib shears

Bethune is also known for a number of medical innovations earlier in his career, while working near Montreal in the late 1920s and 1930s. Bethune pioneered numerous new medical techniques and instruments, one of which—the Bethune rib shears—is still manufactured.

Electronic heart pacemaker

The electronic heart pacemaker was invented in 1949 by Dr. Wilfred Bigelow and Dr. John Callaghan of Toronto, with the help of electrical engineer John Hopps of the National Research Council in Ottawa. In 1958, Arne Larsson was the first person to have an implantable pacemaker. It lasted just three hours. During his lifetime, Larsson had 28 pacemakers before he died at the age of 86.

Artificial kidney ↗

In the 1940s, Dr. Gordon Murray of Toronto independently designed the first artificial kidney in North America, unaware that doctors in Europe were working on a similar invention. It was tested extensively on animals, but after trials on four patients at Toronto General Hospital, his project was abandoned. Dr. Murray's contributions to medicine didn't stop there, however: he was also the first to transplant a human heart valve.

Electric wheelchair

Born in Hamilton, Ontario, George Klein invented the electric wheelchair in 1955 while working for the National Research Council. Originally created for disabled military personnel, the first prototype of the joystick-controlled, battery-operated wheelchair was presented to the United States Veterans Administration.

↑ The first pacemaker, implanted in 1958.

Aerial survey

In 1920, the first experimental aerial survey was taken over Ottawa. The technique became a revolutionary topographical survey method and was eventually used to survey and create an inventory of Canadian forests from the air. Because of the initiative, Canada has one of the world's most extensive collections of aerial photography.

Pablum

The nutritious baby food, Pablum, was created in 1930 by Alan Brown, Theo Drake and Fred Tisdall, to help prevent and treat rickets in children. The popular product improved the health of millions of children around the world and led to ideas for a number of other nutritious foods for infants. The three doctors at Toronto's Sick Kids Hospital donated royalties from the product back to the hospital.

Yukon Gold potato

The Yukon Gold potato naturally was created in Canada. Bred at the University of Guelph in 1966, the Yukon Gold is known for its longevity in storage, as well as being a very good potato for baking, boiling and French frying. It was released to market in 1981.

Canada Dry ginger ale

You knew this! Canada Dry ginger ale was created in Canada, by Toronto chemist and pharmacist John J. McLaughlin. He's said to have perfected the recipe in 1904.

MCINTOSH APPLE

If apple pie is a traditional American dish, the McIntosh apple is as Canadian as it gets. In 1811, John McIntosh discovered an apple sapling on his farm near Dundela, Ontario, which subsequently produced a fruit with a great taste, texture, aroma and appearance. It was also ideally suited for growing in Canada's colder climate. John's son Allan established a nursery for the species and promoted it widely. It has since become one of the most popular apple varieties in Canada and around the world.

Red Fife wheat

Canadian wheat is known as some of the finest in the world. The oldest of the nation's wheat varieties is Red Fife, which was first grown in Peterborough, Ontario on the farm of Dave Fife in 1842. Red Fife was known as a fine milling and baking wheat, and by the 1860s it was being cultivated across the nation. Red Fife was considered the country's wheat standard for more than four decades, from about 1860 to 1900.

First submarine tunnel

The world's first international submarine tunnel, linking Sarnia, Ontario, with Port Huron, Michigan, opened on September 19, 1891. The St. Clair Tunnel, almost 2 km long, was used by the Grand Trunk Railroad.

Largest grain capacity

Ontario's Port of Thunder Bay has the largest grain storage capacity in North America. The port's eight terminals have a capacity of 1.2 million tonnes.

First trolley bus

The first trolley bus (a trackless electric system run by an overhead wire), debuted in Windsor on May 4, 1922.

BIGGEST TRANSIT SYSTEM

The Toronto Transit Commission, or TTC, is the largest public transit system in Canada and the third-largest in North America. More than 450 million passengers use the system annually.

Longest commute

Surprise, surprise. Based on Statistics Canada data from 2010, commuters in the Toronto area have the longest average commute time in the country at 33 minutes. More than 25 percent of commuters in the region travel more than 45 minutes, and another 25 percent travel between 30 and 45 minutes.

First electric transit system

Windsor, Ontario, was the nation's first city with an all-electric transit system. That was inaugurated in 1891, when the city's Sandwich & Windsor Passenger Railway—a series of horse-drawn carts running on rails—was converted to a streetcar system.

First electric car

The buzz these days over electric cars seems a little funny when you consider the nation's first electric car was built more than 100 years ago, in 1893. Using a battery and motor designed by William Still, Frederick B. Featherstonehaugh commissioned the Dixon Carriage Works to build it. The two-person car was capable of moving about 25 km/hour.

First subway ↗

A better way? The city of Toronto unveiled the nation's first subway system on March 31, 1954. The first line ran largely beneath Yonge Street. It encompassed 12 stops, from Union Station on Front Street at the south end to Eglinton Avenue at the north. (Pictured here is a train from 1969.)

First car in production

The nation's first gasoline-powered car to be put into production was the LeRoy, which debuted in 1902. Fewer than 20 of the cars were produced by the LeRoy Manufacturing Co. of Berlin, Ontario (now Kitchener), before the company closed in 1904. The cost of a brand-new LeRoy in 1903? A mere $650 (the average annual income at the time was about $275).

FIRST STREETCAR

The first commercial electric streetcar service in Canada began in Windsor, Ontario on May 28, 1886. The Windsor Electric Railway had just 2.4 km of track.

First international tunnel

The Detroit-Windsor Tunnel, which links the two cities in Michigan and Ontario, respectively, was the world's first international vehicular tunnel. The 1,573-m tunnel opened on November 3, 1930, after more than a year of construction and a cost of $23 million.

The Queen's highway

The Queen Elizabeth Way, a highway from Toronto to Fort Erie, Ontario, was the nation's first four-lane, controlled-access highway. The highway was officially opened by Queen Elizabeth (who later became the Queen Mother) at St. Catharines, Ontario, on June 7, 1939. At the time, the roadway was the longest multi-lane, divided highway in the Commonwealth.

BUSIEST HIGHWAY

If you regularly drive along Highway 401 through Toronto, this may come as little surprise—and may be dismally deflating: the stretch is the busiest highway on the continent. It's estimated that an average of more than 425,000 vehicles travel the route daily, and some days the traffic surpasses half a million vehicles.

Third-longest highway

The Trans-Canada Highway, which runs 7,821 km from St. John's to Victoria, is the one of the world's longest highways, along with the Trans-Siberian Highway and Australia's Highway 1. When the road opened at BC's Rogers Pass on July 30, 1962, more than 3,000 km of it remained unpaved. Eventually completed in 1970, the Trans-Canada cost a total of $1 billion dollars to build.

First traffic lights

The first traffic lights in Canada went up on June 11, 1925, at the intersection of Main and King streets in east Hamilton. The traffic light, which was made in the United States, proved problematic, as it had been designed for use at right-angle intersections, while Main and King crisscross at an angle. As a result, drivers were sometimes confused as to which light was meant for them. Another problem? Local residents weren't fond of the loud bell that accompanied the amber light.

First computerized traffic control

Toronto was the first city in the world with a computerized traffic control system. In 1963, the city implemented the system to automate traffic signals. It required a 4.5-tonne air conditioning unit to keep it cool. Essentially, it was a clock that used predetermined plans to regulate traffic patterns during different parts of the day.

First jetliner

The Avro Canada C102 Jetliner was a first in many respects. Built by Avro Canada in 1949, it was the first Canadian jet to fly and the first commercial jet in North America (and the second in the world: just two weeks behind the first!). The prototype jet's first flight was over Toronto's Malton Airport on August 10, 1949. The following year, the plane was the first to make an airmail delivery by jet on April 18, 1950, on a flight from Toronto to New York.

First intercity flight

The first intercity flight in Canada took place in 1911, when famed pilot J.A.D. McCurdy won an airplane race from Hamilton to Toronto—after giving his competitors a 10-minute head start.

Biggest airport ↑

Toronto's Pearson International Airport is Canada's largest and busiest airport, and as a result, the country's primary air hub. It handles more than 30 percent of the nation's air travel. In 2012, it saw more than 400,000 flights and nearly 35 million passengers pass through. Pearson is the second-busiest gateway to Europe and handles the most United States–Canada air traffic.

Worst Canadian air crash

The year 1985 was a particularly bad year for Canadian air disasters. The worst airline incident associated with Canada, and the third worst in the world, occurred on June 23, when Air India Flight 182 from Toronto crashed into the north Atlantic off the coast of Ireland. It's suspected a terrorist bomb caused the disaster, which killed all 329 passengers, including 280 Canadians.

Instant books

Here's an intriguing first for aspiring authors. The Windsor Public Library in Windsor, Ontario, is the first public library in Canada to offer customers access to an Espresso Book Machine, which prints professionally bound copies of their own work—in just minutes.

First movie star

A Canadian first in Hollywood history: Florence Lawrence, born in Hamilton, Ontario, on January 2, 1886, is believed to be the first movie star known publically by her real name. (Studios didn't use actors' real names for fear they'd demand more money). As part of a publicity stunt for the movie *The Broken Oath* in 1909, her true identity was revealed. Lawrence, who appeared in almost 300 films starting in 1906, is also considered the world's first movie star.

First stars in cement

Early Hollywood actress Mary Pickford, and her husband at the time, Douglas Fairbanks, were the first stars to cast their hands and feet in cement in front of the Grauman's Chinese Theatre in Hollywood, on April 30, 1927. Known as "America's sweetheart," Pickford was born in Toronto on April 8, 1892.

TALLEST MURAL

Who says kids can't do BIG things? A youth-led art project is the world's tallest mural. A 32-storey building in Toronto's St. James Town community, 200 Wellesley Street East to be precise, boasts a painting of a bird that stretches almost the entire height of the building. It was unveiled in September 2012.

Canadian Warner Bros.

How's this for a Canadian connection to Hollywood royalty? Along with his brothers Henry M., Albert and Sam, Jack L. Warner, who was born in London, Ontario, on August 2, 1892, founded Warner Bros. Pictures Inc., the massive Hollywood film studio, in 1923. Jack became one of the most famous and significant film executives of early Hollywood.

Oldest Oscar winner →

Who says you can't teach an old dog new tricks? Canadian actor Christopher Plummer, born in Toronto on December 12, 1929, is the oldest actor to ever win an Oscar. Plummer captured the 2012 Academy Award for Best Supporting Actor for his role in Beginners at the age of 82.

Adults-only theatre

A movie theatre for only adults? That's right! The Cineplex VIP Cinemas Don Mills in Toronto is the nation's first theatre built only for people 19 years old or older. It opened August 15, 2014. The theatres has five screens and only adults are allowed because the theatre serves alcoholic beverages. Coincidentally, among the first films the theatre showed was *Teenage Mutant Ninja Turtles*!

Top film fest

The Toronto International Film Festival, held annually in September, is considered one of the most important film festivals in the world. It's certainly the premiere festival in North America, and internationally it ranks second, after France's Cannes' festival. It will celebrate its 40th anniversary in 2016.

Top docs fest

Not to be outdone, the Hot Docs Canadian International Documentary Festival is North America's largest documentary festival. Each year during its late April/early May run, Hot Docs presents more than 180 Canadian and international documentary films. The festival was founded in 1993.

Highest-grossing movies

Talk about Hollywood North! James Cameron, born in Kapuskasing, Ontario, is the writer and director of the two highest-grossing movies of all time, *Avatar* (2009) and *Titanic* (1997). The two films have combined to gross nearly $500 million dollars, with *Avatar* besting *Titanic* at $2.78 billion to $2.19 billion, as of early 2013.

James Cameron at the 1998 Academy Awards, with his Best Picture and Best Director Oscars for *Titanic*. ↘

Mad television genius

While the rumours of his being the inspiration for Dr. Evil of Austin Powers fame have been denied, there's no question television producer Lorne Michaels is a mad genius, after a fashion. Born in Toronto on November 17, 1944, Michaels' most noteworthy accomplishment is as the creator and executive producer of *Saturday Night Live*, the longest-running and highest-rated late-night television show ever.

Best-selling American debut

Musician Alanis Morissette, born in Ottawa on June 1, 1974, holds the record for the best-selling American debut for a female solo artist, for her 1995 album *Jagged Little Pill*. The album—which won four Grammys, including Album of the Year—has sold more than 33 million copies.

One million records

Singer-songwriter Bryan Adams, born in Kingston, Ontario, on November 5, 1959, was the first Canadian musician to sell one million albums in Canada, for his 1984 album, *Reckless*.

Number One Country

Canadian country music sweetheart Shania Twain, born in Windsor, Ontario, on August 28, 1965, left her mark on the genre. Twain's second album, *The Woman in Me* (1995), holds the record for most weeks at Number One on Billboard's country album chart. It spent 29 weeks at the top and has sold more than 7.7 million copies.

Five Number One Hits ↑

You're likely very familiar with Justin Bieber. Bieber, born in Stratford, Ontario, on March 1, 1994, became the first musician with five number one albums on the Billboard 200 chart before turning 19 years old. He achieved the feat in early 2013 with his Believe Acoustic album. His previous number one albums included *Believe* (2012), *Under the Mistletoe* (2011), *Never Say Never: The Remixes* (2011) and *My World 2.0* (2010).

Legend of Live

Famed concert promoter Michael Cohl, born in Toronto in 1948, was the first recipient of *Billboard* magazine's Legend of Live award, in November 2004, for his significant contributions to the music touring industry.

Youngest supermodel

Considered Canada's first supermodel, Monika Schnarre (see page 49), born in Scarborough, Ontario, May 27, 1971, was the youngest person to win the Ford Modeling Agency's Supermodel of the World competition, in 1986 at age 14.

LARGEST CARIBBEAN FESTIVAL

If you want to celebrate Caribbean culture in Canada, there's nowhere else to be than Toronto in mid-July and early August. The Scotiabank Toronto Caribbean Carnival, formerly Caribana (and still referred to commonly by that moniker), is considered the largest cultural festival of its kind in North America. The highlight of the three-week festival is Parade Day, where Caribbean-inspired acts from around the world celebrate calypso, soca, reggae, hip hop, chutney, steel pan and brass bands.

Most pride

Toronto was the first city in North America to host the World Pride Festival, an international celebration of lesbian, gay, bisexual, transsexual and transgender individuals. The festival, the fourth ever held, ran June 20 to 29, 2014.

Biggest community event

The Canadian National Exhibition, held each year in Toronto since 1879, is the nation's largest annual community event. The CNE is one of the 10 largest fairs on the continent. It attracted 1.36 million visitors in 2013.

Most expensive art

During his life, Toronto painter Alex Colville, who died on July 16, 2013 at the age of 92, held the record for the highest price paid for a work of art by a living Canadian artist. "Man on Verandah," painted in 1953, was purchased at an auction on November 25, 2010, for $1.287 million.

Photo fest

The annual CONTACT Photography Festival is the largest photography event in the world. Held each May in the Greater Toronto Area, it showcases the works of more than 1,500 Canadian and international shutterbugs at at least 175 venues. The festival, which has an estimated audience of 1.8 million, was founded in 1997.

Most maple syrup ↗

Celebrating its 50th anniversary in 2014, the Elmira Maple Syrup Festival, held annually in early April, claims to be the world's largest single-day maple syrup festival (as recognized by Guinness World Records in 2000, when 66,529 people attended the event). The event attracts thousands each year to eat pancakes and sample maple syrup.

Biggest agricultural fair

The Royal Agricultural Winter Fair, held annually in November in Toronto, is the largest combined indoor agricultural fair and international equestrian competition in the world. The first Royal opened on November 22, 1922, with 17,000 entries and drew more than 150,000 visitors. Today the fair takes up nearly 93,000 square m of space and attracts thousands of entries and about 300,000 visitors.

Most Elvis ↘

Elvis lives! At least he does at the Collingwood Elvis Festival, held each July since 1995. It's the world's largest festival celebrating legendary singer Elvis Presley. The highlight of the event is the Elvis impersonator contest, which attracts many of the world's best Elvis tribute artists.

Biggest children's theatre

Toronto's Young People's Theatre is the largest theatre for young audiences in the nation. It was established in 1966 by Susan Douglas Rubes, and the first production was *The Looking Glass Revue*, which was aimed at children aged 3 to 7. Since the start, the theatre has been dedicated to productions written specifically for children.

Most theatres ↑

Toronto has the largest variety of theatres and performing arts companies in Canada, the second-largest in North America after New York City, and the third-largest in the world after London, England. Ten major theatres host the likes of the Canadian Opera Company, the National Ballet of Canada and Mirvish and DanCap Productions, two large private entertainment companies.

First radio symphony concert series

Businessman Henry Thornton inaugurated the first radio transcontinental symphonic series in North America on October 20, 1929. The "All-Canada Symphony Concerts" were performed by 55 members of the Toronto Symphony Orchestra and culminated on April 6, 1930, in a concert entirely of Canadian-composed music.

First opera school

The opera school founded by Canada's Royal Conservatory of Music (known as the Toronto Conservatory of Music at the time) in 1946 was the nation's first school dedicated to the professional training of singers.

Largest classical theatre

Stratford, Ontario, hosts the largest classical repertory theatre in North America. Founded in 1953, the Stratford Festival presents numerous shows spring through fall annually at four theatres in the town. In 2013, the festival attracted 480,000 patrons.

First orchestra concert for children

In 1924–25, its second season, the Toronto Symphony Orchestra performed the first orchestra concert specifically for children. The performance was part of the orchestra's efforts to engage and attract a younger audience.

First National Ballet *Giselle*

The National Ballet of Canada (NBC) was formed in 1951. Its first performance was *Giselle* (considered the *Hamlet* of dance) on November 12 of that year at Toronto's Eaton Auditorium. The ballet has been performed many times since then by the NBC, which is one of the few ballet companies that has always had its own orchestra.

Biggest outdoor show

The Toronto Sportsmen's Show, held annually each spring, is the nation's largest outdoors consumer trade show. The event boasts more than 300 exhibits.

Oldest crokinole board game

Canadian Eckhardt Wettlaufer of Sebastopol, Ontario, built the oldest known crokinole board, in 1876. Crokinole, a table-top disc shooting game, was considered one of the continent's most popular games around the start of the 20th century.

First radio hockey

"He shoots, he scores!" While it's still a matter of debate, the Hockey Hall of Fame reports that the very first radio broadcast of a hockey game took place on February 16, 1923. Legendary announcer Foster Hewitt called the action of the game between Kitchener and Toronto at the Arena Gardens on Toronto station CFCA.

Defenceman top scores

Bobby Orr, born in Parry Sound, Ontario, on March 20, 1948, is the only defenceman to lead the National Hockey League in regular-season scoring. Orr accomplished the feat twice, in 1969–70 (120 points) and in 1974–75 (122 points).

FIRST TABLETOP HOCKEY

The tabletop hockey game was invented in 1932 by Toronto's Don Munro. A bump in the middle of the wooden board kept the steel ball moving, while one lever controlled the goalie and another controlled the other players. Versions of his game were popular until 1954, when a competitor introduced players printed in colour on flat tin cutouts.

OLDEST HORSE RACE

The Queen's Plate, held annually since 1860, is the oldest continuously run horse race in North America. Today, it's run each July at Toronto's Woodbine Racetrack. The race has been attended by reigning monarchs five times in its history, and by representatives of the monarchy another dozen times.

World's largest skating rink ↑

Where else but Canada's capital would you find the world's largest skating rink? Located on the Rideau Canal in downtown Ottawa, the Skateway is 7.8 km long, running from near the Parliament Buildings to Dow's Lake. It's typically open January through February, with the average season lasting 50 days. Its first season of 1971–72 set a record of 90 days.

First sports association

The National Lacrosse Association was Canada's first sports association. It was established on September 26, 1867, in Kingston, Ontario.

First Canadian to win Derby

Racehorse Northern Dancer, born in Oshawa, Ontario, on May 27, 1961, was the first Canadian-bred horse to win the Kentucky Derby, in 1964. Northern Dancer also won the Preakness Stakes in the same year.

Jockey wins 500 +

Jockey Sandy Hawley, born in Oshawa, Ontario, on April 16, 1949, was the first to win 500 races in one year. Hawley eclipsed the record in 1973, totaling 515 first-place finishes. During his career, Hawley won 6,449 races, and stands eighth among jockeys for the most career wins.

Canadian basketball ↗

When it comes to quintessential Canadian sports, basketball doesn't immediately spring to mind. But the sport was invented by a Canadian, Dr. James Naismith, who was born November 6, 1861, in Almonte, Ontario. He came up with the game in 1891 and it was first played on December 21 of that year at Springfield College in Massachusetts.

First NBA game

The first National Basketball Association game was played in Canada. On November 1, 1946, the New York Knickerbockers beat the Toronto Huskies 68 to 66 at Toronto's Maple Leaf Gardens.

Double whammy

Hank Biasatti is the only Canadian to play at the major league level in both basketball and baseball. Aside from playing with basketball's Toronto Huskies in 1946, Biasatti played professional baseball for the Philadelphia Athletics in 1949.

Invention of 5-pin bowling ↗

The invention of 5-pin bowling, a Canadian concept, was the result of dissatisfaction with the American, 10-pin version of the game. Thomas F. (Tommy) Ryan opened the first regulation 10-pin lanes in Toronto in 1905, but customers complained about the size and weight of the balls. Ryan began experimenting with different pin and ball sizes, and in 1909, Canada's 5-pin game was born.

Baseball's mysterious origins

So baseball is America's game, eh? Explain this: a year before the game's accepted creator Abner Doubleday is credited with founding the sport, the first recorded baseball game in North America took place in Beachville, Ontario. Teams from Oxford and Zorra townships played on June 4, 1838.

Babe Ruth's first pro homer

Legendary baseball player Babe Ruth hit his first professional home run in Toronto. On September 5, 1914, as a 19-year-old rookie in the International League, Ruth hit that monumental homer at Maple Leaf Park on the Toronto Islands.

163

First Canadian Cy Young Award

You could call him the ace of Canadian aces. Baseball pitcher Ferguson Jenkins, born in Chatham, Ontario, on December 12, 1942, was the first Canadian to win the Cy Young Award, awarded annually to the game's best pitcher. Jenkins nabbed the honour while pitching for the Chicago Cubs in 1971, and played for four other clubs before retiring in 1983.

FIRST CANADIAN WORLD SERIES WIN

In 1992, the Toronto Blue Jays became the first non-American team to win baseball's World Series championship. They defeated the Atlanta Braves on October 24 to claim the title. The team repeated the feat in 1993.

First alpine gold

Anne Heggtveit, born in Ottawa on January 11, 1939, won Canada's first-ever gold medal in alpine skiing, which was also the first North American gold in slalom. She captured the medal at the 1960 Olympic Games in Squaw Valley, California.

First double Lutz

Figure skater Barbara Ann Scott, born in Ottawa in 1928, was the first woman to land a double Lutz jump in competition in 1942. The feat helped her capture the gold medal at the 1948 Winter Olympics in St. Moritz, Switzerland. Scott was also the first non-European to win a world championship in skating in 1947.

First Olympic gold

George W. Orton of Strathroy, Ontario, won the nation's first Olympic gold medal at the Paris games in 1900, despite the fact that Canada did not send a team to the event. Orton was asked to join the American team, thanks to his many victories at track and field meets throughout the United States, and he reached the top of the podium in the 2,500 m steeplechase. He also won bronze in the 400 m hurdles at the games.

First Commonwealth Games

In 1930, Hamilton, Ontario, was the first host of the British Empire Games, which eventually became the Commonwealth Games. Participating nations included Australia, Bermuda, British Guyana, England, Northern Ireland, Newfoundland, New Zealand, South Africa and Wales. The games featured six sports: athletics, boxing, lawn bowls, rowing, swimming and diving, and wrestling.

Toughest boxer

None other than Muhammad Ali, considered the greatest heavyweight boxer ever, called Canadian boxer George Chuvalo "the toughest man I ever fought." Chuvalo, born on September 12, 1937, in Toronto, was the sport's Canadian heavyweight champion from September 1958 until he retired in 1979. While he never captured the world title, in 97 professional matches, Chuvalo was never knocked out or down – even in two losses to Ali.

World Heavyweight ⚡ Boxing Champion

He's Canada's only world heavyweight boxing champion. Tommy Burns (left), born in Hanover, Ontario, on June 17, 1881, won the world title on February 23, 1906, in a 20-round decision over Marvin Hart in Los Angeles. He held the championship until December 26, 1908, when he was defeated by Jack Johnson – the first black fighter to hold the world heavyweight title – in 14 rounds in Sydney, Australia.

First perfect seven

That first triple Lutz performed by Don Jackson wasn't his only amazing "first." At the end of his performance at the 1962 championship where he unveiled the triple Lutz, Jackson received seven perfect scores (6.0) from the judges, the highest tally ever.

First World Figure Skating Championship

Don Jackson wasn't done there. His perfect score won him the 1962 World Figure Skating Championship, and made him the first Canadian man to do so.

FIRST SWIM ACROSS LAKE ONTARIO

You could call it the first great lake swim. Marilyn Bell, born in Toronto on November 19, 1937, was the first person to swim across Lake Ontario. At just 16 years old, Bell completed the swim from Youngstown, New York, to Toronto on September 9, 1954. It took her 20 hours and 59 minutes to swim the estimated 51.5-km course.

First Canadian to win Boston marathon

Thomas Longboat, born on July 4, 1887, in Six Nations, Ontario, was the first Canadian to win the Boston Marathon, the world's oldest annual marathon (it was first run in 1897). Longboat won the legendary race in 1907.

Oldest marathon run ⬎

When it comes to legendary road running races, one thinks of Boston and New York. But Hamilton, Ontario? One should, as it's home to the oldest marathon in North America (preceding Boston's by three years), the Around the Bay Road Race, which was first run in 1894. The 30 km race has been won by the best in the world, including Olympic medalists and Boston Marathon winners.

Youngest to swim English Channel

Marilyn Bell was the youngest person to swim the English Channel. She achieved that feat on July 31, 1955, at the age of 17.

First to swim the English Channel both ways

There must be something in the water near Toronto. Cindy Nicholas, born on August 20, 1957, in Ontario's capital, was the first woman to swim the English Channel both ways non-stop. She accomplished the record swim on September 8, 1977, in 19 hours and 55 minutes.

Most snowmen

Frosty would be proud. On February 1, 2015, a group of people in Ottawa set a national record for most snowmen built in one hour. A total of 1,299 snowmen—each at least 0.91 m tall, with two eyes, a nose and two arms—were built on the field at TD Place Stadium.

Largest ice cream cake

On May 10, 2011, Dairy Queen Canada served one giant ice cream cake in Toronto. Indeed it was the largest ice cream cake ever. The cake, made of sponge cake, vanilla ice cream, butter cream frosting and Oreo cookie crumb topping, weighed 10.13 tonnes, and measured 4.45 m long, 4.06 m wide and 1 m high.

Largest collection of video games

Like video games? Here's betting your collection isn't as big a Syd Bolton of Brantford, Ontario, who is believed to have the largest known collection of video games in the country. Bolton owns more than 10,000 games, including almost every one created for both the PlayStation 2 and the original Xbox.

Largest collection of computers

Bolton is also the creator and curator of Brantford's Personal Computer Museum. The museum claims to be home to the nation's largest-known collection of computers (at more than 1,000), as well as the largest-known collection of CED video discs.

Most eggs

Like eggs? Ontario is home to the largest percentage of hens that lay table eggs in Canada. Indeed, 38.2 percent of such hens in the country come from Ontario.

Largest orchid colony

This is one special garden! The Purdon Conservation Area, located in Lanark County east of Ottawa, is home to the largest orchid colony in Canada. Between mid-June and early July of each year, more than 16,000 showy lady's slipper orchids bloom in an impressive display.

First surgery by robot ↑

Dr. Mehran Anvari, a professor of surgery at McMaster University in Hamilton, Ontario, and scientific director and CEO of the Centre for Surgical Invention & Innovation, performed the world's first telerobotic-assisted surgery. In 2003, he operated on a patient at North Bay Regional Health Centre from more than 400 km away, at St. Joseph's Healthcare Hamilton. He has since worked with the Canadian Space Agency and NASA on robotic surgical technologies.

FIRST PHOTOGRAPH OF CANADA

What else other than Ontario's Niagara Falls would appear in the first known picture of Canada? It was taken by English industrial chemist H.L. Pattinson during a visit to America. The plate on which the image of Horseshoe Falls appears is marked April 1840 on the back. A total of eight of Pattinson's plates from this trip have been discovered, a number of which show buildings in Niagara Falls, including the Clifton Hotel, which was frequented by dignitaries of the time.

First woman doctor ⤺

The first Canadian woman to practise medicine in Canada was Emily Stowe of Norwich, Ontario, who started working as a doctor in Toronto in 1867. Her daughter, Augusta Stowe Gullen, was the first woman to earn a medical degree in Canada. She studied at the Toronto School of Medicine and graduated from Victoria College in Cobourg, Ontario, in 1883.

First licensed woman doctor

In 1875, Jennie Trout of Stratford, Ontario, became the first woman in Canada licensed to practise medicine. Trout was encouraged in the endeavour by Emily Stowe. Trout practised at Toronto's Therapeutic and Electrical Institute until 1882.

First birth of pre-sexed calf

The world's first calf born with its sex predetermined in a laboratory came into the world on December 25, 1975, at the Animal Disease Research Institute in Nepean, Ontario. The Holstein heifer (named Eugenia Carol) represented a breakthrough in embryo transfer that was later used with other species.

First Women's Institute

The world's first Women's Institute, an organization created to help educate women (especially those living in rural areas) in a wide range of skills, was established in Canada in 1897. After the Stoney Creek Women's Institute was founded in this Ontario community, the concept spread across the nation and the world.

First Labour Day Parade

Power to the people. The world's first Labour Day Parade was held on April 15, 1872, in Toronto. The parade was arranged by the Toronto Trades Assembly to protest federal laws against unions and the imprisonment of 24 Toronto Typographical Union members.

First museum

The first museum in Canada, and the country's oldest, is that of Thomas Barnett, an English "collector" who immigrated to Canada in the early 1820s. He opened a museum of his personal collection of local and foreign artifacts in Niagara Falls in 1827. That museum became today's Niagara Falls Museum.

Most reference materials

It makes sense that Library and Archives Canada has the world's largest and most important collection of Canadian reference materials. The collection includes:

- more than 71,000 hours of films dating back to 1897
- over 2.5 million architectural drawings
- 3.18 million megabytes of electronic materials
- millions of books
- more than 21.3 million photographs
- over 270,000 hours of video and sound recordings
- more than 343,000 works of art
- and much, much more.

Largest art school ↗

The Ontario College of Art & Design University, located in Toronto, is the nation's largest art school. Founded in 1876 as the Ontario School of Art, OCAD now hosts some 3,500 full-time students and about 1,000 part-time students, and has an annual budget of $56 million.

Most vaudeville scenery

What a scene! Or two or three. The Elgin and Winter Garden Theatre Centre in Toronto is home to the world's largest collection of vaudeville scenery. The backdrops (some of which date back to 1913, when the two theatres opened) were discovered during the facility's restoration, which began in 1987 and was completed in 1989. A number of the pieces are on display at the Centre.

Biggest gift

The Art Gallery of Ontario's Thomson Collection, some 2,000 works of Canadian and European art collected by Canadian businessman Ken Thomson, is the largest gift ever made to a Canadian cultural institution.

First nursing school

Canada's first school for nursing was established in 1874 at Ontario's St. Catharines General Hospital. The program inspired similar training initiatives at hospitals throughout the country.

Biggest university

Talk about student life! The University of Toronto is the country's largest university with enough students to create a small city—more than 82,000 students at three campuses (St. George, Mississauga and Scarborough). U of T offers more than 700 undergraduate programs, 215 graduate programs and 63 professional programs. Its operations budget for 2012–13 was $1.8 billion.

Biggest school board

School's in! And a whole lot of it. The Toronto District School Board is the nation's largest. It educates about 259,000 students (172,000 elementary and 87,000 secondary) at nearly 600 schools throughout the city.

MOST CANOES

The Canadian Canoe Museum in Peterborough, Ontario, is home to the world's largest collection of canoes and kayaks. Founded in 1997, the museum has more than 100 watercraft on permanent display, and its total collection of the boats numbers more than 600.

Largest academic library system

The libraries at the University of Toronto constitute the largest academic library system in Canada and the third-largest in North America. U of T has 44 libraries at three campuses that contain more than 12 million publications in 341 languages, 1.5 million electronic resources, 28,000 linear metres of archival material and 500 terabytes of data.

Largest boys school

Located north of Toronto in Aurora, Ontario, St. Andrew's College is Canada's largest all-boys private school. In 2013, 613 students were enrolled in the school in Grades 5 to 12. The campus is 44 hectares and has 17 buildings. First established in Toronto in 1899, the school moved to its current location in 1926.

FIRST QUINTS

They brought a whole new meaning to the phrase "Take five." The Dionne quintuplets, born in Corbeil, Ontario, on May 28, 1934, were the first quintuplets in the world to survive more than a few days. They would become the biggest tourist attraction in the nation at the time, generating an estimated $500 million for the province of Ontario and attracting some three million people to see them in person.

Largest youth-driven charity

Free the Children, founded by brothers Craig and Marc Kielburger in 1995 in Thornhill, Ontario, is the world's largest youth-driven charity.

First forest research centre

Canada's first forest research centre, Ontario's Petawawa Research Forest, was created in 1918. Still in operation today, it is also the country's oldest continuously operated research forest. In its founding year, the nation's first forest inventory was completed and the first forest sample plots were initiated.

Oldest military school

Today, all cadets at the Royal Military College of Canada in Kingston, Ontario, know the names of the "Old Eighteen," the school's first class of students in 1874. The RMC is the nation's oldest military school, which was founded to train Canadian cadets in all aspects of the military profession.

Oldest co-ed boarding school

Albert College in Belleville, Ontario, is Canada's oldest co-educational boarding and day school. Established in 1857, the school educates students from pre-kindergarten to Grade 12 and post graduate. It offers residency to students of both sexes in Grade 7 onward.

First Victoria Cross ↘

Lieutenant Alexander Roberts Dunn was the first Canadian to receive a Victoria Cross, the Commonwealth's highest honour in recognition of military valour. Dunn, born in York (now Toronto), was awarded the medal in 1857 for his role in the Crimean War.

First Canadian spacewoman

On January 22, 1992, Dr. Roberta Bondar, a native of Sault Ste. Marie, Ontario, became the first Canadian woman in space and the second Canadian to leave the planet. During her eight-day mission on the space shuttle Discovery, Bondar conducted experiments to help find ways to allow future astronauts to take prolonged flights.

First black hole

Dr. Tom Bolton was the first to discover a black hole. Bolton discovered Cygnus X-1 from the David Dunlap Observatory, just north of Toronto, in 1971.

First polar dives

You could call him Canada's very own coldwater man. Dr. Joseph MacInnis, born in Barrie, Ontario, on March 2, 1937, led the teams that made the first scientific dives at the North Pole in the 1970s.

Northernmost shipwreck

Dr. Joseph MacInnis wasn't done yet! In 1980, MacInnis led the team that discovered the world's northernmost shipwreck. On August 13, the remains of the Breadalbane—a Royal Navy ship that sank in August 1853 while delivering supplies to another expedition—were found by MacInnis' crew near Nunavut's Beechy Island.

The most immigrants

Ontario is home to the largest proportion of people born outside Canada, according to the latest data from Statistics Canada. About 3.6 million immigrants reside in Ontario, 53 percent of the nation's total.

Most births

Perhaps not surprisingly, given that it's home to the largest provincial population, Ontario leads the country in total births, with 140,135 (based on 2011 data from Statistics Canada).

DEEPEST DIVE

Now here's a story with depth. James Cameron, born in Kapuskasing, Ontario, and the director of the Oscar-winning films *Titanic* and *Avatar*, became the first person to dive solo to the deepest part of the world's oceans. On March, 26, 2012, Cameron visited the Mariana Trench in the Pacific Ocean, some 11 km below the surface, in a custom-built submarine, *Deepsea Challenger*.

Last executions

The last executions in Canada made under the Criminal Code occurred on December 11, 1962. Ronald Turpin, 29, and Arthur Lucas, 54, were hanged at the Don Jail in Toronto. Turpin had been convicted of murdering a Toronto police officer, while Lucas had been convicted of murdering an FBI informant.

Aircraft pulling

Kevin Fast of Cobourg, Ontario, holds the distinction of the heaviest aircraft pull in the world, according to Guinness World Records. Fast pulled a CC-173 Globemaster III, weighing 188.83 tonnes, 8.8 m at Canadian Forces Base Trenton, in Trenton, Ontario, on September 17, 2009.

FIRST TO SCORE 500 GOALS

Maurice "Rocket" Richard, who played his entire career for the Montreal Canadiens, was the first professional hockey player to score 50 goals in 50 games (in 1945–46), but he was also the first professional to score 500 career goals (he tallied his 500th on October 19, 1957). When Richard retired, he'd scored 544 goals.

QUEBEC

As the principle home of French Canadians in Canada, it's somewhat ironic that the origin of the name of the province of Quebec almost certainly comes from First Nations languages, specifically and most likely Algonquin. The name was first applied to the province's current capital in various spellings (Quebecq, Kébec, Quebec) in the 17th century, and is a reference to the Algonquin word for "narrow passage" or "strait," in reference to the narrowing of the St. Lawrence River in the area. The same word is also common to Cree and Micmac.

Largest estuary

With water flowing out from the Great Lakes, the largest source of freshwater in the world, it's little wonder the St. Lawrence maritime estuary (a place where fresh and saltwater mix) is one of the largest and deepest estuaries in the world. Freshwater increasingly mixes with saltwater for nearly 250 km, from Île d'Orléans, near Quebec City, to Pointe-des-Monts, northeast of Baie Comeau on the St. Lawrence River's north shore.

Highest point

The highest point in Quebec is located along its border with Labrador in the province's northeast. Mont d'Iberville lies 1,652 m above sea level in Quebec's parc national Kuururjuaq.

Oldest rocks

The oldest known rocks on Earth—250 million years older than any other known rocks—are found in Canada. Geologists discovered the 4.28-billion-year-old rock in 2001 in an area of exposed bedrock on the eastern shore of Hudson Bay, in northern Quebec.

First lock canal

The canal at Coteau-du-Lac, Quebec, was the first lock canal in North America. Completed in 1781, three locks dropped the level of the canal approximately 2 m. The canal provided a safe way to avoid the rapids, which measured about 2 m from head to bottom.

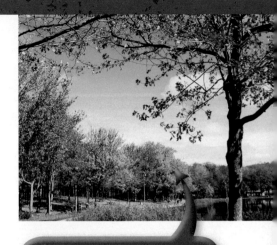

FIRST PROTECTED AREA

Montreal's Mount Royal Park is considered Canada's first protected area. It was inaugurated on Queen Victoria's birthday, May 24, in 1876.

Longest inland waterway

The Great Lakes St. Lawrence Seaway system is the longest inland waterway open to ocean shipping in the world. It extends 3,700 km from the Atlantic Ocean to the head of Lake Superior. The Seaway part of the system stretches from Montreal to the middle of Lake Erie and is considered one of the outstanding engineering feats of the 20th century.

Largest provincial park

More than four times the size of Prince Edward Island, Quebec's Parc national Tursujuq is the largest provincial park in the country. The 26,107-square-km park, located on the eastern shore of Hudson Bay, was created on December 14, 2012.

Windiest day

This was one windy day: on November 18, 1931, in Cape Hopes Advance, Quebec, the nation's highest recorded hourly wind speed, was set at 201.1 km/hour.

Largest snow-removal budget ⤹

Winter and snow are no strangers to those living in the city of Montreal. Indeed, so much snow hits the city—an average of 2 m a year—that it has the largest snow-removal budget of any metropolis in the world. For the winter of 2011–12, the average cost of snow removal for a snowfall of at least 20 cm was $17 million. On December 27, 2012, the city had its largest recorded one-day snowfall: 45 cm.

MONTREAL'S WORST SNOWSTORM

Montreal gets a lot of snow. The worst snowstorm to hit the city happened on March 4, 1971. In total, 47 cm of snow hit the city, and 110-km-per-hour winds created snow drifts as high as two storeys. The storm created power outages that lasted up to 10 days in some areas, and 17 people died as a result of the blizzard.

177

Highest frequency of snow

There's quantity of snow, then there's frequency. The following big Canadian cities had the highest average number of days with at least 2 mm or more snow.

City	mm of snow
Saguenay, Quebec	93
St. John's, NL	79
Sherbrooke, QC	76
Sudbury, ON	75
Quebec City, QC	70
Thunder Bay, ON	62
Kitchener–Waterloo, ON	62
London, ON	60
Montreal, QC	59
Regina, SK	56

Most months of snow

Snow, snow, go away. Ten of the nation's largest cities have at least 1 cm of snow on the ground for at least three months (or more than 120 days).

Average number of days a year when snow is 1 cm or more deep:

City	Days
Saguenay, Quebec	155
Quebec City, Quebec	141
Sudbury, Ontario	136
Trois-Rivières, Quebec	134
Sherbrooke, Quebec	133
Edmonton, Alberta	133
Winnipeg, Manitoba	128
Thunder Bay, Ontario	126
Regina, Saskatchewan	125
Saskatoon, Saskatchewan	124

No change in fall temperatures

Two parts of the country have bucked the warming trend. During autumn in the extreme south of Ontario and Quebec, the average temperature has not changed since 1948.

Ice storm of the century

Some called it "the storm of the century." Whatever you consider it, the ice storm that hit Quebec and Ontario starting on January 5, 1998, was the costliest winter storm in Canadian history. According to the Insurance Bureau of Canada, the six days of freezing rain led to month-long power outages in some locations and worth $2 billion (in 2011 dollars) in insured losses.

Freshwater harbor seals ↘

In the Nunavik region of Quebec, about 250 km east of Hudson Bay, lies a very unique population of harbour seals—the planet's only population of the species that lives year round in fresh water. Known as the Lac des Loups Marins harbour seals, experts believe the animals were separated from their original marine habitat 3,000 to 8,000 years ago. It's estimated that there are 50 to 600 of the seals, which are considered endangered.

Original Canadian fish

Take a male brook trout and cross it with a female lake trout and what do you get? Arguably a uniquely Canadian fish, the splake. While previous records exist of the hybrid, it wasn't until after experiments made in 1947 by J.E. Stenton, a warden at Alberta's Banff National Park, that the first official crosses of the species were made by the Quebec Department of Fish and Game in 1948.

Unique brook trout

The Aurora trout, a unique strain of brook trout, is found only in Ontario and Quebec. The original strain of the fish was extirpated from its original native lakes in Ontario's Temagami region. Captive breeding led to the reintroduction of the species to a select group of lakes in the 1990s.

First billion-dollar disaster ↗

The storm's moniker has a nice ring to it, but there was nothing nice about the disaster. The first billion-dollar disaster in Canadian history was the flood that hit Saguenay, Quebec, from July 18 to 21, 1996. Roads and bridges throughout the area were destroyed, 12,000 residents were evacuated and 10 people were killed.

Deadliest sinkhole

The deadliest recorded sinkhole in Canada happened on May 4, 1971, when heavy rain created a sinkhole 600 m wide and 30 m deep in St-Jean-Vianney, Quebec. The hole and associated mudslide claimed the lives of 31 people and swallowed 35 homes, a bus and several cars.

Biggest church

Saint Joseph's Oratory of Mount Royal is Canada's largest church. The Roman Catholic minor basilica on Westmount Summit in Montreal opened in 1967 and can seat 10,000. More than two million visitors and pilgrims visit the church each year. The building's granite exterior was constructed with blocks cut from Lac Mégantic quarries.

Biggest cemetery

Montreal's Notre-Dame-des-Neiges Cemetery is the largest in Canada and the third-largest on the continent. The Catholic cemetery was founded in 1854 and has more than 65,000 monuments and 71 family vaults. More than 175,000 people visit the cemetery annually.

First movie theatre

Pass the popcorn. The first commercial movie theatre in North America opened on January 1, 1906, in Montreal. The Ouimetoscope was converted from a tavern to a 500-seat cinema with a small screen.

LONGEST CANTILEVER BRIDGE

The Quebec Bridge in Quebec City, which crosses the St. Lawrence River, is the longest span cantilever bridge in Canada, and at the time of its completion in 1917 it was the largest in the world. It is also the longest cantilever railroad span ever. The single span stretches nearly 550 m. The bridge's construction is also famed, as it took three attempts and cost 89 lives before it was finally completed.

First hospital

Quebec City's Hôtel-Dieu was the first hospital in America north of Mexico. It was founded by three Augustinian nuns in 1639.

First public hospital

John Molson, founder of the brewing company, was instrumental in the establishment of Montreal's first public hospital, Montreal General Hospital. It opened on May 1, 1819.

First theatre

More Molson. John Molson also helped build Montreal's first permanent theatre. Molson was a major shareholder of the company that built Theatre Royal, which opened in 1825. The 1,000-seat facility ran 111 full-length plays in one season before the company went bankrupt in 1826.

Longest suspension bridge

The Pierre Laporte Bridge in Quebec City, which crosses the St. Lawrence River, is the longest main suspension bridge in Canada. Located about 200 m west of the Quebec Bridge, the Pierre Laporte has a main span of 667.5 m. It carries Autoroute 73 and was completed in 1970.

Longest bridge

When it officially opened on August 25, 1860, Montreal's Victoria Bridge was the longest bridge in the world. Built as a railway bridge crossing the St. Lawrence River and connecting Montreal and Saint-Lambert, Quebec, the bridge was considered a modern world wonder at the time of its construction. It was the first structure to cross the St. Lawrence.

Busiest bridge

The Champlain Bridge, which crosses the St. Lawrence River in Montreal, is the busiest crossing in Canada. It's estimated that about 50 to 60 million vehicles, 6.2 million trucks, 200,000 buses and 11 million transit users cross the bridge each year. About $20 billion in international trade travels the Champlain annually, and it is vital to regional and national economies.

Oldest French community

Tadoussac, Quebec, is well known as a launching point for great whale watching in the St. Lawrence River. It's also the oldest continuously inhabited French community in America. Known as the cradle of New France, Tadoussac was first settled in 1600.

⤴ Only walled city

Quebec City is the only walled city in North America and the oldest city on the continent north of the Mexico border. It was founded in 1608. The Historic District of Old Quebec is a UNESCO world heritage site, the first city in North America to receive the designation.

Biggest arch and buttress dam

Quebec's Daniel-Johnston Dam, located on the Manicouagan River some 200 km north of Baie-Comeau, is the world's largest multiple arch and buttress dam. The 214-m high dam, which was completed in 1968, boasts 14 buttresses across its 1,310 m length.

Largest hockey arena

The largest hockey arena in Canada? Montreal's Bell Centre, home of the Montreal Canadiens, which has a capacity of 21,273 seats. The arena, known as the Molson Centre when it opened in 1996, is considered one of the most technologically advanced and versatile entertainment facilities in the world. More than one million hockey fans visit the building annually and 650,000 more people attend the arena for other events.

BIGGEST LOG CABIN

Where else in the world would you find the globe's largest log cabin but in Canada? Specifically in Montebello, Quebec. Built in 1930 from 10,000 western red cedar logs and used as a private fishing lodge, the 211-room building is now the Fairmont Le Château Montebello.

Largest stadium ↓

Montreal's Olympic Stadium is the country's largest stadium based on seating capacity. Opened in 1976 for the Summer Olympics, the 56,000-seat stadium has seen more than 67 million visitors since it opened.

First paper mill

Canada's first paper mill was established in 1805 in St. Andrews, Quebec. It created printing, writing and wrapping papers for markets in Montreal and Quebec City.

Oldest brewery

Canada is home to the oldest brewery in North America. Molson was established in Montreal in 1786 by John Molson. The Molson brand is the oldest beer brand on the continent.

✔ Most maple syrup

Canada is the world's leading producer of maple syrup (the United States is the only other country to produce it). Canada produces 82 percent of the globe's maple syrup, valued at more than $177 million. More than 90 percent of Canadian maple syrup comes from Quebec. About 83 percent of the syrup produced in Canada is exported.

Transmission Lines: First 50-kilovolt

North America's first high-voltage (50-kilovolt) transmission line was installed in 1903. It carried electricity 136 km, from the Shawinigan Water and Power Company to aluminum and pulp-and-paper manufacturers in Montreal.

BIGGEST HYDROELECTRIC DEVELOPMENT

The biggest hydroelectric power development in Canada is Quebec's James Bay Project (pictured is its expansion in 1990). It started producing electricity in 1982. Its eight dams and 198 dikes contain five reservoirs covering 11,900 square km, half the size of Lake Ontario. The combined output of its generating stations is 10,283 megawatts.

Transmission Lines: First 220-kilovolt

In 1928, the first 220-kilovolt transmission line ran from Paugan Falls, Quebec, to Toronto, a distance of more than 440 km.

Transmission Lines: First 735-kilovolt

Danger: high voltage! Hydro-Quebec developed the world's first commercial 735-kilovolt power transmission line, along with the earliest equipment designed for the high voltage. It was commissioned in 1965 to link the Manic-Outardes generating stations to Montreal and Quebec.

First credit union

The first credit union in North America, La Caisse Populaire de Levis, was established in 1900 in Levis, Quebec, by journalist Alphonse Desjardins. Nine years later, Desjardins helped organize the first credit union in the United States, the St. Mary's Cooperative Credit Association.

Alphonse Desjardins

✔ First bilingual newspaper

Canada's first bilingual newspaper, *The Quebec Gazette*, was based in Quebec City and was established in 1764 by two Philadelphia printers, William Brown and Thomas Gilmore.

First daily newspaper

The *Montreal Daily Advertiser*, established in 1883, was the nation's first daily newspaper. It went bankrupt within a year of its first edition.

Oldest continuously published newspaper

The Montreal Gazette is the nation's oldest continuously operating newspaper and one of the oldest in North America. Founded by Fleury Mesplet as a French paper in 1778, the paper became bilingual in the late 1700s, then changed to English-only in 1822. Today, *The Gazette* is the dominant newspaper for reaching English speakers in Montreal.

First French radio station

Montreal's CKAC was the first French-language radio station in Canada. It was inaugurated on September 27, 1922.

First commercial radio station

The first commercial radio station in Canada, and some argue, in the world, was XWA Montreal (subsequently known as CFCF, CIQC and AM940). It hit the airwaves in 1919. The first broadcast: "Hello! Hello! This is wireless telephone station XWA at Montreal. Hello! Hello! How are you getting this? Is it clear? Is the modulation okay? XWA at Montreal is changing over." The station stopped broadcasting in January 2010.

First music and voice radio broadcast

Seems as though the impression that all the top musical acts on the radio are Canadian isn't so new. Canadian inventor Reginald Fessenden, born in Knowlton, Quebec, made the first public broadcast of music and voice on December 24, 1906. The broadcast, from Fessenden's headquarters in Brant Rock, Massachusetts, included a Bible passage, a phonograph recording of Handel and a performance of "O Holy Night" on the violin by Fessenden himself.

First voice radio transmission

Reginald Fessenden (see above) is also credited with the first achievement in the creation of what is now radio. On December 23, 1900, he sent the world's first wireless transmission of a human voice at Cobb Island, Maryland. The signal, sent via electromagnetic waves, travelled about 1.5 km.

First television broadcast

The first television pictures in Canada were broadcast in the summer of 1932, using the CKAC radio transmission in Montreal. The broadcasts were experimental and only a handful of people had receivers to view them on.

✓ First television weather report

Canada's first television station, CBC's CBFT Montreal, debuted on September 6, 1952. The first broadcast included the flickering test pattern of native man surrounded by a geometric design (broadcast upside down!), followed by a news item on two men who had just robbed a bank, a puppet show (Uncle Chichimus), and then, finally, a weather report with meteorologist Percy Saltzman.

First text message

It figures a 20-something was the first person to send a text message. What's not so predictable is that the British man who sent it now lives in Montreal. At 22 years old, Neil Papworth typed out the short note that would spawn a new form of communication on December 3, 1992. At the time he was an employee at Sema, a software company in England, and his message was brief, but seasonal: "Merry Christmas."

Peanut butter

Here's something nutty: Montreal's Marcellus Gilmore Edson was the first person to patent modern peanut butter in 1884.

✔ Robertson screwdriver

What do you do when you screw up? Invent a new screwdriver. After

cutting his hand using a spring-loaded screwdriver in Montreal, Peter Lymburner Robertson decided to improve the tool. The result: the Robertson Drive screwdriver, which was patented in 1909. The square-headed driver and screw could be driven more quickly and reduced the slipping common with other screwdrivers.

SNOWMOBILE

While there were patents for snowmobiles that pre-dated his, Joseph-Armand Bombardier is widely considered the inventor of the modern-day snowmobile. Born in Sherbrooke, Québec, on April 16, 1907, Bombardier invented his first B7 snowmobile in 1937, a large vehicle, which was successful primarily because of the front steering skis and the sprocket wheel/ track traction system. In 1959, lightweight compact engines were available on the market so Bombardier could concentrate on his lifelong goal, creating a lightweight vehicle for one or two passengers, the Ski-Doo® Snowmobile was born.

Snow blower

This is hardly a surprise. The snow blower was invented by Canadian Arthur Sicard, born in Saint-Leonard-de-Port-Maurice, Quebec, in 1925. He sold the first commercial self-propelled rotary machine in 1927. The blower was made of a four-wheel-drive truck chassis, a truck motor, a snow-blower head with two adjustable chutes and another motor to drive the snow-blower head.

Short-wave transmitter

Installed in Drummondville, Quebec, in 1926, the Drummondville transmitter was the first short-wave link between England and Canada. At first it only transmitted Morse code, but eventually was modified to carry voice as well.

Methyl methacrylate method

He didn't invent it, but while he was a PhD student at Montreal's McGill University in 1931, William Chalmers devised a new method for creating methyl methacrylate, a previously difficult-to-find ingredient necessary to create Plexiglass. Chalmers sold his patent for the process to Britain's Imperial Chemical Industries, who could then mass-produce the product.

Trivial Pursuit ↖

How else to address this than with a question: Where was the popular game Trivial Pursuit invented? In Montreal, journalists Chris Haney and Scott Abbott came up with the idea on December 15, 1979.

First train

Trains are an important part of the foundation of our nation, and Canada's first railway was opened in 1836 between La Prairie and Saint-Jean-sur-Richelieu, Quebec. It was called the "Champlain and St. Lawrence Railroad," since it connected the St. Lawrence River to Lake Champlain. Prior to the railway's official opening, test runs of the locomotive were conducted at night so as not to frighten locals.

First car ↗

The first car manufactured in Canada was the Taylor Steam Buggy, built by Henry Seth Taylor of Stanstead, Quebec, in 1867. The car was powered by a coal-fired boiler at the back and used a handle to control its speed and a horizontal bar to steer.

187

FIRST AIRSHIP FLIGHT

The *R-100* airship was the first and only rigid-hull airship to ever fly in Canada. After a four-day flight from England, the airship moored at Saint-Hubert, Quebec, on August 1, 1930. It's estimated that more than one million people went to see it there.

First gas car
The first successful gasoline-powered car in Canada was built by George Foote Foss in Sherbrooke, Quebec, in 1896.

First bush plane
The bush plane is synonymous with Canada's hinterland. The first successful, all-Canadian bush plane was the *Noorduyn Norseman*, which first flew in November 1935. More than 900 were built in Montreal by its designer, R.B.C. Noorduyn. The aircraft's large cabin and its ability to take off and land in tight spots made the plane a common workhorse of the nation's north.

First aviation meet
On June 25, 1910, Canada's first aviation meet (and the largest in North America at the time) took flight. The Montreal Aviation Meet boasted 10 airplanes and nine pilots.

First bush pilot

Bush flying was hugely important to the early days of exploring Canada's vast hinterland. It started out as a means to spot forest fires. Stuart Graham was the first to fly such patrols over Quebec's St. Maurice River Valley in 1919, in two war-surplus Curtiss HS-2L flying boats. Thus began a key method of accessing the country's more remote regions.

First forest fire spotted from the air

Fire! On July 7, 1919, Stuart Graham and W. Kahre become the first to spot a forest fire in Canada from the air, while they were flying over Quebec's St. Maurice River.

BUSIEST SUBWAY

The Montreal Metro is the nation's busiest subway system. A total average of 1,241,000 passengers travel through the system's 68 stations daily.

MOUVEMENT COLLECTIF stm

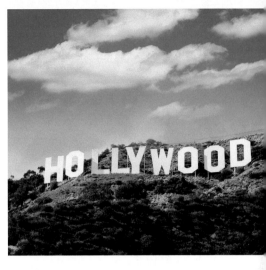

Canadian Hollywood sign ↑

It's quite possibly one of the most recognizable signs in the world—indeed, some call it the most famous sign on the planet. But did you know that the Hollywood sign in Los Angeles, California, was built by Canadian Mack Sennett in 1923? Sennett, born in Richmond, Quebec, on January 17, 1880, became a film actor, director and producer, co-founding the Keystone production company and "discovering" a number of early Hollywood stars, including Charlie Chaplin.

First French Gold Record

Among the many accomplishments of famed songstress Céline Dion, born March 30, 1968, in Charlemagne, Quebec: she was the first Canadian to receive a Gold Record in France. She managed the feat in 1983 at just 15 years old.

Biggest jazz festival

The Montreal International Jazz Festival is considered the largest jazz festival in the world. Held annually in late June/early July since 1982, the modern festival hosts 3,000 musicians from 30 countries, holds more than 1,000 concerts and attracts nearly 2 million visitors.

First symphony

The Quebec Symphony Orchestra, based in Quebec City, is the oldest symphony in Canada. It was officially formed on October 3, 1902, and gave its first performance on November 28 that year. Today, the orchestra attracts an audience of about 100,000 annually.

First Canadian opera

Canada's first original operatic work was composed by Louis-Joseph-Marie Quesnel. *Colas et Colinette* was first performed in Montreal in 1970.

First diva

Emma Albani, born Marie-Louise-Emma-Cécile Lajeunesse on November 1, 1847, in Chambly, Quebec, was the first Canadian opera singer to attain international success. She was a sought-after performer by opera enthusiasts in France, Italy, England, Mexico and Australia.

Polka king ↗

You could call him Canada's greatest musician, if you use Grammy nominations as the measure. Known as Canada's polka king, Walter Ostanek, born in Duparquet, Quebec, on April 20, 1935, has garnered 21 Grammy nominations over the course of his career. He won three times for Best Polka Album. No other Canadian musician has nabbed as many individual Grammy nominations.

Mr. Grammy

Watching events such as the Grammy Awards on live television is second nature these days. But when television producer Pierre Cossette, born in Valleyfield, Quebec, on December 15, 1923, first suggested the idea in 1970, he had a tough job convincing American network executives. Cossette, now known as "Mr. Grammy," was executive producer of the show for 35 years before he retired.

Largest winter carnival ↘

The Quebec Winter Carnival is the largest winter carnival in the world. Held annually from late January through mid-February, the first festival took place in 1894, but the present-day incarnation of the event was established in 1955. The carnival features a variety of winter sports, snow sculptures and activities based on Quebec traditions.

The most laughs ↘

Its mission statement is simple: "Make people happy." The annual Just for Laughs comedy festival in Montreal is the world's largest, with audiences of nearly two million people each July. The Montreal festival has grown into a major comedy business operation, with festivals in Toronto, Chicago and Sydney, Australia; television shows (*Gags*, seen in 135 countries); live tours and talent management.

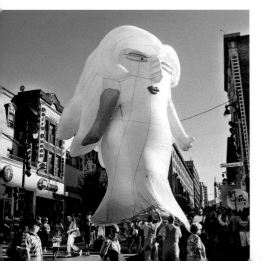

First Canadian Olympics

Here's a medal-worthy accomplishment. The Montreal Olympics, held July 17 to Aug. 1, 1976, were the first Olympic Games held in Canada. The XXI Olympiad hosted 6,084 athletes from 92 nations, and included 198 trials in 23 different sports.

Olympic firsts

The Montreal Olympics (see previous) set some world records themselves. Women participated in basketball, handball and rowing at these Games for the first time in Olympics' history. Romania gymnast Nadia Comaneci scored the first perfect 10 in the uneven bars, and a total of 35 new Olympic records were set at the event.

Olympic lasts

Here's a dubious distinction for Canadians from the Montreal Olympics: It was the first time in the Olympics' history that the host nation did not win a gold medal. Canada finished 27th in the medal count, with five silver medals and six bronze.

Largest night skiing area

Like skiing, but can't get enough during the daylight hours? Visit Stoneham Mountain Resort near Quebec City to take advantage of the country's largest night skiing area. The resort boasts 19 illuminated runs.

First indoor hockey game

The first record of a hockey game played on an indoor ice rink between two teams was on March 3, 1875. It took place at Victoria Skating Rink in Montreal. It's thought that the game as we know it was formed in Montreal according to rules developed by George Aylwin Creighton.

First professional goalie mask

The first professional hockey player to wear a goalie mask was Clint Benedict. Benedict, who played for the Montreal Maroons, is believed to have worn a mask for a game or two in 1929.

Popularizing the goalie mask ↗

Usually one too many shots to the head does not lead to innovation. But for Canadian Jacques Plante, goaltender for the Montreal Canadiens, getting hit in the face by one more puck on November 1, 1959, was the last straw. After getting stitched up, Plante returned to the game wearing a mask and began the popularization of the equipment.

First state funeral

Maurice Richard holds a very unique distinction for a Canadian athlete. After his death on May 27, 2000, Richard was given a state funeral by his home province of Quebec, which was broadcast live across the country—the first time such an honour was bestowed on a Canadian athlete.

Coach with the most Stanley Cups

Legendary hockey coach Scotty Bowman, born in Montreal on September 18, 1933, has won more Stanley Cups than any other coach. His nine championships—five with Montreal (1973, 1976, 1977, 1978, 1979), one with Pittsburgh (1992) and three with Detroit (1997, 1998 and 2002)—also tie him with basketball coach Red Auerbach for the most championships in North America's four major pro sports leagues.

Engraving the Stanley Cup

Engraving the names of the winning team's roster on the Stanley Cup has become a tradition. But the custom only began in 1907, when the Montreal Wanderers became the first to do so. It wasn't until 1924 that the ritual was performed annually.

Team with the most Cups

The Montreal Canadiens have hoisted the Stanley Cup more than any other team in the trophy's history. The team has won the Cup 24 times, first in 1916 and most recently in 1993.

LAST CANADIAN STANLEY CUP

As of this writing, the Montreal Canadians were the last Canadian team to win the Stanley Cup, in 1993. The city has a long tradition of capturing the Cup. Its Montreal AAA team was awarded the trophy the first time it was presented, in 1893. Indeed, it won the championship in each of its first eight years.

First sport club

The first sporting club in Canada was the Montreal Curling Club, which was founded in 1807.

First individual gold

Speed skater Gaétan Boucher, born in Charlesbourg, Quebec, on May 10, 1958, was the first Canadian man to win an individual gold medal at the Winter Olympic Games. In fact, he won two gold medals (one in 1,000 m and one in 1,500 m) on February 14, 1984, in Sarajevo, Bosnia and Herzegovina.

First Canadian team in Major League Baseball

The Montreal Expos were the first Canadian team to join Major League Baseball, in 1969. In 2004, the team was relocated to Washington, D.C. and renamed the Washington Nationals.

First female golf club members

A progressive first: The Royal Montreal Golf Club was the first golf club in North America to allow female members.

Oldest golf club

The Royal Montreal Golf Club is the oldest golf club in North America. Formed as the Montreal Golf Club in 1873 (it received the Royal designation in 1884), the first course was nine holes on Fletcher's Field, part of Mount Royal Park on the outskirts of Montreal.

First World Ski winner

Skier Lucile Wheeler, born on January 14, 1935, in St-Jovite, Quebec, was the first North American to win a World Ski Championship. She captured first in both downhill and giant slalom at the events in Bad Gastein, Austria, in February 1958. She was also the first Canadian to win a medal in downhill at the Olympics—bronze in 1956 at Cortina d'Ampezzo, Italy.

Strongest man in the world

Before weightlifting was a formal sport, Canadian Louis Cyr, born in Saint-Cyprien-de-Napierville, Quebec, on October 10, 1863, was considered one of the strongest men in the world. He was undefeated in lifting competitions, capturing the weightlifting championship of North America in 1885 and the world title in 1892.

First synchronized swimming competition

Ornamental swimming, anyone? Montreal hosted the first synchronized swimming competition ever—called ornamental or figure swimming at the time—in 1924. The event was a provincial championship, which was won by Peg Seller, who was also a top Canadian diver and water polo player.

FIRST CANADIAN GRAND PRIX WIN

Race car driver Gilles Villeneuve, born on January 18, 1950, in Chambly, Quebec, was the first Canadian to win a Grand Prix event. Villeneuve won the Formula One in Montreal, the Canadian Grand Prix, on October 8, 1978. The track is now named after him. Villeneuve died in a crash during a qualifying session for the Belgium Grand Prix on May 8, 1982.

First performance of O Canada

"O Canada" was performed for the first time on June 24, 1880, in Quebec City. The music was composed by Calixa Lavallée and the first lyrics, in French, were written by Adolphe-Basile Routhier. The tune did not become the country's official national anthem until July 1, 1980.

First electric streetlights

Quebec City's Dufferin Terrace was the first area in Canada to have electrical streetlights. The lights debuted in 1883, just three years after the first test of outdoor electrical lighting in North America.

Canada's big birthday

It was a big way to celebrate an important birthday. Canada hosted Expo '67, the "Universal and International Exhibition," in Montreal from April 28 to October 27, 1967, to mark the nation's centennial. It was the first time the World's Fair was held in North America, and more than 50 million people visited the expo.

First Canadian saint

With a nickname like "mother of the poor," it's hardly a surprise that Marie Marguerite d'Youville, was canonized as a saint on December 9, 1990, becoming the first Canadian-born saint. Born in Varennes, Que., on October 5, 1701, d'Youville earned her moniker and her sainthood as founder of Montreal's Sister of Charity organization, where she spent decades helping the city's less fortunate.

First art gallery

Joseph Légaré (see First Canadian landscape painter, next page) opened the first art gallery in Canada. The gallery, which featured his personal collection of art, opened in 1833 in Quebec City.

First YMCA

The first YMCA in North America started in Montreal on November 25, 1851. When it began, the Y had strong ties to Protestant churches, but this soon changed as people from all religions were welcomed. The YMCA of Greater Montreal went on to open the first public library in the city in 1854.

195

First Canadian landscape painter

Canadian art is well known for its landscape paintings. Artist Joseph Légaré, born in Quebec City in 1795, is considered the first Canadian-born landscape painter. Shown here is his *The Fire in the Saint-Jean Quarter, Seen Looking Westward*, painted in 1848.

Oldest French university

The Université Laval in Quebec City is the oldest French-language university in North America. Established in 1663, today the school has nearly 50,000 students and more than 270,000 graduates.

First teaching at patient's bedside

Clinical medical teaching at a patient's bedside was first done in North America at the Montreal General Hospital in 1881.

First medical school

Montreal General Hospital founded the first medical school in Canada. The Montreal Medical Institute was established in 1825 and became the McGill University Faculty of Medicine in 1829.

BIGGEST MUSEUM

The Canadian Museum of History, formerly the Canadian Museum of Civilization, in Gatineau, Quebec, is the nation's largest museum. The museum boasts about 5 million artifacts in its collection, which attracts more than 1.3 million visitors each year.

First Canadian spaceman ↘

Quebec City native Marc Garneau became the first Canadian to fly in space on October 5, 1984. Garneau was a payload specialist on NASA shuttle mission 41-G. He returned to space in 1996 and 2000, and in total logged more than 677 hours in space.

Last fatal duel

Draw! The last fatal duel in Canada occurred on May 22, 1838, in Verdun, Quebec, then part of Lower Canada. Major Henry Warde was fatally shot by lawyer Robert Sweeny. Warde's offence? A love letter to Mrs. Sweeny.

First Christmas tree

O, Canada, O Christmas Tree. The first Christmas tree in Canada was set up on Christmas Eve, 1781, in Sorel, Quebec, north of Montreal. The balsam fir was decorated with fruit and lit with white candles.

Most totem poles

The Canadian Museum of History in Gatineau, Quebec, is home to the world's largest indoor collection of totem poles. Many of the museum's totem poles are housed in the building's dramatic Grand Hall.

Deadliest train wreck

Canada's deadliest train disaster occurred on June 29, 1864, near St-Hilaire, Quebec, on the Grand Truck Railway. It's believed 99 passengers were killed and another 100 injured when the train—carrying 458 people, largely German and Polish immigrants—plunged into the Richelieu River after failing to stop for an open swing bridge.

WORST SHIPWRECK

The worst maritime disaster in Canadian history was the sinking of the *Empress of Ireland* in the St. Lawrence River near Rimouski, Quebec, on May 29, 1914. A total of 1,014 people died when the ship collided with the Norwegian collier *Storstad* in the fog.

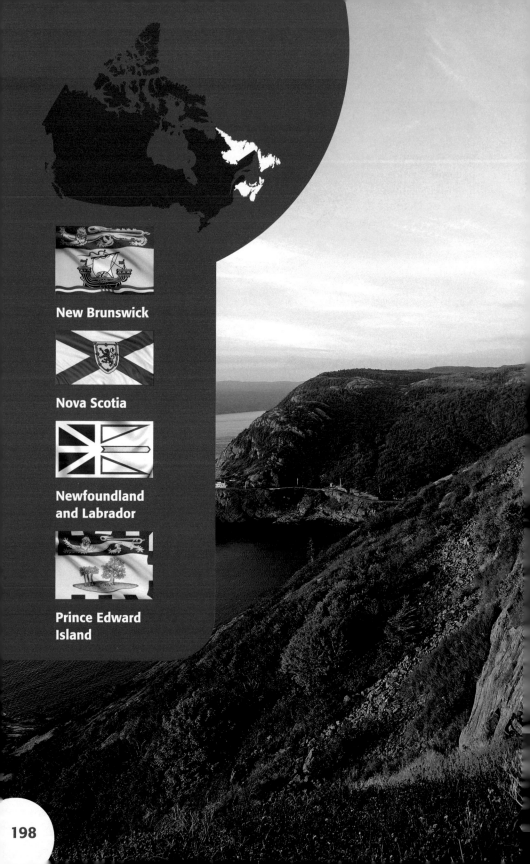

New Brunswick

Nova Scotia

Newfoundland
and Labrador

Prince Edward
Island

ATLANTIC CANADA

FIRST RADIO MESSAGE

It's an apt name. Signal Hill in St. John's, Newfoundland, was the site where the first transatlantic radio telegraphic message was received, by Guglielmo Marconi on December 12, 1901. Marconi used an antenna raised by a kite to transmit and receive that first Morse-code message. The Tower at Signal Hill, now part of a national historic site, was used for signalling until 1960.

New Brunswick

What is present-day New Brunswick was once considered part of Nova Scotia. During the America Revolution (1775 to 1783), many people loyal to Britain (known as Loyalists) moved to the area and pushed to form a new province. New Brunswick was created on Sept. 10, 1784, and the name was chosen in honour of King George III, a descendant of the House of Brunswick.

GEOGRAPHY

Only bilingual province

The nation's only officially bilingual province? New Brunswick, where about 33 percent of people speak French.

HIGHEST POINT

New Brunswick's Mount Carleton is not only the province's highest point, but also the highest point in the Maritimes. From the 817-m elevation located in Mount Carleton Provincial Park, it's estimated you can see some 10 million trees. The mountain is named after the province's first lieutenant-governor, General Thomas Carleton.

Largest whirlpool

The largest natural whirlpool in the Western Hemisphere is located in the Western Passage of Passamaquoddy Bay in the Bay of Fundy, to the west of Deer Island, New Brunswick. Called "Old Sow," the whirlpool infrequently and unpredictably forms a funnel in the water.

Historic island

There are not too many places like this. Saint Croix Island, which lies on the United States' side of the St. Croix River, between Maine and New Brunswick, is recognized as a site of national historic significance to Canada. It is the location of the first attempt at French settlement in North America (1604). An international historic site and a national monument in the United States, there is an interpretation site for the island at Bayside, New Brunswick.

WILDLIFE

Oldest shark fossil

The world's oldest intact shark fossil was discovered in 2003 near Atholville, New Brunswick. The 23-cm-long fossil (from snout to upper trunk), which includes the fish's braincase, scales, calcified cartilage, large fin spines and teeth, is estimated to be more than 400 million years old, which is five million years older than the second-oldest known specimen.

STRUCTURES/COMMUNITIES

Lobster capital of the world

It's hardly an officially designated title, but the town of Shediac, New Brunswick, lays claim to being the "Lobster Capital of the World." Shediac is home to lobster fishermen (naturally), processing plants, live tanks and the famous mid-July Lobster Festival.

Oldest observatory

The Brydone Jack Observatory is the oldest astronomical observatory in the nation. Located in Fredericton, it opened March 19, 1851, and was home to the best instruments of the day at that time.

Longest covered bridge ↗

The longest covered bridge on Earth is the Hartland Covered Bridge in Hartland, New Brunswick. The 391-m bridge was built in 1897 and was covered in 1921–22. Its covering was controversial, as covered bridges were known as "kissing bridges"—horse and wagon traffic would stop half way across so that riders could lock lips. Some locals feared covering the bridge would destroy the morals of their young people.

BUSINESS/INDUSTRY

Most French fries

Get out the ketchup. And lots of it. McCain Foods, whose global headquarters is located in Florenceville-Bristol, New Brunswick, is the world's largest manufacturer of French fries. Indeed, one of every three French fries eaten on Earth is a McCain fry.

INNOVATIONS

Oldest candy company

If you're a Canadian candy connoisseur, you'll appreciate this. Ganong Bros. Limited of St. Stephen, New Brunswick, is Canada's oldest candy company. It was established in 1873. The business is responsible for a number of candy firsts: the first Canadian lollipop in 1895; the first chocolate nut bar in North America in 1910; the first heart-shaped box for chocolates (introduced originally for Christmas) in 1932; and the first fruit snack made from real fruit in purée form, in 1988.

Best potato for French fries

If you eat French fries, there's a good chance you've eaten a Canadian food innovation. The Shepody potato, released by Agri-Food Canada's research lab in Fredericton, New Brunswick, in 1983, quickly became one of the world's most popular potatoes for French fries. The Shepody is known for its short growing season and high yields.

Wind tunnel

Aeronautical engineer Wallace Turnbull, born in Saint John, built Canada's first wind tunnel in Rothesay, New Brunswick, in 1902. He worked at the tunnel, his personal laboratory, for the rest of his life, and collaborated with other aviation pioneers, including Alexander Graham Bell.

POP CULTURE

First Canadian Prix Goncourt

Antonine Maillet, born in Bouctouche, New Brunswick, on May 10, 1929, was the first Canadian, and first non-French citizen, to win the Prix Goncourt, one of France's most important literary awards. Maillet won the prize for her 1979 novel, *Pélagie-la-charette*.

First fiction ↗

Julia Catherine Hart, born on March 10, 1796, in Fredericton, penned the first novel by a Canadian to be published in Canada. Hart's *St. Ursula's Convent*, which explores the dual heritage of French and English cultures in Canada, was published in 1824.

SPORTS & LEISURE

Oldest canoe

What's the big deal about a nearly 200-year-old canoe? Only that it's believed to be one of the oldest known birchbark canoes in the world. Known as the "Grandfather Akwiten canoe," the 6.5-m-long vessel was built by Maliseet aboriginals of present day New Brunswick in the 1820s.

First black hockey player ⬿

Willie O'Ree was the first black player in the National Hockey League. His first game was January 18, 1958. O'Ree, born in Fredericton on October 15, 1935, played two seasons for the Boston Bruins (1957–58 and 1960–61) and scored four goals and tallied 10 assists.

PEOPLE, PLACES & THINGS

Oldest high school

Fredericton High School in Fredericton is the nation's oldest English secondary school. It opened in 1785, and adopted its current name in 1893.

Oldest student newspaper

It's doubtful that anyone would want to be in a school as long as the nation's oldest official student publication, the University of New Brunswick's *Brunswickan*. The student newspaper launched in 1867.

Oldest university building ↗

The oldest university building in Canada still being used as part of a university campus is Sir Howard Douglas Hall (Old Arts Building) at the University of New Brunswick. The building officially opened on January 1, 1829.

Oldest English university

The oldest public English-language university in Canada—and one of the oldest universities in North America—is the University of New Brunswick. Its Fredericton campus was established in 1785 (the Saint John campus was created in 1964).

Oldest bike shop

If you're looking for a bike shop with a long track record, look no further than Savage's Bicycle Centre in downtown Fredericton. Savage's is the nation's oldest bike shop, having opened its doors in 1897.

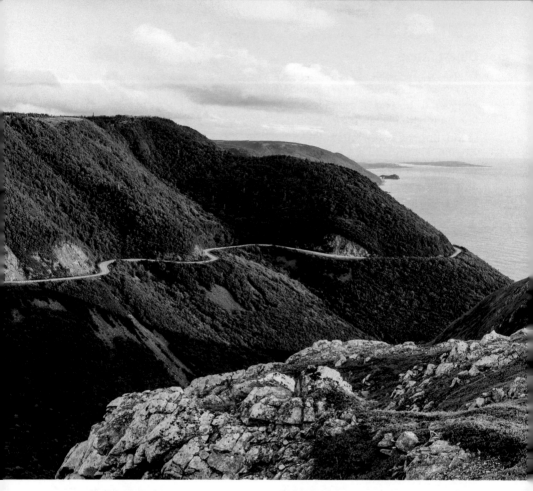

New Scotland

The name Nova Scotia was first used to refer to the area of the modern-day province on September 29, 1621. Sir William Alexander was granted "the lands lying between New England and Newfoundland ... to be known as Nova Scotia, or New Scotland."

GEOGRAPHY

Underwater canyon

Here's some more really special water. The Gully Marine Protected Area, a 65-km-long, 15-km-wide, two-km-deep underwater canyon about 200 km southeast of Nova Scotia is the largest canyon on the east coast of North America. Its so big, it impacts ocean currents.

Highest tides ↑

Sure, Canada's Bay of Fundy has the highest tides in the world, but did you know that depending on the time of day the difference between low and high tide can be taller than a three-storey building? Indeed, Fundy's tides can differ by up to 16.27 m. Part of the reason for Fundy's dramatic tides are the V-shape of the bay, which funnels water into less and less space causing the water to rise.

WILDLIFE

Oldest reptiles

The fossils of the reptiles whose descendents would become dinosaurs and mammals can be found at the Joggins Fossil Cliffs in Nova Scotia. These 315-million-year-old fossils are the world's oldest known reptiles. They come from a time when giant seed fern trees, insects, primitive lobe-finned fish and amphibians roamed the Earth. The fossils are visible simply from a walk on Joggins beach.

HIGHEST POINT

Yet another appropriate name: Nova Scotia's highest point lies in the aptly named Cape Breton Highlands. White Hill Lake in the Cape Breton Highlands National Park has an elevation of 532 m.

Highest variation between tides

The world's highest variation between high and low tide – 16.27 m – was recorded at Burntcoat Head, Nova Scotia, in Minas Basin on the Bay of Fundy. The average tide there is 10 m.

Sable Island, home to horses and seals, viewed from space.

Protected horses

The feral (wild) horses that live on Nova Scotia's Sable Island, located about 300 kilometres south of Halifax in the Atlantic Ocean, were the first animal species in Canada to be federally protected. To ensure the unique population's survival, the horses were granted protection from human interference in 1960 by an amendment to the Canada Shipping Act. Today, the species is also the only terrestrial mammal that calls the island home other than people.

Largest colony of grey seals

Sable Island (see previous), which became Canada's 43rd national park reserve on December 1, 2013, is also home to the world's largest breeding colony of grey seals. It's believed some 16,000 seals have pups on the island between late December and early February each year.

First zoo

The first zoo in North America was opened in Halifax in 1847. Known as Down's Zoological Gardens, the facility was home to the largest collection of birds, animals and plants outside England. The zoo was eventually sold and became the Central Park Zoo in New York.

STRUCTURES/COMMUNITIES

Benjamin Franklin and Canadian mail

Do you know the important Canadian connection to Benjamin Franklin? In 1753, he was named joint deputy postmaster-general for the British colonies and opened the first post office in Canada in Halifax.

First library

The first known library in the Americas was at Port Royal, Acadia (present day Nova Scotia), and was established by Marc Lescarbot in 1606. Lescarbot, a lawyer and writer from France, participated in the first voyage of Samuel de Champlain and Pierre Du Gua de Monts to Acadia that year.

Oldest courthouse

There's been a lot of order in this court. The Argyle Township Court House & Gaol, in Tusket, Nova Scotia, is the country's oldest standing courthouse. Built in 1805, it was a court and jail from its opening until 1944.

Biggest historical reconstruction ↗

The Fortress of Louisbourg, a national historic site located on Nova Scotia's Cape Breton Island, is the largest historical reconstruction in North America. First built in 1713 by the French, the settlement was besieged twice before being destroyed by the British in the 1760s. In 1961, the federal government committed $25 million to restore about one-quarter of the original village, which includes buildings, yards, gardens and streets, as well as part of the fortifications.

First lighthouse

It's no joke. The first documented lighthouse in Canada went into service on April 1, 1734, at Louisbourg, Nova Scotia. The stone tower was about 20 m tall and featured a fire chamber at the top fueled by coal. It was destroyed by the British in 1758, and today a modern lighthouse sits on the same location.

LONGEST DOWNTOWN BOARDWALK

If you advance to this boardwalk, be prepared for a long walk. The Halifax Waterfront Boardwalk is the longest downtown boardwalk in the world. The 3.8-km trail runs from Pier 21 to Casino Nova Scotia and takes about 20 minutes to walk.

BUSINESS/INDUSTRY

First tidal power plant ↗

The first tidal power plant in the Americas, and the only one in North America, was built near Annapolis Royal, Nova Scotia, in 1984. The Annapolis Tidal Station has a capacity of 20 megawatts, and depending on the tides, a daily output of roughly 80 to 100 megawatt hours. It boasts the world's largest straight-flow turbine generator, capable of producing more than 30 million kilowatt hours of electricity per year, enough to power some 4,500 homes.

Oldest farmers' market

The oldest farmers' market in Canada is the Halifax Farmers' Market, which was created by royal proclamation in June 1750, a year after the city was founded. Known today as the Halifax Seaport Farmers' Market, it is also the longest-running farmers' market in North America. Nowadays it hosts more than 250 vendors.

COMMUNICATIONS

First newspaper

It was a humble beginning, but an important one. Printed on half a foolscap sheet, Canada's first newspaper debuted on March 23, 1752. The day's edition of the *Halifax Gazette* boasted news from Europe, Britain and the other British colonies to the south.

First microwave voice transmission system

The world's first commercial microwave relay system for voice transmissions was installed between Nova Scotia and Prince Edward Island on November 19, 1948, ending the need for underwater cables.

INNOVATIONS

↙ Kerosene

Abraham Gesner of Cornwallis, Nova Scotia, is the inventor of kerosene. The geologist started experiments to distill oil in the form of kerosene in 1846, and had created the lamp oil by 1853. Around that time, the fuel became the lighting standard in homes. Thanks to his patents for distilling bituminuous materials, Gesner is also considered a founder of the modern petroleum industry.

Frozen Food

If you're a fan of fish sticks—or any frozen food for that matter—you can thank marine scientist Archibald Huntsman. In 1926, while working for the Biological Board of Canada (later the Fisheries Research Board) in Halifax, Huntsman began work on developing a commercial frozen fish product. The result? Ice Fillets debuted in 1929 in Toronto, marking the first time frozen food was sold to the public. The product was pricey, but popular. Unfortunately, fishing companies lost interest, and the Ice Fillets were abandoned in 1931.

Portable film-developing tank

In 1899, Nova Scotian Arthur Williams McCurdy invented a small portable tank for developing film in daytime, called the Ededec, which was used by photographers for generations. After patenting the device in the United States in 1902, McCurdy sold it to the Eastman Kodak company.

Shatterless rails

Canadian Irwin Cameron Mackie invented the first shatterless rails, which were produced by Nova Scotia's Sydney Steel in July 1931. The new rails, which solved a significant problem of rails cracking under heavy weights, were first used exclusively on the Canadian National Railway.

Hydrofoil

Better known for his invention of the telephone, Alexander Graham Bell is also the co-inventor of the first successful hydrofoil, the wing-like device that lifts a boat above the water to reduce drag from the hull. Along with his wife Mabel and engineer F.W. Casey Baldwin, Bell began to create the machine he called a "hydrodrome" in 1908 in Baddeck, Nova Scotia. The first hydrofoil (the HD-1), unveiled in 1911, was capable of speeds of up to 72 km per hour.

Nova Scotia duck tolling retriever

The Nova Scotia duck tolling retriever, the official dog of Nova Scotia, was the first Canadian dog breed to be named a provincial symbol. Developed in the early 19th century, the species was bred to lure (or toll) and retrieve waterfowl.

TRANSPORTATION

First steam ship across the Atlantic

The HMS *Royal William* was the first Canadian ship to cross the Atlantic completely under steam power. It was first launched in Quebec on April 27, 1831. Later that year, the ship made several voyages between Quebec and Atlantic Canada, but in 1932 it was quarantined because of a cholera epidemic. On August 18, 1833, with seven passengers and a load of coal, it started the 25-day journey from Pictou, Nova Scotia to Gravesend, England. The ship was eventually sold to the Spanish Navy.

FIRST CROSS-CANADA CAR TRIP

Are we there yet? The first cross-Canada car trip took 49 days. Writer Tom Wilby and driver/mechanic Jack Haney left Halifax on August 27, 1912, in an REO The Fifth (the fifth car designed by Ransom E. Olds), and arrived in Vancouver on October 14. During the journey, the duo travelled 298 km on their best day and just 19 on their worst.

Oldest ferry

Halifax is home to the continent's oldest, continuous-running saltwater ferry service, which began in 1752. Known as the "Dartmouth ferry" at the time, the service connected the vast farmland on the Dartmouth side of Halifax Harbour with Halifax, providing the city with fresh food. The original ferry was a rowboat with a sail.

First Naval dockyard

Built in 1759, the Naval Dockyard in Halifax was the first naval dockyard in North America.

First solo voyage around the world

Joshua Slocum, a native of Annapolis County, Nova Scotia, became the first person to sail solo around the world. He departed from Boston on April 24, 1895, in his ship *The Spray* on the 74,000-km voyage, which took three years to complete. His book on the journey, *Sailing Alone around the World*, has been continuously in print since it was published in 1900.

First Canadian flight ↑
The first flight in Canada occurred in Baddeck, Nova Scotia, on February 23, 1909. The silver-winged biplane, called the "Silver Dart," was piloted by J.A.D. McCurdy. It flew 800 m at an average speed of 65 km per hour. The Silver Dart flew 200 flights before it was damaged beyond repair.

POP CULTURE

First famous fiction
Thomas Chandler Haliburton, born in Windsor, Nova Scotia, on December 17, 1796, is considered the first Canadian fiction writer to achieve international recognition for his work. It was Haliburton's *The Clockmaker*, also known as *The Sayings and Doings of Sam Slick of Slickville*, published in book form in 1836, which first gained the writer a serious following in the United States and Britian. The book first appeared in 22 installments in the *Novascotian* newspaper.

First bestseller
Beautiful Joe: An Autobiography of a Dog, by Margaret Marshall Saunders, born on April 13, 1861, in Milton, Nova Scotia, is believed to be the first Canadian book to sell one million copies. It was published in 1894.

First Platinum
Band April Wine, formed in Halifax in 1969, became the first Canadian group to achieve a Platinum album (100,000 sales) in Canada for advance sales: for the record *The Whole World's Goin' Crazy*, released in September 1976.

First million-dollar tour
April Wine's tour in support of its 1976 album *The Whole World's Goin' Crazy* was the first tour to gross $1 million.

↙ First woman to win Gold Album
Born in Springhill, Nova Scotia, on June 20, 1945, Anne Murray was the first solo Canadian female artist to be awarded an American Gold album (500,000 sales), in 1970, with her second album *This Way is My Way*. It featured the hit "Snowbird."

First agricultural fair
The first agricultural fair in North America was held in Windsor, Nova Scotia, in May 1765. The Hants County Exhibition still takes place each September, making it the oldest, continuously run agricultural exhibition on the continent.

Biggest tattoo

Billed as the world's largest annual indoor show, the Royal Nova Scotia International Tattoo is held annually during the first week of July and features a variety of entertainment, including bagpipes, highland dancers, military displays, acrobats and more. The Tattoo has been held yearly since 1979.

First theatre production

The first European theatrical production in North America was performed in Port-Royal, Nova Scotia, in 1606. French poet and playwright Marc Lescarbot presented *Théâtre de Neptune*.

First Canadian play

Acadius, the story of a wealthy Boston businessman's extramarital affairs and how his black servants dealt with their exploitation, is considered the first original Canadian play. It was performed in Halifax in 1774, and its author is unknown.

PEOPLE, PLACES & THINGS

Biggest gourd

What a long gourd you have! In 2013, the Great Pumpkin Commonwealth, an international organization that sets standards and regulations for recognizing world-record-sized fruits and vegetables, declared a new world-record gourd. The 3.5-m-long vegetable was grown by Nova Scotian Fred Ansems.

Largest pumpkin

Charlie Brown take note! Here's one great pumpkin: According the to Great Pumpkin Commonwealth (see previous), John MacKinnon of Strathlorne, Nova Scotia, grew the world's largest ever field pumpkin. It weighed 95.708 kg (211 pounds).

✔ Official blueberry

Nova Scotia is home to what must surely be the nation's best-tasting official provincial symbol. On January 11, 1996, the province declared the wild blueberry its provincial berry. Wild blueberries are grown in five regions throughout Canada, though Nova Scotia is the country's largest producer of the produce.

Official fossil

Nova Scotia is the nation's only province with an official provincial fossil. The fossil of *Hylonomous lyelli*, the oldest known reptile in the world, which predated dinosaurs and lived about 315 million years ago, was discovered in the province by geologist Sir William Dawson in the 1800s. The slender-bodied, 20-cm-long, insect-eating lizard was named Nova Scotia's official provincial fossil in 2002.

First social club

L'Ordre de Bon Temps ("Order of Good Cheer") was North America's first social club. It was founded in 1606 in Port-Royal, Nova Scotia, by explorer Samuel de Champlain.

Youngest supernova-spotter

How do you top finding a supernova—the most luminous type of cataclysmic explosion of a dying star—as a 10-year-old? You keep looking for more. That's exactly what Nathan Gray of Greenwood, Nova Scotia, vowed to do after spotting potential supernova PGC 61330 in the constellation of Draco on October 30, 2013. If the International Astronomical Union confirms Gray's discovery, he'll become the youngest known person to locate a supernova—besting the previous record holder, his sister Kathryn, by just 33 days.

WORST EXPLOSION

The world's largest accidental explosion (and Canada's worst disaster) was the Halifax Explosion of December 6, 1917. Some 1,600 people were killed, another 9,000 injured and 6,000 left homeless in the disaster, caused when the French munitions carrier, *Mont Blanc*, and the Belgian relief vessel, *Imo*, collided in the harbour's Narrows.

A very old new name

The name Newfoundland comes from England's King Henry VII, who referred to the island as "New Found Launde" by 1852. (Its French name, Terre Neuve, was used as early as 1510.)

A Portuguese connection

Experts aren't certain, but most suspect that the name Labrador came from a Portuguese explorer and *lavrador* or "landowner" named João Fernades. It's believed the name was first given to the coast of modern Greenland, then later used to refer to the northeastern coast of North America by cartographers.

GEOGRAPHY

Richest sea harvest

Considered one of the world's largest and richest resource areas, the Grand Banks off the southeast coast of Newfoundland have been plumbed for resources since at least the 1400s. The banks are actually a series of raised underwater plateaus ranging between 36.5 m and 185 m deep. The relatively shallow water allows a range of marine and plant life to thrive. Fishermen from around the Atlantic harvest haddock, ocean perch, crabs, clams and scallops, as well as hundreds of other species from these waters.

Highest point – Newfoundland

About 20 km north of Stephenville, Newfoundland, on the island's west coast, you'll find the Rock's highest elevation, the Lewis Hills. Located along the coast at Port au Port Bay, the Hills sit 814 m above sea level.

Highest point – Labrador

It would seem that a mountain by any other name would still be as high. The highest point in Labrador is the same as Quebec's, although on the Labrador side of the border Mont d'Iberville is known as Mount Caubvik, at an elevation of 1,652 m.

Easternmost point

The most easterly point in Canada and North America is Cape Spear, Newfoundland.

Easternmost point of North America

The most easterly point of continental North America is Cape St. Charles, Labrador.

Oldest European funeral mound

Newfoundland is home to the oldest known funeral mound on the continent, the burial site of a child that dates to approximately 7,500 years ago.

RAINIEST, FOGGIEST, WINDIEST

Cold, foggy and windy. Sounds like St. John's? Okay, it may be an unfair generalization, but of all Canadian cities, St. John's has the most days per year with freezing rain (38) and fog (121), and the most wind (an average annual wind speed of 24 km/hour).

WEATHER

Snowiest communities

Canada's snowiest communities based on average annual snowfall records.

Days	Place	cm	inches
89	Woody Point, NL	637.9	251.1
117	Forêt Montmorency, QC	619.9	244.1
125	Cape Dyer, NU	554.2	218.2
85	Murdochville, QC	547.8	215.7
103	St. Anthony, NL	543.7	214.0
51	Main Brook, NL	515.0	202.8

Community with the highest snowfall

A snow blower must be standard equipment for a homeowner in Woody Point, Newfoundland. Located on Bonne Bay on the province's west coast, Woody Point is the Canadian community that receives the highest recorded average snowfall. Over 89 days, 638 cm of snow falls each year.

Snowiest cities

When it comes to snow in Canada's largest cities, 10 of them receive an average of more than 2 m of the white stuff annually (based on urban centres with more than 100,000 population in 2011 and snow data averages between 1981 and 2010).

Annual average snowfall a year:

City	cm	inches
St. John's, NL	335.0	131.9
Saguenay, QC	321.7	126.6
Quebec City, QC	303.4	119.4
Sherbrooke, QC	286.5	112.8
Moncton, NB	282.0	111.0
Sudbury, ON	263.4	103.7
Trois-Rivières, QC	259.0	102.0
St. John, NB	239.6	94.3
Barrie, ON	223.0	87.8
Montreal, QC	209.5	82.5

Foggiest place in the world

The Grand Banks off Newfoundland is considered the foggiest place in the world. The area experiences 40 percent fog cover in the winter and up to 84 percent in the summer.

Cold summers

It could claim the title of "bad summer capital of Canada."
St. John's has the nation's lowest average daily summer temperature (at just 13.9°C) and the fewest hot days (an average of only 0.2 days during June, July and August when the temperature exceeds 30°C.). Vancouver could be considered a close second for that ominous title. It has a daily average summer temperature of 16.8°C and 0.2 days of summer temperatures over 30°C.

City with the worst climate

Based on the Climate Severity Index, developed by Environment Canada to rate an area's climate based on human comfort and well being, St. John's is the major Canadian city with the worst climate. The city scores 56 out of 100 on the index's scale.

WORST RIG DISASTER

The worst disaster involving an offshore drilling rig in Canada (and the third-worst in the world) was the sinking of the Ocean Ranger on February 15, 1982. At the time, it was the largest semi-submersible drilling rig in existence. The Ocean Ranger sank 300 km off the coast of Newfoundland in winds of 145 km per hour and waves 21 m high. Eighty-four people were killed.

Biggest wave

This is one seriously big wave! On September 11, 1995, the *QE2* ocean liner was caught in Hurricane Luis off the coast of Newfoundland and was hit by a 30-m wave. This is the largest wave height ever recorded. The storm was also gigantic: it covered almost the entire north Atlantic.

The Independence hurricane

A horrid hurricane. The Newfoundland Hurricane of 1775 was probably part of the same storm that was dubbed the "Independence Hurricane" in the United States. It was by far the most deadly to have occurred in what is present-day Canada. The storm killed more than 4,000 mariners, destroying the entire Newfoundland fishing fleet as well as some British warships. It also killed hundreds and wreaked havoc along the eastern seaboard of present-day United States. It came at a crucial point at the beginning of the American War of Independence—hence its name.

WILDLIFE

⌁ Largest puffin colony

The largest colony of Atlantic puffins in North America is found in Newfoundland's Witless Bay Ecological Reserve. The reserve, made up of four islands—Gull, Green, Great and Pee Pee—sees more than 260,000 pairs of puffins nest there in late spring and summer. The puffin is Newfoundland and Labrador's official bird.

Largest storm-petrel colony

The Witless Bay Ecological Reserve (see above) is also home to the continent's largest colony of Leach's storm-petrel, a small black seabird. The second largest such colony in the world, it is home to more than 620,000 pairs that nest on the island each year.

Regulated walrus fishery

In September 1770, the government of St. John's Island (modern-day Prince Edward Island) regulated the sea cow (walrus) fishery as its first legislative act. The move was aimed to protect the species' population.

Biggest Quebec-Labrador caribou

And yet another world-best 'bou: the world-record Quebec-Labrador caribou was taken near Nain, Labrador, by Zack Elbox in 1931, and scored 4746/8, according to the Boone & Crockett Club.

A recreated long house at the location of the first European settlement.

Biggest woodland caribou

In 1910, an unknown hunter in Newfoundland took the world-record woodland caribou. It scored 4195/8, according to the Boone and Crockett Club.

STRUCTURES/COMMUNITIES

First English colony

There are some great place names in Newfoundland and Labrador (Come By Chance and Heart's Content, for instance). Cupids is another. But the town on Conception Bay is significant for more than just its unique name. It was the first English colony in Canada and also the oldest continuously occupied English settlement in the country. In 1610, English colonist John Guy established a plantation at was then known as Cuper's Cove.

Oldest European settlement ↗

It's a relatively unassuming site today, but L'Anse aux Meadows at the northern tip of Newfoundland's Great Northern Peninsula is the oldest European settlement in the New World. Leif Erickson and crews of Norse explorers settled the spot in 1000 AD. The encampment was the source of myth and folklore until archaeologists discovered the site in 1968. In 1978, it was named a world heritage site by UNESCO.

Oldest city

St. John's, Newfoundland, is the most easterly city in North America. But it also claims to be the continent's oldest city. St. John's has long been a centre of fisheries in the New World — the earliest records of battles over control of the city's port date back to 1555.

Oldest lighthouse

Cape Spear, Newfoundland, Canada's easternmost point, is home to the oldest surviving lighthouse in the province. Built in 1836, the Cape Spear Lighthouse is now a national historic site.

BUSINESS/INDUSTRY

Biggest towed object

The Hibernia oil platform, located in the waters of the Grand Banks off Newfoundland, is believed to be the largest object ever towed. It took 13 days—from May 23 to June 5, 1997—to tow the 1.08 million tonne structure from Bull Arm, Newfoundland, to the Grand Banks.

COMMUNICATIONS

First transatlantic telephone cable

A cooperative effort of the General Post Office of the United Kingdom, American Telegraph and Telephone and the Canadian Overseas Telephone Corporation, TAT-1 was the first transatlantic telephone cable. Actually there were two cables, laid side by side (one running in each direction) in the summer of 1955 and 1956. TAT-1 linked Scotland near Oban to London and to Clarenville, Newfoundland, then across the Cabot Strait to Nova Scotia.

INNOVATIONS

Labrador retriever

The Labrador retriever, which originated on the island of Newfoundland, was first recognized as a breed by England's Kennel Club in 1903, though records describing the breed date from as early as the mid-18th century. Known as a "water dog," Labs were appreciated for their intelligence and outgoing nature.

Newfoundland dog

The Newfoundland dog is another made-in-Canada dog species. Little is known of the breed's exact origins, though the species was first named in the late 17th century. Nearly as at home in the water—if not more so—than the land, the Newfoundland was originally used as a ship dog (to carry lines to shore or for water rescues).

GAS MASK

There's a saying that necessity is the mother of invention. This may never have been more true than when it came to the invention of the first military gas mask, which was invented by Dr. Cluny Macpherson of St. John's in 1915. Macpherson attached a canvas hood with eyeholes and a breathing tube to a helmet that had been treated with chemicals to absorb chlorine used in German gas attacks.

TRANSPORTATION

Worst air crash in Canada

The worst air crash in Canadian history occurred December 12, 1985, when an Arrow Airlines DC-8 enroute to Kentucky crashed just after takeoff, after refuelling at Gander, Newfoundland. All 256 passengers, including 248 members of the United States 101st Airborne Division, were killed.

SPORTS & LEISURE

Oldest sporting event

Here's betting you didn't know that the Royal St. John's Regatta is the oldest sporting event in North America. It's also known as "the largest garden party in the world," thanks to the socializing that accompanies the rowing races. The first record of the event is from 1818, however, crews were known to compete in the St. John's Harbour since the 1700s. Today, the event, held annually in August, draws 50,000 spectators to the shores of Quidi Vidi Lake.

PEOPLE, PLACES & THINGS

Only official game bird

Newfoundland and Labrador is the nation's only province with an official game bird species. The partridge (*Lagopus* sp) or ptarmigan, including both the willow and rock species, is found throughout the province.

Ode to Newfoundland

Newfoundland and Labrador is one of three provinces with an official anthem or song. The provincial anthem, Ode to Newfoundland, was written by Governor Sir Cavendish Boyle in 1902, and was composed by Sir Hubert Parry.

> When sunrays crown thy pine-clad hills
> And Summer spreads her hand
> When silvern voices tune thy rills
> We love thee smiling land
> We love thee, we love thee,
> We love thee smiling land.

> When spreads thy cloak of shimm'ring white
> At Winter's stern command
> Thro' shortened day and starlit night
> We love thee frozen land
> We love thee, we love thee,
> We love thee frozen land.

> When blinding storm gusts fret thy shore
> And wild waves lash thy strand
> Thro' spindrift swirl and tempest roar
> We love thee wind-swept land
> We love thee, we love thee,
> We love thee wind-swept land.

> As loved our fathers, so we love
> Where once they stood we stand
> Their prayer we raise to heav'n above
> God guard thee Newfoundland
> God guard thee, God guard thee
> God guard thee Newfoundland.

Highest median age

Newfoundland and Labrador has the nation's highest median age, at 43.8 years, based on Statistics Canada data from 2011. The median age is the exact age where half the population is older and half is younger.

WORST ENCOUNTER WITH AN ICEBERG

The world's worst iceberg accident? The reportedly "unsinkable" *Titanic* hit an iceberg on April 14, 1912, 700 km southeast of Newfoundland, and 1,500 people died in the waters of the north Atlantic. The disaster is considered one of the planet's worst maritime disasters ever.

Most varieties of spoken English

What did you say? Was that English? Newfoundlanders are known for their distinctive way of speaking. The province is home to more varieties of spoken English than anywhere else on Earth. The province's English dialects are so distinct that there's even a dictionary of Newfoundland English.

Deadliest earthquake

The deadliest recorded earthquake in Canadian history claimed 27 lives, all of whom drowned in the resulting tsunami that hit Newfoundland's Burin Pennisula. Centered near the Laurentian slope, offshore between Newfoundland and Nova Scotia, the 7.2 magnitude quake struck on November 18, 1929.

First recorded avalanche

The first recorded avalanche in Canada and possibly North America, occurred near Nain, Labrador, in 1782. It's believed 22 people died in the snow slide, an account of which was discovered by historian Wallace J. McLean. A postscript in a letter from the Moravian Mission reported the event as "a monstrous body of snow which shot all at once down and pressed the winter hauss even with the ground, with all the people in it excepting one man who was buried in the snow without. Out of 31 only 9 got out alive."

The island first known as Île de Saint Jean

Modern-day Prince Edward Island had a couple of different names before it received its current name in 1798 in honour of Prince Edward, Duke of Kent, and the father of Queen Victoria. The island was first known as Île de Saint Jean in the 17th century, then as St. John's Island after it became British property in 1759.

GEOGRAPHY

Highest point

It's little surprise that Canada's smallest province has its lowest highest point. This spot, located at Springton in Queen's County, Prince Edward Island, lies 142 m above sea level.

Most densely populated

Despite being Canada's smallest province, Prince Edward Island is the nation's most densely populated. It's estimated there are 23.9 individuals per square km on the island.

STRUCTURES/COMMUNITIES

Longest bridge over icy waters ⬎

Opened on May 31, 1997, at a cost of $1 billion, the Confederation Bridge (linking Prince Edward Island and New Brunswick) is the largest bridge in the world that crosses ice-covered waters. Prince Edward Islanders voted to replace the ferry service connecting the island to the mainland with the curved, 12.9-km bridge. In a plebiscite in 1988, 59.4 percent of voters preferred the fixed link.

COMMUNICATIONS

First submarine telegraph cable

The first submarine telegraph cable in North America was laid by Frederick N. Gisborne between New Brunswick and Prince Edward Island in 1852, most of it by a machine he devised himself. He also engineered the first link between Cape Breton and Cape Ray, Newfoundland, in 1856.

TRANSPORTATION

No cars allowed

Can you imagine banning cars? Prince Edward Island did it in 1908. The government instituted the prohibition because many islanders thought the automobile was too noisy and scared horses. In 1913, the restriction was reduced and driving was banned on Tuesdays, Fridays, Saturdays and Sundays. It wasn't until 1918 that the province rescinded the ban entirely.

PEOPLE, PLACES & THINGS

Largest great white

Think you won't find big sharks in Canadian waters? Think again. The largest great white shark caught in Canada was caught near P.E.I. in 1983 and was more than 5 m long.

Official anthem

Prince Edward Island also has an official provincial anthem, which was adopted on May 7, 2010. The Island Hymn was written by novelist Lucy Maud Montgomery in 1908. The music was composed by Lawrence W. Watson. It also has a French version, *l'hymne de l'Île*, that was adapted by Raymond J. Arsenault.

> Fair Island of the sea,
> We raise our song to thee,
> The bright and blest;
> Loyally now we stand
> As brothers, hand in hand,
> And sing God save the land
> We love the best.

> Upon our princely Isle
> May kindest fortune smile
> In coming years;
> Peace and prosperity
> In all her borders be,
> From every evil free,
> And weakling fears.

> Prince Edward Isle, to thee
> Our hearts shall faithful be
> Where'er we dwell;
> Forever may we stand
> As brothers, hand in hand,
> And sing God save the land
> We love so well.

✔ First European flag in Canada

The first recorded European flag to fly in North America had the flag of England on one side and the winged-lion pennant of St. Mark of Venice on the opposite side. It flew on St. John's Island (present-day Prince Edward Island) on June 24, 1497, planted by the crew of John Cabot.

Yukon

Northwest
Territories

Nunavut

224

THE TERRITORIES

MARS ON EARTH

About the closest environment to Mars that exists on the Earth is that of the Haughton Crater in Nunavut. It is a polar desert that undergoes little erosion because of the relative lack of water or vegetation. NASA has used this area to prepare for Mars expetiions and test its Mars rovers, like the K10 Rover "Red," pictured here.

Our land
The territory of Nunavut is named after the Inuktitut term meaning "our land."

GEOGRAPHY

Highest northern waterfall
Canada's Far North is filled with impressive geographical landmarks. Among them is Nunavut's Wilberforce Falls on the territory's Hood River, which runs to the Arctic Ocean. With a vertical drop of 50 m in two sections, Wilberforce Falls is the world's highest waterfall north of the Arctic Circle—so iconic it's been immortalized by Canada Post on a stamp.

Widest strait
Davis Strait, part of the Arctic Ocean that runs between Nunavut's Baffin Island and Greenland, is the broadest strait in the world. At its widest, it stretches more than 950 km.

Largest lake on an island ↑
Baffin Island is not only Canada's largest island, but it's also home to the world's largest lake on an island. Measuring some 5,542 square km, Nettilling Lake is the largest lake in Nunavut and the 11th largest in Canada. It is located toward the island's south end, about 110 km southwest of Auyuittuq National Park. Covered by ice for most of the year, the lake is known to host only three fish species: Arctic char and two species of stickleback.

LONGEST CLIFF FACE
It really is a picture that speaks louder than words. It's difficult to describe the impressive sight of Mount Thor, a peak in Nunavut's Auyuittuq National Park. It has the world's longest uninterrupted cliff face, measuring approximately one km. The mountain, named after the Norse god of thunder, soars 1,675 m above sea level.

Largest island

With millions of lakes across the country and the longest coastline in the world, Canada is also home to thousands, if not millions, of islands. Most Canadians, however, are unlikely to ever see the nation's largest island, Nunavut's Baffin Island, which lies in the Arctic Ocean north of Labrador. At 507,451 square km, Baffin is also the fifth-largest island in the world. Nunavut's capital, Iqaluit, is located on the island's southern coast on Frobisher Bay.

Largest uninhabited island

Nunavut's Devon Island claims to be the largest island on Earth uninhabited by people. Located just north of Baffin Island, about one-third of Devon's 55,247 square km is covered by ice, while the rest of the island is largely barren.

Island-lake-island-lake-island

Okay, follow closely: Canada is home to the world's largest island, in a lake, on an island, in a lake, on an island. About 120 km inland from the southern coast of Nunavut's portion of Victoria Island, the one-hectare, nameless island is found on a small lake that's on an island surrounded by a smaller lake.

Northernmost point of North America

It's certainly aptly named. Zenith Point, Nunavut, is the northern-most point of continental North America.

Northernmost land

Cape Columbia, Nunavut, is Canada's most northerly point of land.

Northernmost community

Grise Fiord, Nunavut, lays claim to the title of most northerly community in North America. Only about 150 people, mostly Inuit, live in the hamlet, which was established in 1953 when the federal government relocated Inuit families from northern Quebec and northern Baffin Island to this spot to strengthen Canadian claims to the High Arctic.

Northernmost inhabited place

Alert, Nunavut, at latitude 82° 30′ N, is the world's northernmost permanently inhabited place. Located on the northeastern coast of Ellesmere Island on the Lincoln Sea, Alert is the site of an Environment Canada weather station, an atmosphere observatory and a military station, which is occupied year-round by an unknown number of personnel. The settlement experiences 106 days of full darkness each year, and an average annual temperature of −18°C.

First Arctic national park

The country's first national park north of the Arctic Circle is Nunavut's Auyuittuq National Park. Located on Baffin Island's Cumberland Peninsula, the 19,089-square-km park was created as a national park reserve in 1976 and became a national park in 2001, as part of the Nunavut Land Claims Agreement.

WEATHER

Longest-lasting snowfall

Canada's south typically sees more snow, but it lasts longer in the north. Indeed, the nation's northernmost settlement, Alert, Nunavut, is covered in snow for longer on average than anywhere else—at least one cm of snow covers the ground for an average 304 days annually.

WILDLIFE

Largest national wildlife area

The Ninginganiq National Wildlife Area in Nunavut is the largest national wildlife area in Canada. It protects more than 336,000 hectares on the northeast coast of Baffin Island.

First bowhead whale sanctuary

The Ninginganiq National Wildlife Area (see above) was the world's first bowhead whale sanctuary. It was established in 2010.

LARGEST BOWHEAD WHALE POD

Here's a whale of a place. The Ninginganiq National Wildlife Area in Nunavut is home to the nation's largest known concentration of bowhead whales. As many as 100 of the animals have been spotted in the area's Isabella Bay at one time.

Largest walrus herd

It's called the Foxe Basin, but maybe it should be called the Walrus Basin. The ocean basin north of Hudson Bay and between mainland Nunavut and Baffin Island, is home to Canada's largest walrus herd. More than 6,000 walruses call the area home.

Largest bird sanctuary

If birds have a heaven on Earth, it must be the Queen Maud Gulf Migratory Bird Sanctuary on the Arctic Ocean coast in Nunavut. It's the country's largest migratory bird sanctuary and Canada's largest federally protected area, measuring some 61,765 square km. There are about 60 goose colonies in the area. One contains 90 percent of the world population of Ross's Geese and another has more than 30 percent of the Western Canadian Arctic population of lesser snow geese.

Largest goose colony

By the sound of all the honking, you'd think it was one serious traffic jam. But no, it's just the world's largest goose colony, home to an estimated 1.7 million lesser snow geese. The federal Dewey Soper Migratory Bird Sanctuary on Nunavut's Baffin Island has an estimated one third of all lesser snows on the planet, along with significant populations of other birds.

Zinc bars ↗

BUSINESS/INDUSTRY

Northernmost mine ↗

The planet's northernmost mine was the Polaris lead and zinc mine on Little Cornwallis Island in Nunavut. Before it closed in 2002, more than one million tonnes of ore were extracted annually. Its operators undertook 22 years of exploration before opening the mine in 1981. Along with the nearby Nanisivik lead and zinc mine, Polaris was one of the lowest-cost producers of zinc on the planet and made Nunavut the largest producer of zinc in Canada.

INNOVATIONS

↙ Canadian Eskimo dog

This is one old dog. The Canadian Eskimo Dog is considered the oldest indigenous dog species still in existence. The breed, often used to pull sleds, is believed to have originated around 1100 to 1200 AD in what is now the Canadian Arctic. The breed, also known as the Canadian Inuit Dog, is the official animal of Nunavut.

229

TRANSPORTATION

Fly or swim

There are no communities in Nunavut that are accessible by road or rail. Everything arrives by air or sea.

PEOPLE, PLACES & THINGS

Youngest skier to the South Pole

In 2004, when she was 18, Iqaluit native Sarah McNair-Laundry became the youngest person in the world to ski to the South Pole. The more than 1,100-km trek took her 52 days to complete.

Highest birth rate

Based on 2011 data from Statistics Canada, Nunavut has Canada's highest birth rate, at an average of 2.97 children per woman.

Canadian birth rate

Here's how all of Canada's provinces rank on birth rate, based on 2011 data from Statistics Canada:

	Fertility rate*
Canada	**1.61**
Nunavut	2.97
Saskatchewan	1.99
Northwest Territories	1.97
Manitoba	1.86
Alberta	1.81
Yukon	1.73
Quebec	1.69
Prince Edward Island	1.62
Ontario	1.52
New Brunswick	1.54
Nova Scotia	1.47
Newfoundland and Labrador	1.45
British Columbia	1.42
*Average number of children per woman	

YOUNGEST TERRITORY

Nunavut has Canada's lowest median age, 24.8 years, based on 2011 data from Statistics Canada. Nearly one-third (31.5 percent) of the territory's residents are under the age of 15.

GEOGRAPHY

Highest point

Seems a fitting name for this remote, spectacular mountain. Mount Nirvana is the highest point in the Northwest Territories, rising to 2,773 m above sea level.

The most pingos

Our pingos are bigger than yours. The Northwest Territories' Mackenzie Delta region is home to the world's greatest concentration of pingos (some 1,350) and the largest. A pingo is an ice-cored hill, usually conically shaped, that grows only in permafrost. They're formed when water freezing under the surface is forced up by pressure, and they range from a few metres to several tens of metres high.

HIGHEST PINGO

The Ibyuk Pingo, near Tuktoyaktuk, Northwest Territories, is the highest pingo (a unique ice-core formation) in Canada and the second largest in the world. It pokes up 49 m above the surrounding terrain.

Deepest lake

At 614 m deep, Great Slave Lake in the Northwest Territories is North America's deepest lake. The 27,000-square-km lake is also the second-largest lake in Canada and the ninth largest in the world.

Biggest lake inside Canada

The Northwest Territories' Great Bear Lake is the biggest lake wholly in Canada, and the eighth-largest lake in the world. It has an area of 31,792 square km and is 446 m deep at its deepest spot.

231

Largest national park ↗

It seems fitting that Canada's largest national park (and the second-largest in the world) is named after North America's largest terrestrial animal. Wood Buffalo National Park, pictured here in a satellite photo in which forest fires can be seen, straddles the Alberta-Northwest Territories border and spans 44,807 square km. It was established in 1992 to protect the last remaining herds of the continent's wood bison.

Largest dark-sky preserve

Wood Buffalo National Park (see above) is the world's largest dark-sky preserve. The park was officially granted the dark-sky preserve designation in August 2013 by the Royal Astronomical Society of Canada for its work to preserve dark skies for the benefit of visitors and ecology.

Largest freshwater delta

The globe's largest inland freshwater delta is found in Wood Buffalo National Park.

WEATHER

Northernmost lightning

The farthest north a lightning flash was detected in Canada over the eastern Beaufort Sea, north of Tuktoyatuk, Northwest Territories on August 11, 2013.

Coldest wind chill

Canadians know that frigid temperatures are one thing, but wind chill is another. The nation's record wind chill was set on January 28, 1989, at Pelly Bay, Northwest Territories. The temperature was a nippy −51°C. The wind chill? A super-frosty −91°C!

Most sunshine ever

"Get out the suntan lotion," isn't a commonly heard refrain in Canada's Far North. But the most sunshine any community in Canada ever observed in one month was 621 hours in Eureka, Ellesmere Island, Northwester Territories, during May 1973. SPF 50, anyone?

↙ Place with the worst climate

Based on the Climate Severity Index, the nation's worst climate was in a place that no longer exists. The weather station at Isachsen, Northwest Territories, which was closed in 1978, registered 99 out of 100 on the index's scale.

WILDLIFE

Largest herd of wood bison ↗

When it comes to world wildlife records, Wood Buffalo National Park, which straddles the Alberta/ Northwest Territories border, claims quite a few. For starters, it's home to the world's largest herd of wood bison.

Only nesting whooping cranes

Wood Buffalo National Park is home to the world's only nesting site of the endangered whooping cranes.

Oldest fossils

Canada is home to three of the world's known examples of the oldest fossils on the planet—signs of the earliest life on Earth. Known as stromatolites, these fossils, which date back 3 to 3.5 billion years ago, are very rare. Examples have been found near Red Lake and Steep Rock Lake, Ontario and near Yellowknife, Northwest Territories.

Biggest lake trout

The sport angling world-record lake trout also came from Canadian waters: a 32.7-kg fish caught in Great Bear Lake, Northwest Territories in 1995.

Biggest arctic char

The International Game Fish Association all-tackle world record for Arctic char was caught in the Northwest Territories' Tree River on July 31, 1981. The char weighed 14.77 kg.

Biggest waterfowl

Cue the horns. The trumpeter swan is the largest species of native waterfowl in North America. Males weigh an average 12 kg, while females are slightly smaller, averaging 10 kg. In Canada, trumpeters are found in British Columbia, the Northwest Territories and the Yukon.

Biggest Arctic grayling

Perhaps it should come as little surprise, given our expanse of Arctic, that the International Game Fishing Association all-tackle world record for Arctic grayling was caught in Canada. The record grayling was nabbed on August 16, 1967 in the Katseyedie River, Northwest Territories, and tipped the scales at 2.69 kg.

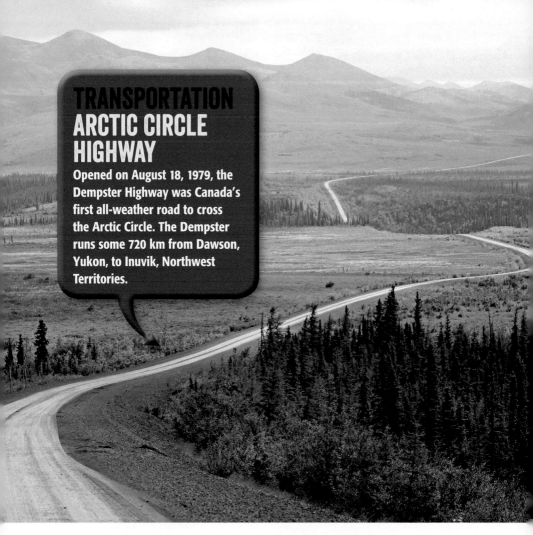

TRANSPORTATION
ARCTIC CIRCLE HIGHWAY

Opened on August 18, 1979, the Dempster Highway was Canada's first all-weather road to cross the Arctic Circle. The Dempster runs some 720 km from Dawson, Yukon, to Inuvik, Northwest Territories.

Biggest Central Canada barren-ground caribou

Another big 'bou: according to the Boone and Crockett Club, the world-record, Central Canada barren-ground caribou, which scored 4334/8, was taken by Donald J. Hotter III in 1994 near Humpy Lake, Northwest Territories.

BUSINESS/INDUSTRY

Biggest diamond mine

Canada's largest diamond mine, Diavik, is located 300 km north of Yellowknife, Northwest Territories. Run as part of the Rio Tinto group of companies, the reserves are located in three diamond ore bodies. Since production began in 2003, more than 50 million carats of rough diamonds have been extracted.

Great river

The name of the Yukon territory is believed to have come from the Amerindian term *Yu-kun-ah*, which means "great river." It was first officially recorded by a Hudson's Bay Company employee for what he thought was the area's Aboriginal name.

GEOGRAPHY

Newest lake

Canada is home to millions of lakes, many with no name. But did you know in the fall of 2014 the nation got a new one? A landslide in the Yukon's Kluane National Park and Reserve in the fall of that year blocked the Vulcan Creek and created a lake about 350 m long and 80 m wide.

Highest mountains

Look up, way up … to Canada's highest mountains!

Name	Height
Mount Logan, Yukon	5,959 m
Mount Saint Elias, Yukon	5,489 m
Mount Lucania, Yukon	5,226 m
King Peak, Yukon	5,173 m
Mount Steele, Yukon	5,067 m
Mount Wood, Yukon	4,880 m
Mount Vancouver, Yukon	4,812 m
Fairweather Mountain, British Columbia	4,671 m
Mount Slaggard, Yukon	4,663 m
Mount Hubbard, Yukon	4,577 m

Largest non-polar icefield

The Yukon's Seward Glacier and Alaska's Bagley Icefield together form the largest non-polar icefield in the world. The area is home to some of the world's longest and most spectacular glaciers. The icefields are a United Nations Educational, Scientific and Cultural Organization (UNESCO) world heritage site that combines Kluane National Park and Reserve in the Yukon and Tatshenshini-Alsek Provincial Park in British Columbia with Wragell-St. Elias National Park and Glacier Bay National Park in Alaska.

Westernmost point

Canada's westernmost point is Boundary Peak in the Yukon, along the Yukon-Alaska border.

Westernmost community

The nation's most westerly community is the Yukon's Beaver Creek. Located on the Alaska Highway at the 141st meridian, the community is home to the White River First Nations and considered to be Canada's gateway to Alaska.

First people in North America

The earliest known signs of humans in North America have been found in the Yukon's Bluefish Caves. Butchered mammoth bones and primitive tools were discovered that date to 15,000 and 12,000 years ago and evidence suggests these peoples migrated from Asia. The tools are made with a stone technology reminiscent of the Dyuktai culture of Siberia.

WEATHER

Lowest temperature

Brrr. The lowest temperature ever recorded in Canada and North America? The village of Snag, Yukon, registered −63°C on February 3, 1947.

Fastest rising temperatures

Need proof that climate change is a problem? Average winter temperatures in the Yukon and northern British Columbia went up by 4.9°C between 1948 and 2007 — the fastest rising temperatures in the country.

World's smallest desert

When you think of Canada, and when you think of the North, you naturally think of deserts — or maybe not! But Canada is home to what's called the world's smallest desert, the Carcross Desert in the Yukon. The area's dry climate and strong winds have created a small, 260-hectare series of sand dunes — but it's not technically a desert.

WILDLIFE

Biggest polar bear

This is one big bear. The wildlife museum at the Caribou Crossing Trading Post in Carcross, Yukon, is home to the world's largest mounted polar bear.

Biggest mountain caribou

Canada is renowned for its caribou populations, and it's home to some of the largest antlered caribou ever recorded. The world-record mountain caribou, according to the Boone and Crockett Club, was taken in the Yukon's Pelly Mountains in 1988 by Paul T. Deuling. It scored 4593/8.

BIGGEST MOOSE

If there's a critter synonymous with Canada's hinterland, it's undoubtedly the moose. Not only is the moose the largest member of the deer family, but the subspecies (giant moose), found in western Yukon, is the largest of the species. Adult males measure up to 2.1 m tall at the shoulder, are about 2.7 m long and can weigh up to 725 kg. Indeed, on September 25, 2013, hunter Heinz Naef from Dawson City took a moose weighing in at more than 560 kg, which is now a new world record.

TOUGHEST SLED DOG RACE

The Yukon Quest 1,000 Mile International Sled Dog Race, is the self-proclaimed "toughest sled dog race in the world." The 1,600-km competition runs each February between Whitehorse, Yukon, and Fairbanks, Alaska, along the historical Klondike gold rush route. Besides the great distance, racers face temperatures plunging to –40°C, winds up to 160 km per hour and steep mountain summits.

PEOPLE, PLACES & THINGS

Fewest births

The Yukon Territory has the lowest number of births, based on 2011 data from Statistics Canada, at just 431 in that year.

BUSINESS/INDUSTRY

Biggest gold rush ⬉

The biggest gold rush in Canadian history was the Klondike Gold Rush from 1897 to 1899. During that time, 40,000 fortune seekers made their way to gold fields near Dawson, Yukon. By the end of the rush, prospectors spent an estimated $50 million reaching the Klondike, an amount essentially equal to the value of the gold extracted during those years.

↑ The first steamer, *Excelcior*, leaves San Francisco for the Yukon after news of the discovery of gold.

PHOTO CREDITS

b = bottom; t = top; l = left; m = middle;
bi = background image; ip = inset photo

Associated Press

p. 36 t: © PR NEWSWIRE/AP Images; p. 44: © Bettmann/CORBIS/AP Images; p. 54: © AP Photo/Mary Altaffer; p. 55: © ASSOCIATED PRESS/Rick Eglinton; p. 56: © ASSOCIATED PRESS; p. 61 b: © ASSOCIATED PRESS; p. 63 t: © AP Photo/Mikhail Metzel, Pool; p. 84 br: © AP Photo/The Canadian Press/Darryl Dyck; p. 121: © ASSOCIATED PRESS/Tom Hanson; p. 124 b: © Bettmann/Corbis/AP Images; p. 162 tr: AP Photo/The Canadian Press/Frank Gunn; p. 164: AP Photo/Ed Reinke; p. 166 © Bettmann/CORBIS/AP Images; p. 178 t: © AP Photo/Jacques Boissinot; p. 183 b: © AP Photo/ Jeffrey Ulbrich; p. 188 t: © AP Photo/Staff/Putnam; p. 203 m: © Bettmann/CORBIS/AP Images; p. 211 bm: © AP Photo/Marty Reichenthal; p. 216 b: © Bettmann/CORBIS/AP Images; p. 230: © Kike Calvo via AP Images

Can Stock Photo

p. 231: © Can Stock Photo Inc./Eppic

Corbis

p. 48: © John Springer Collection/CORBIS; p. 50: © Neal Preston/CORBIS; p. 53: © Bettman/CORBIS; p. 58 b: ANDY CLARK/Reuters/CORBIS; p. 101 b: © Gilbert Lundt, Jean-Yves Ruszniewski/TempSport/ CORBIS; p. 123: © Paul A. Souders/CORBIS; p. 173 br: © Stephen Kraly/Splash News/CORBIS; p. 174 bi: © Bettmann/CORBIS; p. 192: © Bettmann/CORBIS

Dreamstime

p. 16 t: © Vismax/Dreamstime.com; p. 17: © Leaf/ Dreamstime.com; p. 25 t: © Splosh/Dreamstime. com; p.132 b: © Jason A. Paul/Dreamstime.com; p. 159 tl: © Marcus Miranda/Dreamstime.com; p. 159 tr: Matthew Bamberg /Dreamstime.com ; p. 228 t: (c) Corey A. Ford/Dreamstime.com

iStock

p. 41 t: © alicat/iStock; p. 42: © Lokibaho/iStock; p. 45 b: © DavidBukach/iStock; p. 122 l: © rappensuncle/iStock; p. 136 bi: © kertlis/iStock; p. 187 b: © Lokibaho/iStock; p. 219 b: © pongky.n/iStock

Miscellaneous

p. 2 bi: Courtesy of NASA; p. 13 b: Public Domain; p. 25 b: Courtesy of Library Archives Canada; p. 28 br: Toronto Public Library/Toronto Star/Frank Lennon; p. 34 b: Courtesy of Library and Archives Canada; p. 37 t: Courtesy of Library and Archives Canada; p. 38 bl: Courtesy of Nobel Prize; p. 38 br: Canada History; p. 39 bi: Courtesy of NASA; p. 45 t: Public Domain courtesy of the City of Vancouver Archives; p. 49 b: Courtesy of Scholastic Canada; p. 104 b: (c) Kraay Family Farm/Engadget; p. 105 m: Public Domain Courtesy of National Film Board of Canada; p. 115 r: (c) Trackie Group Inc.; p. 137 m: Courtesy of Michael Mouland; p. 152 b: Manitoba University/David A. Wyatt; p. 155: Demotix; p. 177 t: www.flickr.com; p. 186 b: © L. Armand Bombardier Museum; p. 187 m: Courtesy of Colby Curtis Museum & The Stanstead Historical Society; p.196 t: Courtesy of AGO; p. 196 b: Canadian Museum of History Building/ Steven Darby/Canadian Museum of History; p. 200 t: © Brian Atkinson/NB government tourism; p. 202 mr: Courtesy of Brock University/Hugh C. Thompson; p. 206 t: Courtesy of NASA; p. 210 t: St. Catherines Museum; p. 224 bi: Courtesy of NASA; p. 232 t: Courtesy of NASA; p. 237: Public Domain courtesy of Library of Washington University

Reuters

p. 57: © Reuters/Jim Young; p 103: © Reuters/Patrick Price; p. 190: © Reuters/Reuters Photographer

Shutterstock

p. 3: © SurangaSL/Shutterstock.com; p. 6: © Jeff Whyte/Shutterstock.com; p. 12 t: © Josef Hanus/ Shutterstock.com; p. 16 b: © Carolina K. Smith MD/ Shutterstock.com; p. 24 t: © RRuntsch/Shutterstock. com; p. 26 l: AndreAnita/Shutterstock.com; p. 27 t: © Robert L. Kothenbeutel/Shutterstock.com; p. 27 br: © Xavier gallego morel/Shutterstock.com; p. 27 bl: © Modfos/Shutterstock.com; p. 28 l: © Chris Frost/ Shutterstock.com; p. 29 t: © Pete Spiro/Shutterstock. com; p. 29 m: Piotr Krzeslak/Shutterstock.com; p. 31 b: © Elena Elisseeva/Shutterstock.com; p. 31 r: © antidesign/Shutterstock.com; p. 32 t: © SpaceKris/ Shutterstock.com; p. 32 bl: © meunierd/Shutterstock. com; p. 32 br: © Mike Loiselle/Shutterstock.com; p. 33: © Sebastian Knight/Shutterstock.com; p. 34 t: © ziviani/Shutterstock.com; p. 35 m: © vita khorzhevska/Shutterstock.com; p. 37 m: © Marie C. Fields/ Shutterstock.com; p. 40 l: © Geo-grafika/Shutterstock. com; p. 43 tr: © Alessandro Tumminello/Shutterstock. com; p. 47 tr: Sergey89rus/Shutterstock.com; p. 47 tl: © Rawpixel/Shutterstock.com; p. 47 t: © Bildagenture Zoonar GmbH/Shutterstock.com; p. 47 tr: © Piotr Marcinski/Shutterstock.com; p. 47 m: © LaiQuocAnh/ Shutterstock.com; p. 48 b: © Veronica Louro/Shutterstock.com; p. 49 t: © s_bukley/Shutterstock.com; p. 51: © Jamie Roach/Shutterstock.com; p. 52 t: © Jason Kasumovic/Shutterstock.com; p. 59: © Nucharee Tubthong/Shutterstock.com; p. 64 t: rhfletcher/ Shutterstock.com; p. 64 b: © Elena Elisseeva/Shutterstock.com; p. 65 b: © alexskopie/Shutterstock.com; p. 66: Yanas/Shutterstock.com; p. 67 r: © Dennis Jarvis/Shutterstock.com; p. 72 bi: © Roberto Caucino/ Shutterstock.com; p. 74 t: © puttsk/Shutterstock. com; p. 75: © JamesChen/Shutterstock.com; p. 76 t: © Christopher Gardiner/Shutterstock.com; p. 79 t: © Serjio74/Shutterstock.com; p. 79 b: © Lightspring/ Shutterstock.com; p. 80 b: © kzww/Shutterstock. com; p. 81 tr: © Steve Norman/Shutterstock.com; p. 82: © Max Lindenthaler/Shutterstock.com; p. 83 t: © Josef Hanus/Shutterstock.com; p. 84: © Christian Delbert/Shutterstock.com; p. 85: © Lissandra Melo/ Shutterstock.com; p. 86: © Volt Collection/Shutterstock.com; p 87: © Albert Pego/Shutterstock.com; p. 90/91 bi: © Constantine Androsoff/Shutterstock. com; p. 92 t: © Ray Yang/Shutterstock.com; p. 93 b: © Jeff Whyte/Shutterstock.com; p. 93 m: © Artifan/ Shutterstock.com; p. 94 b: © Jeff Whyte/Shutterstock. com; p. 94 t: © David P. Lewis/Shutterstock.com; p. 95: Ryan Morgan/Shutterstock.com; p. 96 b: Ian Maton/Shutterstock.com; p. 96 t: © Dennis W. Donohue/ Shutterstock.com; p. 98 t: 2009fotofriends/Shutterstock.com; p. 98 b: © 2009fotofriends/Shutterstock. com; p. 99 t: Constantine Androsoff/Shutterstock. com; p. 99 b: © Jeff Wasserman/Shutterstock.com; p. 103 t: © Christopher Gardiner/Shutterstock.com; p. 105 t: © Ronnie Chua/Shutterstock.com; p. 106 bi: © Blaze986/Shutterstock.com; p. 108 b: © Andrew Park/Shutterstock.com; p. 109 b: © Blaze986/Shutterstock.com; p. 111 bi: © Pictureguy/Shutterstock. com; p. 113 t: Gyorgy Bama/Shutterstock.com; p. 114 bl: adriaticfoto/Shutterstock.com; p. 114-115 t: Scott Prokop/Shutterstock.com; p. 119 t: © Cindy Creighton/Shutterstock.com; p. 120 r: © siraphat/Shutterstock.com; p. 120 l: © Jostein Hauge/Shutterstock.com; p. 125 t: © Henryk Sadura/Shutterstock.com; p. 126 tl: © corund/Shutterstock.com; p. 126 bi: © A

Cotton Photo/Shutterstock.com; p. 128: © M.M.G./
Shutterstock.com; p. 130 t: © Chris Hill/Shutterstock.
com; p. 131 t: © shipfactory/Shutterstock.com; p. 133
br: ©Martchan/Shutterstock.com; p. 133 l: © Tom
Middleton/Shutterstock.com; p. 134 t: © Alexander
Erdbeer/Shutterstock.com; p. 134 b: © Viacheslav
V. Fedorov/Shutterstock.com; p. 135 br: © njene/
Shutterstock.com; p. 136 bl & t: © dreamcatcher/
Shutterstock.com; p. 139 tl: © mikecphoto/Shutter-
stock.com; p. 140 bi: © David C. Rehner/Shutterstock.
com; p. 141 t: © Lester Balajadia/Shutterstock.com;
p. 143 t: © Randi Scott/Shutterstock.com; p. 144 l: ©
Paul McKinnon/Shutterstock.com; p. 146 b: © goir/
Shutterstock.com; p. 146 t: © SF photo/Shutterstock.
com; p. 147 t: © javarman/Shutterstock.com; p. 149
t: © keki/Shutterstock.com; p. 150 t: © rj lerich/Shut-
terstock.com; p. 151 t: © Kiev.Victor/Shutterstock.
com; p. 154 t: © rmnoa357/Shutterstock.com; p.
156 t: ©Jaguar PS/Shutterstock.com; p. 156 b: ©
Featureflash/Shutterstock.com; p. 157 t: © JStone/
Shutterstock.com; p. 158: igor kisseleve/Shutterstock.
com; p. 160 t: © ValeStock/Shutterstock.com; p. 161
b: © Evan Fariston/Shutterstock.com; p. 162 tl: ©
Paul McKinnon/Shutterstock.com; p. 163 tl: © Everett
Collection/Shutterstock.com; p. 166 b: © Matthew
Jacques/Shutterstock.com; p. 169: © Pete Spiro/
Shutterstock.com; p. 173 r: © Marjan Apostolovic/
Shutterstock.com; p. 174 tl: © CGinspiration/Shut-
terstock.com; p. 176 t: © Horst Petzold/Shutterstock.
com; p. 177 b: © Paul Vaserhelyi/Shutterstock.com;
p. 179 tr: © Randimal/Shutterstock.com; p. 180
t: © Andre Nantel/Shutterstock.com; p. 181 b: ©
meunierd/Shutterstock.com; p. 182 b: © meunierd/
Shutterstock.com; p. 183 m: © Norman Pogson/
Shutterstock.com; p. 184 t: © I. Pilon/Shutterstock.
com; p. 186 t: © Michael C. Gray/Shutterstock.com;
p. 188 b: © Benoit Daoust/Shutterstock.com; p. 189
t: © holbox/Shutterstock.com; p. 191 t: © Maridav/
Shutterstock.com; p. 191 b: © meunierd/Shutter-
stock.com; p. 198 bi: © Norman Pogson/Shutterstock.
com; p. 198 lt: © yui/Shutterstock.com; p. 198 lm: ©
corund/Shutterstock.com; p. 198 lb: © Niyazz/Shut-
terstock.com; p. 201 r: © gvictoria/Shutterstock.com;
p. 202 ml: © Paul Binet/Shutterstock.com; p. 204
m: © Colin D. Young/Shutterstock.com; p. 205 t: ©
Alberto Loyo/Shutterstock.com; p. 206 m: © Georgios
Kollidas/Shutterstock.com; p. 207 t: © LunaseeStu-
dios/Shutterstock.com; p. 207 m: © Paul McKinnon/
Shutterstock.com; p. 208 t: © V.J. Matthew/Shutter-
stock.com; p. 208 b: © Olivier Le Queinec/Shutter-
stock.com; p. 212 m: © Binh Thanh Bui/Shutterstock.
com; p. 215 t: © Elena Elisseeva/Shutterstock.com;
p. 217 t: © Chiyacat/Shutterstock.com; p. 219 t: ©
Eric Isselee/Shutterstock.com; p. 219 m: © cynoclub/
Shutterstock.com; p. 221 t: © Everett Historical/Shut-
terstock.com; p. 223 b: vesilvio/Shutterstock.com; p.
223 b: © smcfeeters/Shutterstock.com; p. 224 tm: ©
Ronnie Chua/Shutterstock.com; p. 224 tl & bl: © yui/
Shutterstock.com; p. 226: © Catmando/Shutterstock.
com; p. 229 b: © Nancy Bauer/Shutterstock.com; p.
229 t: © SARIN KUNTHONG/Shutterstock.com; p. 233
t: © Pi-Lens/Shutterstock.com; p. 233 b: © aleksandr
hunta/Shutterstock.com; p. 234: © oksana.perkins/
Shutterstock.com; p. 236 b: © Michal_K/Shutterstock.
com; p. 237 t: © Gary Whitton/Shutterstock.com

The Canadian Press

p. 8 bi: The Canadian Press/Winnipeg Free Press/Joe
Bryksa; p. 35 ip: The Canadian Press/Peter Bregg; p.
37: The Canadian Press; p. 57: The Canadian Press/
Toronto Star/Jim Young; p. 58 t: The Canadian Press/
Winnipeg Free Press/Christian Laforce; p. 61: The
Canadian Press/Toronto Star; p. 124 t: The Canadian
Press/Winnipeg Free Press; p. 132: The Canadian
Press/Tim Clark; p. 138 tr: Deborah Baic/The Globe
and Mail/The Canadian Press; p. 167: © The Cana-
dian Press/The Globe and Mail/Tiber Kolley; p. 193:
The Canadian Press/Frank Gunn

Wikipedia

p. 11 t: Public Domain; p. 11 b: Public Domain; p. 15
b: Public Domain; p. 19 l: McKay Savage CC BY-SA
2.0/Wikipedia; p. 20 b: Public Domain; p. 21 b: Public
Domain; p. 22 b: Public Domain; p. 23 bl: Public
Domain; p. 23 br: Wikimedia Creative Commons
Attribution 2.0 Generic/Thomas Fisher Rare Book
Library; p. 25 b: Public Domain; p. 28 bl: Public
Domain; p. 28 br: Public Domain; p. 29 bl: Public
Domain; p. 30 b: Public Domain; p. 33 br: Public
Domain; p. 34 b: Public Domain/Wikipedia; p. 35 t:
© George Granthan Bain Collection/Wikipedia; p. 35
b: Public Domain; p. 36 b: Public Domain; p. 37 b:
Public Domain; p. 37 br: Public Domain/Wikipedia;
p. 38 bm: Public Domain/Wikimedia; p. 39 b: Public
Domain; p. 39 b: Skcdoenut CC BY-SA 3.0/Wikipedia;
p. 40: Andrew Rusk CC BY-SA 2.0/Wikipedia; p. 40 br:
Remy Steinegger CC BY-SA 2.0/Wikipedia; p. 41 br:
CC BY-SA 3.0/Wikimedia; p. 43 b: CC BY-SA 3.0/Mat-
tnad at English Wikipedia; p. 46 m: Public Domain; p.
46 b: Public Domain; p. 61 tr: Arthur S. Goss/Public
Domain; p. 63 b: Public Domain/Wikimedia; p. 68 &
front cover: Antony Stanley CC BY-SA 2.0/ Wikipedia;
p. 69: Canoe1967 CC BY-SA 3.0/Wikimedia; p. 70:
Public Domain/Wikipedia; p. 71: Myke CC BY-SA 4.0/
Wikipedia; p. 88 l: Jeff Seiferd CC BY-SA 2.0/Wikipe-
dia; p. 89: CC BY-SA 3.0/Wikimedia; p. 100 b: Brian C.
Passifiume CC BY-SA 3.0/Wikimedia; p. 112 b: Turgan
CC BY-SA 3.0/Wikipedia; p. 118 t: Public Domain; p.
119 l: (c) Mike Beauregard CC BY-SA 2.0/Wikipedia;
p. 122 r: Public Domain; p. 125 b: Public Domain;
p. 138 bl: Public Domain; p. 145 t: Public Domain/
Wikipedia; p. 145 m: Public Domain; p. 148 b: Public
Domain/Wikipedia; p. 149 b: Professor Marko Turina/
University Hospital, Zurich CC BY-SA 3.0/Wikipedia; p.
152 t: Frank Denardo CC BY-SA 2.0/Wikipedia; p. 153
m: © Danielle Scott CC BY-SA 2.0/Wikimedia; p. 163
tl: D'Arcy Norman CC BY-SA 2.0/Wikipedia; p. 165 tr:
Public Domain/George Grantham Bain Collection; p.
168 t & b: Public Domain; p. 170 b: P199 CC BY-SA
3.0/Wikipedia; p. 171: Public Domain; p. 172 b: ©
Mike Weston ABIPP/MOD; p. 182 t: Pierre Bona/
Wikipedia; p. 184 b: Public Domain/Wikipedia; p.
185 m: Public Domain/Wikipedia; p. 194 b: ideogibs
CC BY-SA 2.0/Wikipedia; p. 195 b: Denis Jacquerye
CC BY-SA 2.0/Wikipedia; p. 197 t: Public Domain/Wikipedia; p.
197 b: Public Domain/Wikimedia; p. 203 t: Public
Domain; p. 211 t: Public Domain/ Wikipedia; p. 213
t: Public Domain/Wikimedia; p. 218 t: © D. Gordon E.
Robertson/Wikipedia; p. 226 b: Ansgar Walk CC BY-SA
2.5/Wikipedia; p. 232 b: © Randy Dueck/Wikipedia

INDEX

Page numbers in bolded italics refer to illustrations.

INDEX

INDEX

INDEX

INDEX